Beach... WordPerfect 5.0 Handbook

Beacham's WordPerfect 5.0 Handbook

Walton Beacham
and
Deborah Beacham

BANTAM BOOKS
TORONTO • NEW YORK • LONDON • SYDNEY • AUCKLAND

Trademarks

WordPerfect is a Registered Trademark of WordPerfect Corporation.
Lotus, 1-2-3, and Symphony are Registered Trademarks of Lotus Development Corporation.

BEACHAM'S WORDPERFECT 5.0 HANDBOOK
A Bantam Book / July 1988

ISBN 0-553-34493-5

Published simultaneously in the United States and Canada

Bantam Books are published by Bantam Books, a division of Bantam Doubleday Dell Publishing Group, Inc. Its trademark, consisting of the words "Bantam Books" and the portrayal of a rooster, is Registered in U.S. Patent and Trademark Office and in other countries. Marca Registrada, Bantam Books, Inc., 666 Fifth Avenue, New York, New York 10103.

PRINTED IN THE UNITED STATES OF AMERICA

BH   0   9   8   7   6   5   4   3   2   1

Table of Contents

Introduction

The Modern WordPerfect

When word processing was first developed for the personal computer, it resembled word processing systems that had been designed for mainframe environments. Mainframe users felt at home with software like WordStar; many other users simply felt intimidated. WordPerfect's idea was to design software that was fun to use and that did not require a computer programmer's skills to enter commands in exact syntax. Thus, WordPerfect developed the function key concept as a means to give the software commands. Over a million users worldwide have attested to WordPerfect's success in creating professional word processing software that is also fun.

The functions that WordPerfect could perform in the early days seem rudimentary compared to the sophisticated word processing environment today. Figure I.1 shows earlier WordPerfect template back in the days when WordPerfect Corporation was named Satellite Software International (SSI):

Being able to cut, copy, and move text were the principal features users wanted from their word processors then. Today, we expect miracles and are impatient when our software can't do everything. WordPerfect 5.0 is a new generation of software, although it operates very much like Word-

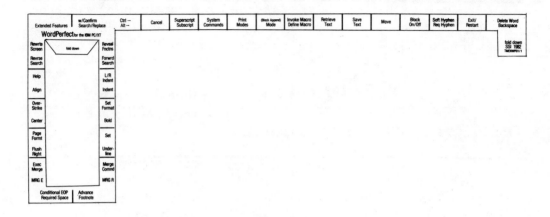

Figure I.1 *Template for WordPerfect 3.0*

Perfect 4.2. Users of 4.2 will notice little difference in the operation, but they will be pleased by the additional features. From a user viewpoint, the principal differences pertain to printer support and desktop publishing features, especially graphics.

What is Desktop Publishing?

How people define desktop publishing is really a function of how much they want their work to look like a typeset document. A minimum set of features would include good hyphenation and kerning; automatic footnotes, lists, and tables; automatic indexing; and columns. On the upper end of the scale, desktop publishing means perfectly integrated bit-mapped images combined with sophisticated page layout capabilities. Printer support is an essential ingredient in how the document will look when printed. If your software can't take full advantage of your printer's features, you're not going to get the best document.

WordPerfect 5.0 offers many features that make it possible to produce extremely good quality professional documents, but it is not designed to be a true page layout editor, such as PageMaker and Ventura. This is not to say that you can't lay out pretty fancy pages, including rotating graphics, wrapping text around boxes, and creating your own color palate. You can import bit-mapped images and can select from some 30 "clip-art" images that come with the software. And the best news is that all of these features are presented in WordPerfect's friendly, fun-to-use format. You don't have to learn more software to produce high-quality pages.

New Features in Release 5.0

File, Printing, and Hardware Management

Auxiliary File Location allows you to specify path locations to other drives and files.

Banners and Form Numbers set up documents for Nouvelle networks.

Beep Options alert you to certain errors.

Locked Documents and all associated files are secured with a password.

Fast Save saves files in an unformatted format that speeds up the Save function.

Initial Fonts and Initial Settings allow you to change the defaults for all the features.

Keyboard Setup maps specialized keyboard needs.

Language tells WordPerfect what language the dictionary, hyphenation, and thesaurus should use.

Master Document combines two or more files and allows you to expand or collapse them.

Mnemonic menus allow you to select choices either by a number or by the first letter of the menu item.

Quality of Print sets draft- medium- or high-quality printing, which often speeds up the process.

Select Printer defines the printer driver for 150 different printers.

Setup permits you to change backup options, screen format, fast save, default settings, and other features.

Formatting and Managing Documents

Advance moves the cursor to specified positions.

Automatic Reference cross-references pages and paragraphs, footnotes, and graphics boxes.

Document Compare illustrates any changes between different versions of the same document.

Endnote Placement allows you to collect and print endnotes anywhere in the document.

Extended Parallel Columns span a page break.

Top and Bottom Margins are now measured in inches from the top and bottom of the page rather than by the number of lines on a page as in the older versions.

Ordinary Tabs allow you to bypass the tab set process when resetting left tab markers.

Advanced Printing and Desktop Publishing Features

Appearance of attributes include italics, shadows, outlines, small caps, and redline.

Base Fonts allow you to change font style and size anywhere in the document.

Downloadable Fonts enter font files that you want to download to the printer.

Fonts is a menu that automatically determines the capabilities of your printer and allows you to select the options available.

Fonts and Carriages allow you to mark the fonts you've selected for your printer.

Force Odd/Even Pages assures that pages will print on the side you want them to.

Forms is a list of standard form sizes and stock that streamlines your printing specifications.

Kerning sets more precise spacing between pairs of letters.

Leading precisely adjusts the line height.

Line Spacing more precisely judges the proportions of the distance between lines.

Overstrike permits overstriking two or more characters with font attributes.

Size/Position select sub- and superscripts as well as the size of text.

Style sheets streamline formatting text.

Width Adjustment measures precisely the width of characters.

Word Spacing offers additional control for the amount of space between letters and words.

Graphics

Graphics is now a function key entry for creating various types of graphics boxes and importing images from other software.

Graphic Screen Type allows you to set graphics drivers for different monitors run by the same computer.

Graphics, Text, or Both permits you to print either or both.

View Document allows you to see on the screen the entire page, including graphics, as it will be printed.

Screen Display Features

Colors/Fonts/Attributes offer a wide variety of choices for displaying text *on the screen*, which can be captured with WordPerfect's resident *screen capture utility*.

Display Pitch helps eliminate overlapping characters.

Display Setup determines message and status line appearance.

Formatting Text

Compose creates digraphs and diacritical marks.

Decimal Character sets the alignment character.

Underline Spaces/Tabs turn off continuous underlining from word to word.

Who Benefits from the New Features?

Actually, everyone in the long run. WordPerfect contains not only improved features, but it also contains updated architecture in anticipation of new generations of software.

Specifically, specialized and power users, as well as people moving toward desktop publishing, will find the new features attractive. WordPerfect 5.0 has been designed with the legal, business, and military communities in mind. Because of its foreign language features, European users will fit WordPerfect easily into their current word processing environment.

What WordPerfect Does Best

All professional-quality word processors today handle the basics of text management easily, but WordPerfect's advantages are the power and flexibility of managing an address database, sorting and merging the database, easy-to-build macros that manage complex operations, creating columns and graphics boxes and integrating with third-party graphics software. WordPerfect 5.0 also supports an amazing number and variety of printers. Where WordPerfect is weakest is in using outline features to help construct a document and in creating long documents.

Primarily, what WordPerfect does best is to make friends with the user, but you probably already know that. What else the WordPerfect Corporation shines at is supporting its product and the people who use it. You'll find the customer support staff unusually responsive to your problems. You may call toll free: 800-321-5906 or 801-226-6800 for phone systems that do not accept toll free calls.

The customer-support line is open 7 a.m. to 6 p.m. for users with IBM/compatibles and from 8 a.m. to 5 p.m. for users of all other computers.

Requirements for Using WordPerfect 5.0

An important difference between WordPerfect 4.2 and 5.0 is that WordPerfect 5.0 require 512K of memory while 4.2 required only 256K. This not only means more expensive hardware but also less working space in RAM, even if your computer is fully loaded. Because an entire document must be able to reside in memory, the more limited RAM restricts the length of documents. You can, of course, store different chapters under different file names, but editing text between chapters is difficult.

WordPerfect 5.0 Learn Tutorial

For a quick introduction to WordPerfect's features, you will find the Learn Tutorial useful and easy. The tutorial explains a feature, then gives you an opportunity to try it. **Learn** will not allow you to make a mistake. If you try a procedure incorrectly, WordPerfect explains what you did wrong.

There are seven lessons in all. As you complete each leason, WordPerfect places a check mark. You can interrupt a lesson and return to it, and you can repeat lessons as often as you wish. The end of each lesson offers a review summary. You might want to print these using Print Screen (Shift-PrtSc).

CHAPTER 1

Basic Concepts

1.1 Function Keys

All operations for WordPerfect are performed with the 10 keys numbered F1 through F10 along the side or top of your computer. These keys are gateways to all the features you'll use. Look at the templates in Figures 1.1 and 1.2 that lay out the function keys. (IBM-AT keyboards have 12 keys.) Notice that each function key is used for four different operations. If you press **F1** you invoke **Cancel**, but if you press **Shift F1** you invoke **Setup**. By using **Shift, Alt,** and **Ctrl** the 10 function keys can control 40 operations. All operations listed in black, such as **Cancel** (F1) and **Search** (F2) are started by pressing the function key. Operations listed in green, such as **Setup** and **Search**, are started by pressing **Shift** and the function key. Operations listed in blue, such as **Thesaurus** and **Replace**, are started with **Alt** and the function key. Red operations are started by pressing **Ctrl** and the function key.

Some function keys, such as F6 (Bold), Shift F6 (Center), and F8 (Underline) immediately perform the operation. Other function keys will bring up a menu from which you'll make selections. For example, if you press Shift F7 (Print), the menu in Figure 1.3 appears. WordPerfect does not have as many menus as many word processors, which makes it more convenient once you get the knack of what each of the keys does. Throughout this book we'll introduce you to all of the keys, their functions, and attached menus.

1

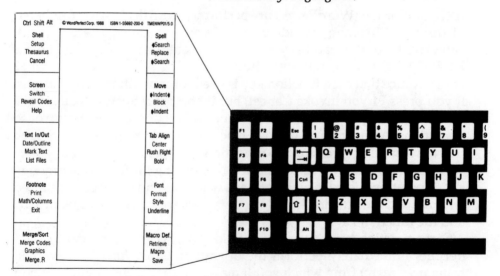

Shell	Spell	Screen	Move	*Ctrl*	Text In/Out	Tab Align	Footnote	Font	*Ctrl*	Merge/Sort	Macro Define
Thesaurus	Replace	Reveal Codes	Block	*Alt*	Mark Text	Flush Right	Math/Columns	Style	*Alt*	Graphics	Macro
Setup	◆Search	Switch	◆Indent◆	*Shift*	Date/Outline	Center	Print	Format	*Shift*	Merge Codes	Retrieve
Cancel	◆Search	Help	◆Indent		List Files	Bold	Exit	Underline		Merge R	Save
F1	F2	F3	F4		F5	F6	F7	F8		F9	F10

Figure 1.1 *IBM AT Keyboard and Template*
(Function Keys Highlighted)

Figure 1.2 *IBM XT Keyboard and Template*
(Function Keys Highlighted)

1.2   Cancel

The first key to remember is F1 (Cancel). If you press a function key by mistake, or change your mind, do not press any key other than F1. If you

```
Print

     1 - Full Document
     2 - Page
     3 - Document on Disk
     4 - Control Printer
     5 - Type Through
     6 - View Document
     7 - Initialize Printer

Options

     S - Select Printer          Standard Printer
     B - Binding                 0"
     N - Number of Copies        1
     G - Graphics Quality        Medium
     T - Text Quality            High




Selection: 0
```

Figure 1.3 *Print Menu (Shift F7)*

do, you could start an operation you don't want. F1 (Cancel) simply negates all orders you've given to that point and returns you to the screen. No harm can come from using this key. When in doubt, use it and start your commands again.

1.3   Help

This feature assists you in remembering the many features available in WordPerfect without having to look them up. While in the typing area, press **F3 (Help)** which brings up the screen in Figure 1.4. If you want an explanation of a feature, such as **Bold, Tab Set, Search,** or **Page Numbering,** just enter the first letter of the feature. WordPerfect then produces an explanation of all the features that begin with that letter. If you enter **B,** for example, WordPerfect gives you what is shown in Figure 1.5. If you want an explanation of how a function key works, just press the key, such as **Alt F7** (see Figure 1.6).

You can also ask for Help for some other special keys: Esc, Del, Ins, Backspace, Tab, Home, Cursor, Arrows.

```
Help                                                    UP 4.9    03/09/88


      Press any letter to get an alphabetical list of features.

           The list will include the features that start with that letter,
           along with the name of the key where the feature is found.  You
           can then press that key to get a description of how the feature
           works.


      Press any function key to get information about the use of the key.

           Some keys may let you choose from a menu to get more information
           about various options.   Press HELP again to display the template.

      Press Enter or Space bar to exit Help.
```

Figure 1.4 *Help Screen (F3)*

```
Function Key    Feature                  Key Name

Shft-F1         Advance Up, Dn or Ln     Super/Subscript
Ctrl-F6         Align on Tabs            Tab Align
Shft-F8         Alignment Character (Set)   Line Format - 6
Ctrl-F3         Alt/Ctrl Key Mapping     Screen - 3
Ctrl-F3         Auto Rewrite             Screen - 5

Shft-F7         Binding Width            Print - 3 or 4 Select Options
Ctrl-F4         Block Append             Move - 3
Alt -F4         Block On/Off             Block
Alt -F8         Block Protect (Block On)    Page Format
     F6         Bold                     Bold
```

Figure 1.5 *Help for Features Beginning with B*
(F3, Select 1, Type B)

1.4   Getting Started

The procedures for starting depend on whether you are using Word-Perfect on a computer that has a hard (fixed) disk or one with floppy disk drives. Because the WordPerfect system requires eight floppy disks, it is

```
Math and Columns

     This defines math and text columns, turns math or columns mode on and off,
     or calculates the math operations already defined and entered.

     One of the following menus will appear on the status line:
with Math on:

     1 Math Off; 2 Calculate; 3 Column On/Off; 4 Column Def; 5 Column Display:
with Math off:

     1 Math On; 2 Math Def; 3 Column On/Off; 4 Column Def; 5 Column Display:


     Type one of the menu numbers for more help: 0
```

Figure 1.6 *Help for the Function Key for Math/Columns*
(F3, Select 2, Press Alt F7)

more convenient to run it from a hard disk. The following sections describe installation for both types of computers.

1.4.1 *Hardware Requirements*

WordPerfect 5.0 requires 512K of memory, runs under DOS versions 2.0 and higher, and has been written for IBM PC, XT, AT and compatibles, and IBM PS/2 series of personal computers.

1.4.2 *Installing WordPerfect On a Hard Disk*

There are two ways of installing WordPerfect on your hard disk drive: **Auto-Install** and **Disk Copy**. If you are using Word Perfect for the first time, you'll use the Auto-Install utility, which automatically creates a subdirectory, changes the buffers if necessary, and leads you through steps to copy the program files into your computer.

To begin Auto-Install, insert the **Learn** diskette into the **A** drive and by the A: type **INSTALL** Type

```
C>:A
```

```
A>:Install
```

When you tell it that you're ready to begin, WordPerfect instructs you to insert the diskette labeled **Wordperfect 1** into the **A** drive. When it has copied the system files, WordPerfect follows with instructions to insert the diskettes: **WordPerfect 2, PTR Program, Fonts/Graphics, Speller, Thesaurus** and **Learn**

Notice that the Auto-Install does not copy the 4 Printer diskettes. Because WordPerfect supports so many printers, the drivers would occupy too much space on the hard disk.

Before you will be able to print, you msut specify the printer you will be using. Section 5.1 will tell you how to do this, but for now you can continue working with the system.

If you already have some version of WordPerfect installed on your hard disk, you can copy the files from the six diskettes directly into the WorkPerfect directory with the DOS command:

```
C:copy A:*.* C: \WP
```

Be sure to store the original system disks in a warm, dry, dust-free place away from sunlight and any substance that might contaminate them. It's not a bad idea to make backup copies of the original program disks (see Section 1.4.4 if you need instructions for making backups.)

1.4.3   *Starting WordPerfect from Floppy Disks*

Of the eight floppy disks there are two that you'll use constantly, the ones labeled **WordPerfect 1** and **WordPerfect 2**. These contain the system files that run the programs. Whenever you start or exit the program, you'll use these disks. Disks that you'll use less frequently are the **Speller, Thesaurus,** and **Learn**. WordPerfect will tell you when to remove the system disk from the disk drive and insert one of these. Disks that you'll use infrequently are the two **Printer** disks and the **Font/Graphics** disk. In fact, once you specify your printer, you may not use the **Printer** disks again until you buy a different printer.

1.4.4 *Formatting Disks and Copying WordPerfect's Disks*

Don't be tempted to start WordPerfect on a floppy drive computer using the original disks. Although WordPerfect Corporation will replace damaged disks, you'll lose valuable time. Disks are vulnerable to magnetic environments, such as cigarette ashes, paper clip dispensers, and dust, as well as to moisture, sunlight, and bending.

Before you can copy on to a blank disk, you must first format it. The following process codes the disk with DOS' specifications:

1. With the DOS disk in drive **A:**, turn on your computer and wait for the **B:** to appear.

2. Insert a blank disk (or an old one which you can reformat) into the **B:** drive, then type:

   `B:FORMAT B:/s`

   and press **Enter**.

3. After this disk has been formatted, DOS will ask if you want to:

   `Format another (Y/N)?`

   Press **N** for No.

4. Even though you need to format seven more disks, you will not use the **/s** command, which is why you told DOS not to continue. Remove the formatted disk from the B: drive and label it **WordPerfect 1 Backup**. *Do not use a ball point pen to label your disks.* It might penetrate the cover and damage the disk. Use some type of soft tip pen or write on the label before you stick it to the disk.

5. Insert another blank disk into the B: drive and type:

   `B: FORMAT B:`

Press **Enter** and follow instructions. This time when the prompt appears:

`Format another (Y/N)?`

Select **Y**.

DOS will instruct you to remove the newly formatted disk and insert another blank disk. Repeat this process until you have formatted all your blank disks. You'll need more formatted disks than those required to back up WordPerfect; so format a few extras, which you'll use to store the work you create.

When you've formatted all your disks, select **N** for **Format another (Y/N)?** and DOS will return to the **B:** prompt.

1.4.5   *Copying the System Disks*

To copy the WordPerfect program disks, follow these steps.

1. Insert the disk labeled **WordPerfect 1** into the **A:** drive and the formatted disk which you labeled **WordPerfect 1 Backup** into drive **B:**.

2. Type **COPY A:*.* B:** and press **Enter**. The ***.*** tells DOS that you want to copy all the files found on the disk in drive **A:** to the disk located in drive **B:** When DOS has copied the files, it will tell you how many were copied.

3. Remove both disks, insert the disk **WordPerfect 2** into the **A:** drive and **WordPerfect 2 Backup** disk into the **B:** drive. Repeat the steps for each of the WordPerfect program disks. It doesn't matter what order you copy them in, but be sure to label the backup copies appropriately.

4. Store the original program disks in a warm, dry, dust-free environment. You will not be using them again unless something happens to your backup copies.

1.5   Starting the Program

If you are starting the program from a hard disk computer, type:

```
C: CD WP50
Enter
C\WP50 : WP
```

and press **Enter**

If you are starting the program from floppy disks, insert **WordPerfect 1 Backup** into the **A:** drive and type:

```
A:WP
```

Press **Enter**. WordPerfect will instruct you to then insert the second program disk, labeled **WordPerfect 2 Backup**, into drive **A:**. Press **Enter** again.

1.6 The Typing Area

As you'll see, WordPerfect takes you directly to a screen that is blank except for the bottom line (see Figure 1.7). The information in the lower right corner tells you which document you are working on (this is useful if you are using WordPerfect's dual document feature and are switching from one document to another), followed by the page, line, and cursor position numbers. Although the lower left corner is blank now, it serves as a message center. For example, press **Ins** and you'll see the word "Typeover";

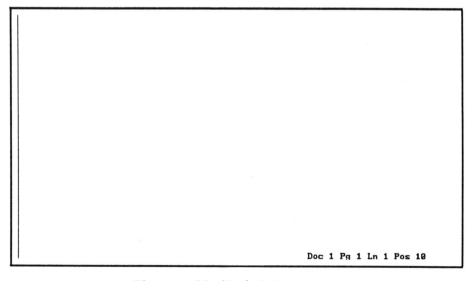

Doc 1 Pg 1 Ln 1 Pos 10

Figure 1.7 *WordPerfect's Typing Area*
(A:WP or C:WP, Enter)

press **Esc** and the message says "Repeat value = 8." Once you have created and **Saved** a document, the name of the document file will appear in the message center.

1.7   WordPerfect's Screen

WordPerfect attempts to create a screen that will look like the page when you print it. You can use the status line in the right corner to keep track of the length of your document. Since most computer monitors display 24 lines of text, a screen holds about half of a text page.

Take a minute to practice with the function keys. Press **Shift F7** to enter the Printer Control menu (see Figure 1.8).

Now press **F1** to **Cancel** the command and return to the typing area.

Press **Shift F6 (Center)**. Notice that the cursor has moved from the upper left corner to the center of the top line (see Figure 1.9). Type your name (see Figure 1.10.).

Using the **Backspace** key, erase your name. Notice that when you erase the last letter on the screen, WordPerfect asks if you want to delete the **Center** command as well (see Figure 1.11). Press **Y**. The cursor returns to the left margin.

```
Print

        1 - Full Document
        2 - Page
        3 - Document on Disk
        4 - Control Printer
        5 - Type Through
        6 - View Document
        7 - Initialize Printer

Options

        S - Select Printer          Standard Printer
        B - Binding                 0"
        N - Number of Copies        1
        G - Graphics Quality        Medium
        T - Text Quality            High




Selection: 0
```

Figure 1.8 *Printer Control Menu (Shift F7)*

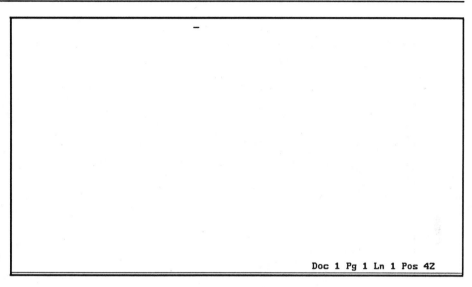

Doc 1 Pg 1 Ln 1 Pos 42

Figure 1.9 *Center Command (Shift F6)*

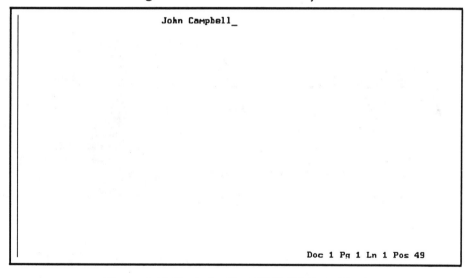

John Campbell_

Doc 1 Pg 1 Ln 1 Pos 49

Figure 1.10 *Centering Text (Shift F6, Enter Text)*

1.8 Entering Text and Moving the Cursor

Whenever you're ready, begin working. You can move through a blank document only by entering text, by scrolling across a line using the Space Bar, or moving down the page with the Enter key. Until you enter text or

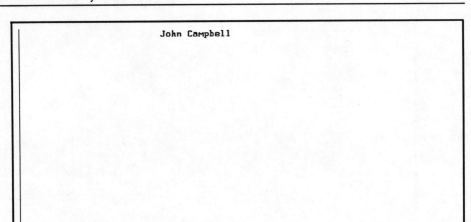

Figure 1.11 *Deleting the Center Command*
(Backspace to Erase All Text)

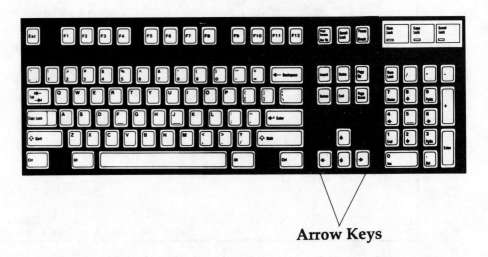

Arrow Keys

Figure 1.12 *IBM Keyboard Showing the Position*
of the Arrow Keys

spaces, the screen is a void you can't penetrate. Once you have entered
text, you move through it using the four Arrow keys (see Figure 1.12).

Look at the document in Figure 1.13. The cursor is positioned one space
beyond the last character entered (the period). If you press the **Down
Arrow** or the **Right Arrow** keys, nothing happens because there is no text

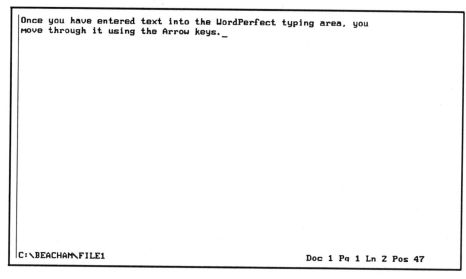

Figure 1.13 *Sample Document (File1)*

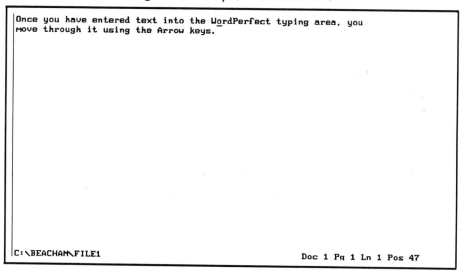

Figure 1.14 *Repositioned Cursor (File1, Up Arrow)*

or spaces in that area. However, the **Left Arrow** key causes the cursor to move one space to the left; if you press the **Up Arrow** key, the cursor moves to the same position on the line above (see Figure 1.14).

As you can imagine, once you have created a longer document, moving the cursor with the Arrow keys could be tedious, so WordPerfect offers faster ways to move the cursor. By pressing the Home key first, then the

```
Once you have entered text into the WordPerfect typing area, you
move through it using the Arrow keys.




























C:\BEACHAM\FILE1                              Doc 1 Pg 1 Ln 1 Pos 10
```

Figure 1.15 *Moving the Cursor to the Left Margin*
(Home, Left Arrow)

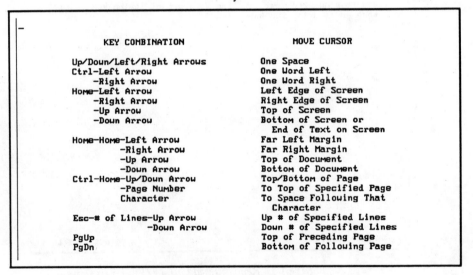

```
          KEY COMBINATION                 MOVE CURSOR

    Up/Down/Left/Right Arrows       One Space
    Ctrl-Left Arrow                 One Word Left
        -Right Arrow                One Word Right
    Home-Left Arrow                 Left Edge of Screen
        -Right Arrow                Right Edge of Screen
        -Up Arrow                   Top of Screen
        -Down Arrow                 Bottom of Screen or
                                       End of Text on Screen
    Home-Home-Left Arrow            Far Left Margin
            -Right Arrow            Far Right Margin
            -Up Arrow               Top of Document
            -Down Arrow             Bottom of Document
    Ctrl-Home-Up/Down Arrow         Top/Bottom of Page
        -Page Number                To Top of Specified Page
        Character                   To Space Following That
                                       Character
    Esc-# of Lines-Up Arrow         Up # of Specified Lines
                  -Down Arrow       Down # of Specified Lines
    PgUp                            Top of Preceding Page
    PgDn                            Bottom of Following Page
```

Figure 1.16 *Keys that Move the Cursor*

Arrow key, the cursor moves all the way to the left, right, top, or bottom of the screen. In our example document, we can move the cursor to the beginning of the line by pressing **Home** and **Left Arrow** (see Figure 1.15).

Figure 1.16 gives a summary of the different ways you can move the cursor. As you'll see, you can efficiently move the cursor one space, one word, to the beginning and end of lines, to the left, right, top, bottom of the screen, to another page, or to the top or bottom of the document.

1.9 Automatic Word Wrap and the Enter Key

WordPerfect recognizes when you've come to the end of the line and calculates if the next word is too long to fit the space. If it is, WordPerfect "wraps" around to the next line. WordPerfect is also preset not to hyphenate words, so depending on the typeface and type size of your printer, what you see on the screen may closely resemble how it will look when printed. Later sections will discuss how to turn on automatic hyphenation and how to alter the appearance of the ragged right edge.

Because of the automatic word wrap, you never use the Enter (Return) key to move to the next line unless you want to create a blank line. Use Enter only at the end of paragraphs. Press Enter twice if you want a blank line between paragraphs.

1.10 The Space Bar and Inserting Text

Unlike a typewriter, the Space Bar is not used to move the cursor across a line. The Arrow keys and the cursor movements listed in Figure 1.16 do that. The Space Bar inserts a blank space just as if it were a character. If you position the cursor on the p in "Space Bar" and hit the Space Bar, you get "S pace Bar."

Similarly, you can insert new text anywhere within existing text simply by positioning the cursor and typing. If you want to edit the sentence:

```
Now is the time for men to aid their party.
```

Position the cursor on the m in "men" and begin typing:

```
Now is the time for all good men to aid their party.
```

Now position the cursor on the a in "aid" and type

```
Now is the time for all good men to come to the aid of their
party.
```

1.11   Typing Over Existing Text

You can replace any character or string of characters with a feature called **typeover**. To use typeover, position the cursor on the first letter you want to replace and press **Ins**. The message center will say "**Typeover**." Begin typing and the existing text will be replaced. To turn off the typeover feature, press **Ins** again. The message center will return to normal.

1.12   Correcting Mistakes

The two keys used to correct smaller mistakes are **Del** and **Backspace**. If you've misspelled a word, for example, you would move the cursor to the incorrect character and press **Del** to remove it. Leaving the cursor in the same position, you type the correct letter.

1.12.1   *To Remove a Character from a Misspelled Word*

Position the cursor on the letter(s) to delete:

```
missppeled
```

Press **Del** to remove the character

```
misspeled
```

If you hold the Del key down, it will continue to erase all the characters to the right of the cursor until you release the key.

1.12.2   *To Add a Character*

Position the cursor:

```
mispeled
```

Type the letter:

```
misspelled
```

1.13 Backspace Key

The **Backspace** key is also used to erase both characters and words. Position the cursor one space beyond the character you want to erase and press **Backspace**.
Position the cursor:

```
misspell|ed
```

Press **Backspace**:

```
misspelled
```

To erase an entire word, or any portion of a word, position the cursor one space beyond the word and press **Ctrl-Backspace**.
Position the cursor:

```
misspelled
```

Press **Ctrl-Backspace**

```
spelled ("mis" has been erased)
```

If you hold the **Backspace** key down, it will delete one character after the next to the left of the cursor until you release pressure.

1.14 Deleting Lines and Portions of Lines

You can delete an entire line or a portion of a line with the keys **Ctrl-End**. Position the cursor on the first character of the line (or part of a line) you want to delete:

```
Now is the time for all good men to come to the aid of their
```

Press **Ctrl-End** to get:

```
Now is the time for
```

Note that you will erase all text to the end of the line. You cannot select a few words from the middle of the line using the Ctrl-End keys. Using the same procedure, you can delete a specified number of contiguous lines with just a few keystrokes. For example, if you want to delete a paragraph that is five lines long, position the cursor on the first character to be deleted and press **Esc**. The message center will say:

```
repeat value = 8
```

This "repeat" function can be used for several operations, but for now we want to delete five lines, so we enter the number 5. The prompt changes to:

```
repeat value = 5
```

Now press **Ctrl-End**. Rather than deleting one line as we did in the example above, WordPerfect deletes five lines. Actually, what happens is that it deletes one line five times.

1.15 Deleting Entire Pages and Portions of Pages

You can also use the **Ctrl** key to delete from the cursor's position to the end of the page. If you want to delete the entire page, position the cursor at the top left margin; otherwise position the cursor on the first character you want deleted. Then press **Ctrl-PgDn**. Because deleting a page is a pretty serious decision, WordPerfect asks:

```
Delete remainder of page (Y/N)?
```

If you press **Y**, all text from the position of the cursor to the end of the page will be deleted.

The **Ctrl-End** and **Ctrl-PgDn** keys are very useful and efficient, and you'll use them often. The only disadvantage to them is that you cannot cut text from the middle of lines, only from the cursor position to the end of the line or end of the page.

The **Cut, Copy,** and **Move** features require more keystrokes, but they overcome this obstacle. **Cut, Copy,** and **Move** are described in Section 2.3.

An important feature of WordPerfect's **Delete** function is that if you delete text and decide later that you want it, you can restore it through a feature called **Undelete**. See Section 2.4.1 for directions.

1.16 Clearing the Screen

If you have started a document and decide that you want to delete the entire document and start again, WordPerfect provides an easy way to do it. But remember, you are deleting the entire document, no matter how many pages, from the computer's memory. This procedure does not affect any of the files stored to disk, but it does eradicate forever the text on the screen.

To clear the computer's memory of your work, press **F7 (Exit)**. WordPerfect will ask:

```
Save Document (Y/N)?
```

Because you want to delete your work, answer **N**. Then WordPerfect will ask:

```
Exit WordPerfect (Y/N)?
```

Again the answer is **N**. WordPerfect will delete the current text and return you to an empty typing area. Remember, if you begin a procedure with **F7** (or any other function key) and you change your mind, the *only key you should press is* **F1**. The following is a keystroke summary to clear the screen:

F7
Save Document (Y/N)? **N**
Exit WordPerfect (Y/N) > **N**

1.17 Saving Your Work

If you're new to computers, there's an essential concept which you must respect: how information is stored. The computer has two kinds of data storage, external and internal. All of the files stored on a floppy disk or hard disk are in permanent storage and will not be changed unless you give specific instructions to do so. Data that resides on the screen is very fragile, subject to change and destruction. If a power failure occurs, everything on the screen will be lost; nothing on the disk will be affected. Therefore, it is essential that you frequently transfer the data on the screen to permanent storage on the disk. WordPerfect makes this easy to do in one of two ways.

1.17.1 *Manually Saving Your Work*

When you press the **F10 (Save Text)** function key, the message center in the lower left corner will prompt:

```
Document to be saved:
```

If this is the first time you have saved this document, you must enter a name for the file. File names can be from one to eight characters in length and may contain numbers, although they cannot begin with a number. They cannot contain spaces or special characters. Although in the beginning it might not seem important, you should give your files logical names which will help identify their content.

```
Document to be saved:B:Staffmem
```

WordPerfect Saves work to the default (preset) drive, which is the B: drive for floppy disk computers. If your computer is equipped with a hard disk, the message center will say:

```
Document to be saved:C:\WP\
```

Unless you want to use another drive, you need enter only the file name.
    When you have typed in the file name, press **Enter**. WordPerfect will begin "writing to disk." The message center will tell you that the file is being Saved, and you might see a red dot light up on your computer. When the message center changes again, it will give the name of the file which has been Saved as well as the disk drive location. The file name will remain in the message center permanently.

```
B:Staffmem or C:\WP\Staffmem
```

The keystroke summary for Saving a file for the first time is:

Format your disk (see Section 1.4.4) if you are using floppy disks
Press **F10**

Document to be saved: Type **Drive location, file name**
Press **Enter**

The message center will permanently show the file name.

1.17.2 *Saving a File the Second Time*

There is one important difference between Saving a file the first time and the second. The first time you Save it, there is no file by that name in storage and WordPerfect knows there is no danger in Saving it to disk. However, the second time you Save your work under the same file name, WordPerfect wants to make sure it is obeying your intentions as well as your command. What happens when you Save is that the version of your file that is stored on the disk will be *replaced* by the version on the screen. Normally, this is what you want to do because you have edited or expanded the old version. If you replace the old version with the new version, the old version is gone forever. WordPerfect adds a safeguard by asking if you want to replace the existing file.

Keystroke summary for saving a file the second time:

Press **F10**
Document to be saved:C:\WP\STAFFMEM appears in the message
   center
Press **Enter**
Replace C:\WP\STAFFMEM (Y/N)? appears in the message center
Press **Y** if you want to replace the existing file

1.17.3 *Saving an Existing File Under a New Name*

If you do not want to replace the existing file, you can easily Save the work on the screen under a different file name:

Press **F10**
Document to be Saved:C:\WP\STAFFMEM appears
Begin typing in a new file name. The name of the current file in the
   message center is replaced, which now reads:
Document to be saved:C:\WP\REV1MEM
Press **Enter**

1.17.4 Automatic Backup

Saving your file and creating emergency copies of it are so important that WordPerfect provides ways to perform backups automatically. See Section 3.1.2 for instructions.

1.18 Looking at Your Directory

Now that you have Saved a file to disk, the file name will appear in the directory. Just as an introduction to a feature you'll use frequently, press **F5 (List Files)**. The message center will suggest that you want to look at the default directory, either B: or C:. Press **Enter** and the directory will appear on the screen (see Figure 1.17). The information provided by this directory helps you manage your disk space and gives you a list of all the files contained on your disk. In addition to the file name, you can see the size of the file as well as the date and time it was created. The date is especially useful for keeping track of different revisions or continuing correspondence.

The List Files feature allows you to work with files in several ways (see Chapter 6), but for now the feature that interests you is **6-Look**. If you have forgotten the content of a file, you can see the first 24 lines to refresh your memory. To look at a file in storage:

```
03/16/88  11:43              Directory C:\WP5\*.*
Document size:         0    Free: 10633216   Used:   3185974      Files:  83

.  <CURRENT>       <DIR>                  .. <PARENT>        <DIR>
AND      .WPG      1466  02/06/88 07:17   APPLAUSE.WPG      1774  02/06/88 07:17
ARROW1   .WPG       342  02/06/88 07:17   ARROW2   .WPG      352  02/06/88 07:17
ARROW3   .WPG       340  02/06/88 07:17   ARROW4   .WPG      404  02/06/88 07:17
ARROW5   .WPG       698  02/06/88 07:17   AWARD    .WPG     1746  02/06/88 07:17
BADNEWS  .WPG      4167  02/06/88 07:17   BOMB     .WPG      950  02/06/88 07:17
BOOK     .WPG      1904  02/06/88 07:17   BORDER   .WPG    13662  02/06/88 07:17
CH1FIG3  .SCR      8128  03/16/88 09:36   CH1FIG4  .SCR     8128  03/16/88 09:37
CH2FIG1  .SCR      8128  03/15/88 12:44   CH2FIG2  .SCR     8128  03/15/88 12:53
CH2FIG3  .SCR      8128  03/15/88 12:57   CHARACTR.DOC     52559  02/24/88 15:38
CHECK    .WPG      1070  02/06/88 07:17   CLOCK    .WPG     6038  02/06/88 07:17
COMPASS  .WPG      2126  02/06/88 07:17   CONFID   .WPG     2242  02/06/88 07:17
EGA51Z   .FNT      7168  02/06/88 07:16   EGAITAL  .FNT     3584  02/06/88 07:16
EGASMC   .FNT      3584  02/06/88 07:16   EGAUND   .FNT     3584  02/06/88 07:16
FACTORY  .WPG       972  02/06/88 07:17   FATARROW.WPG       342  02/06/88 07:17
FC       .DOC      1906  02/06/88 07:17   FC       .EXE    23552  02/06/88 07:17
FEET     .WPG      1384  02/06/88 07:17   FLAG     .WPG      554  02/06/88 07:17
GAVEL    .WPG       912  02/06/88 07:16   GLOBE    .WPG     2542  02/06/88 07:16
GOODNEWS.WPG       4494  02/06/88 07:16   GRAB     .COM    12747  02/06/88 07:16

1 Retrieve; 2 Delete; 3 Rename; 4 Print; 5 Text In; 6 Look;
7 Change Directory; 8 Copy; 9 Word Search; N Name Search: 6
```

Figure 1.17 *Directory of Files (F5, Enter)*

Press **F5**
With the Arrow keys, move the cursor to the file you want to see
Press **Enter**
To Exit press **F7**

If you want to Retrieve the file, select item 1; if you want to return to the typing area, press **F1**.

1.19 Exiting WordPerfect

It is important that you Exit WordPerfect properly. First, WordPerfect assists in making certain you have Saved your work. Second, if you simply turn off your computer, you'll create "lost clusters" which may eventually cause you to run out of disk space. The proper way to Exit is to press **F7**. WordPerfect will ask:

```
Save Document (Y/N)?Yes
```

To Save your document, press **Enter**. To bypass Saving the document on the screen, press **N**. Now WordPerfect will ask:

```
Exit (Y/N)?N
```

Since you want to Exit the system, type **Y**. WordPerfect will shut itself off and return to the B: or C: in DOS.

If you Exit without using **F7** or if there is a power failure, the next time you use WordPerfect, it will ask:

```
System already in use?
```

Enter **N** for No, or **Y** for Yes if you are networked and someone else is online.

1.20 Retrieving Files from Disk

There are two ways to recall files from disk storage into memory. With an empty typing area on the screen, press **Shift F10**. The message center will ask:

```
Document to be retrieved:
```

If the file resides on the B: drive in a dual floppy drive computer, or the C: drive in a hard disk computer, you need only to enter the file name, such as:

```
Document to be retrieved:Staffmem
```

Press **Enter** and WordPerfect retrieves the file. If no file exists by that name, the message center tells you:

```
Error. File not found--
```

and gives you the incorrect file name you entered. Remember, file names must be entered exactly as they were saved. Upper- and lowercases make no difference, but the exact spelling is mandatory.

1.20.1 *Can't Remember File Name*

After creating several files, it will be difficult for you to remember their names, but by using **List Files (F5)** you can see all your file names and even look at the first 24 lines. See Section 1.18 for instructions.

CHAPTER 2

Working with Text

2.1 Blocking

Using the **Block** feature, you can designate the beginning and end of any amount of contiguous text. Once you have defined the "block," you can perform many operations with it, including:

Boldface
Cut and Copy
Moving
Saving
Printing
Holding Text Together

Blocking is one of the most useful features WordPerfect offers.

2.1.1 *How to Block*

You can start Blocking from any place in the text and can Block as little as one character or as many pages as you wish. Position the cursor on the first character or space you want to Block. Press **Alt-F4** or F12 on IBM-AT keyboards. The message center will advise **Block On**. Using any of WordPerfect's keys for moving the cursor (see Section 1.8), move the cursor **one character beyond** the last character or space where you want the

25

```
STAFF MEMO

Date: April 1, 1988

To: Senior Marketing Reps

From: Bob Williams

Re: Marketing to the Government

In January we submitted a proposal to the Department of Defense
to bundle our file security software with 50,000 units of Zenith
183 lap top computers. We have now received a reply from the
Office of Contracts stating that the Army and Navy must justify
their need for security software. It is very important that we
follow up on our proposal immediately.

Once source of justification can come from the end users
themselves, and I want you to contact all of your major accounts
during the next week to make certain they understand why file
security is particularly important for lap top computers which
are more vulnerable to loss and theft..


                                          Doc 1 Pg 1 Ln 13 Pos 13
```

Figure 2.1 *Blocked Text*
(Position Cursor, Alt-F4, Move Cursor)

Block to end. The text that is included in the Block is highlighted (see Figure 2.1). While the message **Block On** is still flashing, perform one of many operations. To **turn off** the Block feature, press **Alt-F4** again.

2.2   Blocking Features

Almost any operation you can perform with text can be performed on a portion of text that has been Blocked. Some of the important features are described in the next sections.

2.2.1   *Bold and Underline*

The function keys **F6** and **F8** allow you to Bold and Underline while you are entering text (see Section 2.2.2), but to make existing text Bold or Underlined, you'll use Block as follows:

Position the cursor and turn on **Block (Alt-F4)**
Define the Block using the **Arrow** keys
Press **F6 (Bold)**

As soon as you press F6, the text is made Bold and the Block command is released. The **Block On** prompt in the message center disappears.

If you want to perform another operation using the same text, you have to Block it again (see Figure 2.2). Notice that while the cursor is positioned in the Bold zone, the status line in the lower right corner has highlighted the Pos numbers.

To Underline existing text, use the same procedure:

Position the cursor and turn on **Block (Alt-F7)**
Define the Block
Press **F8 (Underline)**

You can Underline and Bold the *same* text using Block.

2.2.2 *Bold and Underline New Text*

As you are typing text and come to a word(s) you want to make Bold or Underline, press **F6 (Bold)** or **F8 (Underline)**. Continue typing your text. Notice that the Pos indicator in the status line has been highlighted. When you have typed the last character that you want to make Bold or Underline, press the function key again to turn it off. Notice how the status line changes again. WordPerfect has placed a Bold command marker [B][b] on either side of the Bold text. Everything within the [B][b] markers will be highlighted. (Italics are created with the Ctrl-F8 font key.)

```
STAFF MEMO

Date: April 1, 1988

To: Senior Marketing Reps

From: Bob Williams

Re: Marketing to the Government

In January we submitted a proposal to the Department of Defense
to bundle our file security software with 50,000 units of ████
████ lap top computers. We have now received a reply from the
Office of Contracts stating that the Army and Navy must justify
their need for security software. It is very important that we
follow up on our proposal immediately.

Once source of justification can come from the end users
themselves, and I want you to contact all of your major accounts
during the next week to make certain they understand why file
security is particularly important for lap top computers which
are more vulnerable to loss and theft..


C:\BEACHAM\FILE2                              Doc 1 Pg 1 Ln 13 Pos 13
```

Figure 2.2 *Completed Use of Bold Using Block*

You can move the cursor into the Bold zone and edit or expand the text. If, for example, you have made the following bold:

```
Jane  Monroe  will  meet  with  the  Navy  brass  in  Norfolk  and
Charleston.
```

You can add another city by positioning the cursor within the Bold zone and beginning typing. You do not need to tell WordPerfect to make it Bold:

```
Jane  Monroe  will  meet  with  the  Navy  brass  in  Norfolk,  Panama
City,  and  Charleston.
```

2.2.3   *Turning Off Bold or Underline*

You must delete the command markers in order to change Bold or Underline to normal type. See Section 3.2 for instructions.

2.2.4   *Changing to Upper- or Lowercase*

Position the cursor and turn on **Block (Alt-F7)**
Define the Block
Press **Shift-F3 (Switch)**
Select **1** for uppercase letters or **2** for lowercase letters

The Block function will automatically turn itself off.

2.2.5   *Cut, Copy, and Move (Cut and Paste)*

This is one of the features you'll use most often as you edit text. Using **Block**, you can Cut or Copy any amount of text and, if you wish, reposition the Cut or Copied text anywhere else in this document or in another file. The keystrokes to Cut and Copy are:

Position the cursor and turn on **Block (Alt-F7)**
Define the Block
Press **Ctrl-F4 (Move)**

The menu choices in Figure 2.3 appear along the bottom of the screen. Since we are dealing with a block of text, we'll select **1-Block** to bring up a second menu (see Figure 2.4).

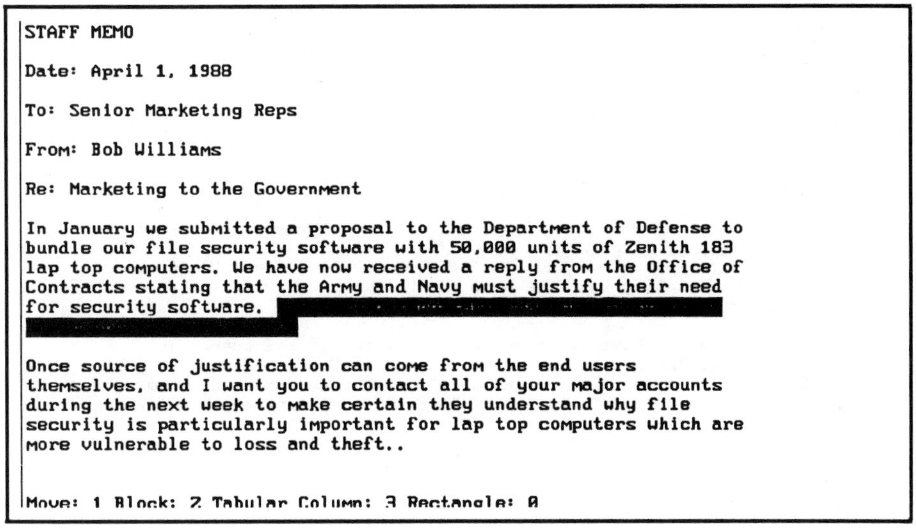

```
STAFF MEMO

Date: April 1, 1988

To: Senior Marketing Reps

From: Bob Williams

Re: Marketing to the Government

In January we submitted a proposal to the Department of Defense to
bundle our file security software with 50,000 units of Zenith 183
lap top computers. We have now received a reply from the Office of
Contracts stating that the Army and Navy must justify their need
for security software.

Once source of justification can come from the end users
themselves, and I want you to contact all of your major accounts
during the next week to make certain they understand why file
security is particularly important for lap top computers which are
more vulnerable to loss and theft..

Move: 1 Block: 2 Tabular Column: 3 Rectangle: 0
```

Figure 2.3 *Move Text Menu Items*
(Alt-4, Define Block, Ctrl-F4)

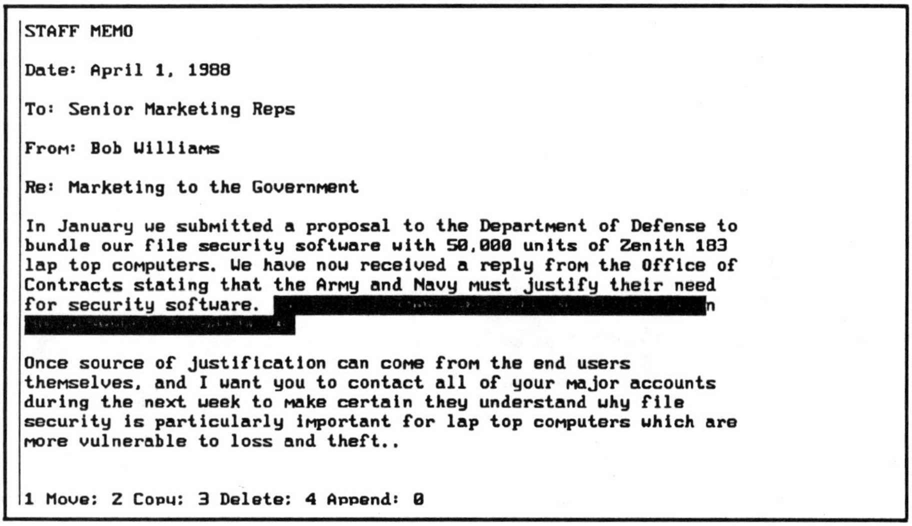

```
STAFF MEMO

Date: April 1, 1988

To: Senior Marketing Reps

From: Bob Williams

Re: Marketing to the Government

In January we submitted a proposal to the Department of Defense to
bundle our file security software with 50,000 units of Zenith 183
lap top computers. We have now received a reply from the Office of
Contracts stating that the Army and Navy must justify their need
for security software.                                           n

Once source of justification can come from the end users
themselves, and I want you to contact all of your major accounts
during the next week to make certain they understand why file
security is particularly important for lap top computers which are
more vulnerable to loss and theft..

1 Move: 2 Copy: 3 Delete: 4 Append: 0
```

Figure 2.4 *Staff Memo with Text Cut*

If we elect to Move text, WordPerfect Cuts the block and the message center tells us to position the cursor where we want the moved text to be placed (see Figure 2.5).

When we press **Enter** the text is restored. **Copying** text is the same procedure (see Figure 2.6).

```
STAFF MEMO

Date: April 1, 1988

To: Senior Marketing Reps

From: Bob Williams

Re: Marketing to the Government

In January we submitted a proposal to the Department of Defense to
bundle our file security software with 50,000 units of Zenith 183
lap top computers. We have now received a reply from the Office of
Contracts stating that the Army and Navy must justify their need
for security software. _

Once source of justification can come from the end users
themselves, and I want you to contact all of your major accounts
during the next week to make certain they understand why file
security is particularly important for lap top computers which are
more vulnerable to loss and theft..


Move cursor: press Enter to retrieve.              Doc 1 Pg 1 Ln 15 Pos 33
```

Figure 2.5 *Retrieve Text Menu Items (Ctrl-F4)*

```
STAFF MEMO

Date: April 1, 1988

To: Senior Marketing Reps

From: Bob Williams

Re: Marketing to the Government

In January we submitted a proposal to the Department of Defense
to bundle our file security software with 50,000 units of Zenith
183 lap top computers. We have now received a reply from the
Office of Contracts stating that the Army and Navy must justify
their need for security software.

Once source of justification can come from the end users
themselves, and I want you to contact all of your major accounts
during the next week to make certain they understand why file
security is particularly important for lap top computers which
are more vulnerable to loss and theft..

It is very important that we follow up on our proposal
immediately.
C:\BEACHAM\FILE3                                   Doc 1 Pg 1 Ln 1 Pos 10
```

Figure 2.6 *Staff Memo with Text Restored*
(Follow Figure 2.5, then Ctrl-F4, Item 5)

2.2.6   *Deleting and Restoring Text*

If you want to Cut text, either permanently or to restore it later on, select item **3-Delete** from the menu (see Figure 2.4). Section 2.4 explains this function.

2.2.7 *Saving Blocked Text with Cut and Paste*

Section 1.17 described how to Save a document. When you use the **F10** function key to **Save**, you Save the entire text, whether it is one sentence or 10 pages. There may be times when you want to extract a portion of your document and Save it as a different file. For example, in a long sales report, some portions might be suitable for circulation to certain departments and other sections to other departments. Using Block, you can easily create two files.

> Position the cursor and turn on **Block (Alt-F4)**
> Define the Block
> Press **F10 (Save Text)**

The message center will prompt:

`Block name:`

Type any new file name and press **Enter**. The Block is Saved and Word-Perfect returns to the typing area (see Figure 2.7).

Block Save can be a useful method for transferring text to another document or permanently Saving it for later use. Since a Saved Block resides on the disk as a separate file, you can insert it into any document whenever you wish.

2.2.8 *Block Print*

Using WordPerfect's standard Print features, you can Print only the entire document or specified pages (see Chapter 5). Using Block, you can print any portion of a page or from the middle of one page to the middle of the next. Follow these steps:

> Position the cursor and turn on **Block (Alt-F4)**
> Define the Block
> Press **Shift-F4 (Print)**

The message center will prompt: "Print block (Y/N)?No." Change the No to **Y** to print the Block (see Figure 2.8).

```
STAFF MEMO

Date: April 1, 1988

To: Senior Marketing Reps

From: Bob Williams

Re: Marketing to the Government

In January we submitted a proposal to the Department of Defense
to bundle our file security software with 50,000 units of Zenith
183 lap top computers. We have now received a reply from the
Office of Contracts stating that the Army and Navy must justify
their need for security software.

Once source of justification can come from the end users
themselves, and I want you to contact all of your major accounts
during the next week to make certain they understand why file
security is particularly important for lap top computers which
are more vulnerable to loss and theft..

It is very important that we follow up on our proposal
immediately.
```

Figure 2.7 *Saving a Block of Text*
(Alt-F4, Block Text, F10)

```
STAFF MEMO

Date: April 1, 1988

To: Senior Marketing Reps

From: Bob Williams

Re: Marketing to the Government

In January we submitted a proposal to the Department of Defense
to bundle our file security software with 50,000 units of Zenith
183 lap top computers. We have now received a reply from the
Office of Contracts stating that the Army and Navy must justify
their need for security software.

Once source of justification can come from the end users
themselves, and I want you to contact all of your major accounts
during the next week to make certain they understand why file
security is particularly important for lap top computers which
are more vulnerable to loss and theft..

It is very important that we follow up on our proposal
immediately.
```

Figure 2.8 *Printing a Block of Text*
(Alt-F4, Block Text, Shift-F7)

2.2.9   *Block Protect*

If you have lines of text that you want to appear together at all times, one method for assuring that they will never be broken up because of page formatting is with **Block Protect**. Formulas, tables, and quotations are just a few examples of text you don't want separated. To protect blocks:

Position the cursor and turn on **Block (Alt-F4)**
Define the Block
Press **Shift-F8 (Format)**
Select **Y**

You can alter or add as much text as you wish within the block and the entire block will still be glued together. For other methods of gluing text, see Conditional End of Page (Section 13.1.2), Hard Spaces (Section 13.1.4) and Widows/Orphans (Section 13.1.1).

2.3 Cut, Copy, or Move Sentences, Paragraphs, and Pages

Although Blocking is easy enough to do, WordPerfect has built in a kind of automatic blocking for Cutting or Copying sentences, paragraphs, and pages that is a joy to use. You can position the cursor anywhere in the sentence, the paragraph, or page that you want to Cut, Copy, or Move and WordPerfect knows where to block the beginning and ending characters:

Position the cursor in the sentence, paragraph, or page
Press **Ctrl-F4**
Select item **1-Sentence, 2-Paragraph, or 3-Page**
Select item **1-Cut, 2-Copy, or 3-Delete**

If you select **1-Sentence**, WordPerfect blocks the entire sentence in which the cursor resides. Selecting **2-Paragraph** blocks the full paragraph.

To restore this text to another part of the document (or to another file), position the cursor where you want to text to be brought in and press **Ctrl-F4** again. Select item **5-Text** (see Figure 2.9). The text will be restored within the existing text, which will be reformatted correctly to fit the space.

2.4 Delete and Undelete

Using the **Delete** function you can Cut or Move up to three blocks of text. When you Delete, the text is stored on a clipboard. You can restore that text to your document at anytime prior to exiting the program. The prin-

```
STAFF MEMO

Date: April 1, 1988

To: Senior Marketing Reps

From: Bob Williams

Re: Marketing to the Government

In January we submitted a proposal to the Department of Defense
to bundle our file security software with 50,000 units of Zenith
183 lap top computers. We have now received a reply from the
Office of Contracts stating that the Army and Navy must justify
their need for security software.

Once source of justification can come from the end users
themselves, and I want you to contact all of your major accounts
during the next week to make certain they understand why file
security is particularly important for lap top computers which
are more vulnerable to loss and theft..



Retrieve: 1 Block: 2 Tabular Column: 3 Rectangle: 0
```

Figure 2.9 *Menu to Retrieve Text*
(Position Cursor, Ctrl-F4)

cipal way to access the Delete menu is to block the text (**Alt-F4**), and select
1-Block. When you press **3-Delete,** the text is removed from the document and stored on the clipboard. There are, however, other keys that will delete text:

Ctrl-End	Delete to end of line
Esc-Ctrl-End	Delete specified number of lines
Ctrl-PgDn	Delete to end of page
Backspace	

Backspace Delete offers three options: word, word boundary, and block. To Delete a word, position the cursor one space beyond the last character. Press **Ctrl-Backspace.** To Delete a portion of a word, position the cursor anywhere in the word and press **Home-Backspace.** This deletes all the characters from the cursor to the beginning of the word; press **Home-Del** to erase from the cursor to the end of the word.

Deleting a Block can, of course, be accomplished with the steps outlined in Section 2.2.5, but a quicker method is to define the Block, then press **Backspace** (see Figures 2.10 and 2.11):

Position the cursor and turn on **Block (Alt-F4)**
Define the Block
Press **Backspace**
Delete Block (Y/N)?**Y**

Move key deletions are the easiest if you are Deleting a sentence, paragraph, or page rather than a Block. Position the cursor *anywhere* within the sentence, paragraph, or page and press **Ctrl-F4**. Select item **1-Sentence, 2-Paragraph**, or **3-page**. The message center will then prompt: "1-Cut, 2-Copy, 3-Delete." Select **3-Delete**. The text will be stored on the clipboard and you can Retrieve it anytime *until you turn off the computer or exit WordPerfect*. This text resides in the internal memory, not in permanent storage. If you think you might use the text another day, Save it to disk using the Block method described in Section 2.2.5.

2.4.1   *Undelete*

If you Delete text using any of the methods described in Section 2.4, you can Restore it by pressing **F1 (Cancel)**, which produces the menu shown in Figure 2.12.

The text that resides on the clipboard appears at the position of the cursor. If this is the text you want to Undelete, select **1-Restore** and the text

```
STAFF MEMO

Date: April 1, 1988

To: Senior Marketing Reps

From: Bob Williams

Re: Marketing to the Government

In January we submitted a proposal to the Department of Defense
to bundle our file security software with 50,000 units of Zenith
183 lap top computers. We have now received a reply from the
Office of Contracts stating that the Army and Navy must justify
their need for security software.

Once source of justification can come from the end users
themselves, and I want you to contact all of your major accounts
during the next week to make certain they understand why file
security is particularly important for lap top computers which
are more vulnerable to loss and theft..

It is very important that we follow up on our proposal
immediately.
```

Figure 2.10 *Deleting Blocks with the Backspace Key*
(Position Cursor, Alt-F4, Define Block, Backspace, Y)

```
STAFF MEMO

Date: April 1, 1988

To: Senior Marketing Reps

From: Bob Williams

Re: Marketing to the Government

In January we submitted a proposal to the Department of Defense
to bundle our file security software with 50,000 units of Zenith
183 lap top computers. We have now received a reply from the
Office of Contracts stating that the Army and Navy must justify
their need for security software.


It is very important that we follow up on our proposal
immediately.




C:\BEACHAM\FILE3                                    Doc 1 Pg 1 Ln 17 Pos 10
```

Figure 2.11 *Staff Memo with Text Deleted*

```
STAFF MEMO

Date: April 1, 1988

To: Senior Marketing Reps

From: Bob Williams

Re: Marketing to the Government

In January we submitted a proposal to the Department of Defense
to bundle our file security software with 50,000 units of Zenith
183 lap top computers. We have now received a reply from the
Office of Contracts stating that the Army and Navy must justify
their need for security software.

Once source of justification can come from the end users
themselves, and I want you to contact all of your major accounts
during the next week to make certain they understand why file
security is particularly important for lap top computers which
are more vulnerable to loss and theft..

It is very important that we follow up on our proposal
immediately.
Undelete: 1 Restore: 2 Previous Deletion: 0
```

Figure 2.12 *Undelete Text Menu*

will be inserted in your document at the position of the cursor. If there
are two or three deleted sections on the clipboard and you want to Restore one of them, select **2 Previous Deletion**. The text of the second deletion appears on the screen at the position of the cursor. Press **1** to Restore
it or press **2** again to see the third item on the clipboard. You can also use

the **Up and Down** Arrow keys to scroll through the three items of clipboard text.

WordPerfect knows the order of each item you placed on the clipboard. When you have filled the clipboard with three items, the fourth item will replace the first text you Deleted. However, before throwing that first text away, WordPerfect will ask if you want to store it for further use:

```
Delete without saving for Undelete?(Y/N) N
```

If you want to keep the first text, press **Enter** or **N** and WordPerfect stores the text. If you don't want to keep it, press **Y** and WordPerfect discards it for good.

2.5   Setting Margins

WordPerfect has preset the margins to leave 1 inch at the left and right margins. The left margin begins on space 11; the right margin ends at 75. You can change margins anywhere in the document, and you may enter as many different margin settings as you wish. Just as with Blocking, WordPerfect enters a margin code *at the position of the cursor* and maintains that margin until you enter another margin code.

For example, you are entering text using WordPerfect's default 1-inch margins. You come to a special portion of the document which requires 1.5-inch left and right margins. To accomplish this, you position the cursor at the left margin of the first line where you want the 1.5-inch text to begin. Set the margin (see Section 2.5.1). When you have ended the special text, position the cursor once again at the left margin, one line past the last line of the special text. Set the margin again. This places a second code marker that tells WordPerfect to return to 1-inch margins. (These steps can be accomplished automatically with macros. See Chapter 15.)

There are two settings — margin width and paper size — that control margins, and both are accessed through **Shift-F8 (Format)** (see Figure 2.13). When you set the margins using item **1-Line**, you enter the margins in inches. WordPerfect then measures that number of inches (see Section 16.1.5 for changing the unit of measurement to metric) from the left and right edges of your paper. As long as you do not change the paper size, you need enter only this setting. However, if your paper is a different width from the default of 8 1/2 inches, you must also tell WordPerfect the new paper width. This is accomplished with item **2-Page**.

```
Format

    1 - Line
                Hyphenation                  Line Spacing
                Justification                Margins Left/Right
                Line Height                  Tab Set
                Line Numbering               Widow/Orphan Protection

    2 - Page
                Center Page (top to bottom)  New Page Number
                Force Odd/Even Page          Page Number Position
                Headers and Footers          Paper Size/Type
                Margins Top/Bottom           Suppress

    3 - Document
                Display Pitch                Redline Method
                Initial Settings             Summary

    4 - Other
                Advance                      Overstrike
                Conditional End of Page      Printer Functions
                Decimal Characters           Underline Spaces/Tabs
                Language

Selection: 0
```

Figure 2.13 *Format Menu Selections (Shift-F8)*

2.5.1   *Setting Left and Right Margins*

Position the cursor at the left margin where you want the new margin to begin. If you want to change the margin for the entire document, the cursor is positioned at the top left margin of the document. Home-Home-Up Arrow will assure this location (see Figure 2.14).

Press **Shift-F8**
Select **1-Line**
Select **7-Left and Right**

The cursor will jump to the left margin setting. If you want to change it, enter a number. You may also enter decimals (but not fractions). If you don't want to change the left margin, press **Enter** or **Down Arrow** and the cursor jumps to the right margin setting. Type a number and press **Enter**. This returns you to the main menu. Press **Enter** again to return to the typing area with the new margins now set.

Following this same logic, if you want to set new margins for only one page, position the cursor at the top of that page and enter your settings. Then move to the top of the next page and enter the default settings. Remember, WordPerfect resets the margins from the code markers you enter. This is an important concept that you'll need for Deleting margin settings (see Section 3.2).

```
Format: Line

    1 - Hyphenation                        Off

    2 - Hyphenation Zone - Left            0.7"
                          Right            0.25"

    3 - Justification                      Yes

    4 - Line Height                        Auto

    5 - Line Numbering                     No

    6 - Line Spacing                       1

    ███████████████████████                ███

    8 - Tab Set                            0", every 0.5"

    9 - Widow/Orphan Protection            No


Selection: 0
```

Figure 2.14 *Line Format Menu*
(Shift-F8, 1-Line, 7-Margins)

2.5.2 Changing the Form Size

For legal documents, mailing labels, ledger paper, special stationery, and other nonstandard-sized paper, you must tell WordPerfect the dimensions. As with new margin settings, you are changing the specifications for *this document only*. WordPerfect files your specifications with the document when you store it to disk, and whenever you recall that document, the revised specifications are used; for other documents, the default settings remain intact. If you want to permanently change specifications, you must go to the Setup program (see Section 16.1.2). To change Form size, with the cursor positioned anywhere in the document:

Press **Shift F-8 (Format)**
Select **2-Page**
Select **3-Form**

These keystrokes bring up the choices shown in Figure 2.15.

If your document size is listed in items 1 through 9, enter the associated number. Otherwise, you can enter any size you wish by selecting O-Other ("o", not zero). When you press O, you'll be asked for Width, then Height. Enter any decimal value.

```
Format: Paper Size

    1 - Standard                  (8.5" x 11")

    2 - Standard Landscape        (11" x 8.5")

    3 - Legal                     (8.5" x 14")

    4 - Legal Landscape           (14" x 8.5")

    5 - Envelope                  (9.5" x 4")

    6 - Half Sheet                (5.5" x 8.5")

    7 - US Government             (8" x 11")

    8 - A4                        (210mm x 297mm)

    9 - A4 Landscape              (297mm x 210mm)

    0 - Other

Selection: 0
```

Figure 2.15 *Form Size Selection Menu*
(Shift-F8, 2-Page, 3-Form)

When you have made a selection from the Form Size menu, Word-Perfect will shift you to a Form Type menu. This does not pertain directly to specifying the form size, so bypass it by pressing **Enter** three times to return to the typing area (see Section 13.5, a discussion of Form Types).

2.5.3   *Setting Top and Bottom Margins*

The **Page Format** settings sheet (see Figure 2.16) is also the gateway for changing the top and bottom margins:

Press **Shift-F8**
Select **2-Page**
Select **5-Margins Top/Bottom**
Type desired margins
Press **Enter** twice

As with changing left and right margins, if the length of your paper is different from the 8.5- x 11-inch default, you must give WordPerfect the new dimensions (see Section 2.5.2).

```
Format: Page

    1 - Center Page (top to bottom)          No

    2 - Force Odd/Even Page

    3 - Headers

    4 - Footers

    5 - Margins - Top                        1"
                  Bottom                     1"

    6 - New Page Number                      1
          (example: 3 or iii)

    7 - Page Numbering                       No page numbering

    8 - Paper Size                           *8.5" x 3.42"
                  Type                       *Standard
                                             (*requested form is unavailable)
    9 - Suppress (this page only)

Selection: 0
```

Figure 2.16 *Page Format Menu*
(Shift-F8, 2-Page, 5-Margins)

2.6 Setting Tabs

As with left and right margins, you can change tab settings anywhere in the document. WordPerfect respects the new setting until you change it again. You can change one tab at a time and place tabs at any interval you want, or you can set all the tabs at the same time with evenly spaced intervals.

2.6.1 *Changing Tabs with Equal Intervals*

Press **Shift-F8**
Select **1-Line**
Select **8-Tab Set**

These keystrokes produce a tab ruler that shows the current tab settings (see Figure 2.17).

The first step is to clear the existing tab settings. To do this press **Home-Home-Left Arrow**, which moves the cursor to the far left margin. Then press **Ctrl-End**, which erases all tabs.

As you see, there are four types of tabs: left, center, right, and decimal. Using the **Arrow** keys, position the cursor at the location where you want

```
STAFF MEMO

Date: April 1, 1988

To: Senior Marketing Reps

From: Bob Williams

Re: Marketing to the Government

In January we submitted a proposal to the Department of Defense
to bundle our file security software with 50,000 units of Zenith
183 lap top computers. We have now received a reply from the
Office of Contracts stating that the Army and Navy must justify
their need for security software. It is very important that we
follow up on our proposal immediately.

Once source of justification can come from the end users
themselves, and I want you to contact all of your major accounts
during the next week to make certain they understand why file
L....L.....L....L....L....L....L....L....L....L....L....L....L....
T        ^        |        ^        |        ^        |        ^        |        ^        |        ^
1"        2"        3"        4"        5"        6"        7"
Delete EOL (clear tabs); Enter Number (set tab); Del (clear tab);
Left; Center; Right; Decimal; .= Dot Leader
```

Figure 2.17 *Tab Ruler (Shift-F8, 1-Line, 8-Tab Set)*

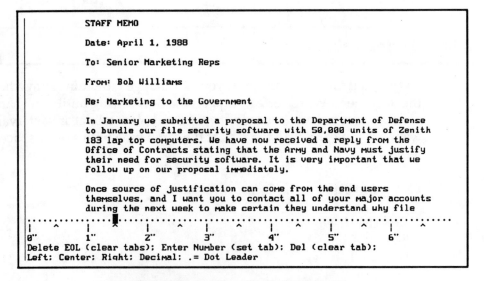

```
        STAFF MEMO

        Date: April 1, 1988

        To: Senior Marketing Reps

        From: Bob Williams

        Re: Marketing to the Government

        In January we submitted a proposal to the Department of Defense
        to bundle our file security software with 50,000 units of Zenith
        183 lap top computers. We have now received a reply from the
        Office of Contracts stating that the Army and Navy must justify
        their need for security software. It is very important that we
        follow up on our proposal immediately.

        Once source of justification can come from the end users
        themselves, and I want you to contact all of your major accounts
        during the next week to make certain they understand why file
...............................................................
|        ^        |        ^        |        ^        |        ^        |        ^        |        ^
0"        1"        2"        3"        4"        5"        6"
Delete EOL (clear tabs); Enter Number (set tab); Del (clear tab);
Left; Center; Right; Decimal; .= Dot Leader
```

Figure 2.18 *Entering the First Tab Position*
(Shift-F8, 1-Line, 8-Tab Set, Home-Home-Left Arrow,
Ctrl-End, Position Cursor, Enter Tab Type)

the first tab to appear. Type the first letter of the tab type, such as **L** for **left**. WordPerfect enters an L at that position (see Figure 2.18).

If you wanted to set only one tab or a few random tabs, you would use this manual method for placing tabs on the ruler. Then press **F7 (Exit)** to record the new tab settings. To generate multiple tabs with equal intervals requires one more step.

The ruler also shows corresponding inches to tab positions. To set multiple tabs, you must first enter the numerical position of your first tab. In our example, we have positioned the first tab at 1.5 on the ruler; so type in 1.5 followed by a comma (**1.5,**) (see Figure 2.19).

Now type the distance in inches between tabs, such as **1.5,1** where 1.5 is the position of the first tab and 1 inch is distance between them (see Figure 2.20). Press **F7** to record your new tab settings. Then press **Enter** twice to return to the typing area. At any time while setting tabs, you can cancel your order by pressing **F1**.

2.6.2 *Setting Tabs with Unequal Intervals*

Bring up the tab ruler:

> Press **Shift-F8**
> Select **1-Line**
> Select **8-Tab Set**

You can clear all existing tabs by pressing **Home-Home-Left Arrow**, then **Ctrl-End**, or you can eliminate tabs individually with the **Del** key.

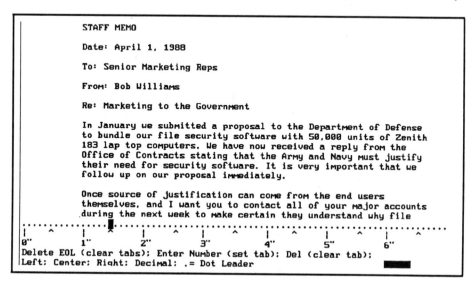

Figure 2.19 *Entering the Numerical Position*
(Same as Figure 2.18 with the Number Entered)

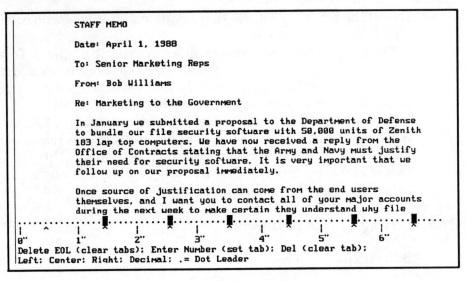

Figure 2.20 *Tabs Set to Intervals of 1 Inch*

Using the **Arrow** keys, move to the tab you want to delete and press **Del**. To insert a tab, position the cursor along the tab ruler and enter the first letter of the kind of tab you want: L(eft), R(ight), C(enter), D(ecimal). You may set up to 40 tabs on a line, and you can mix the types of tabs (see Figure 2.21).

2.7 Centering Text

You can center text as you enter it or you can center existing text. When you enter a **Center** command, WordPerfect places a code equally between the margins. You can center within columns as well as in a standard text document.

To center new text, position the cursor at the left margin and press **Shift-F6 (Center)**. The cursor jumps to the middle. As you enter text, it will be centered on either side of the code marker.

You can place the center code marker anywhere, not just equally between the margins. If the cursor is not at the left margin when you evoke the center command, the marker will be placed at the position of the cursor, so you can place a center code anywhere you wish.

```
        STAFF MEMO

        Date: April 1, 1988

        To: Senior Marketing Reps

        From: Bob Williams

        Re: Marketing to the Government

        In January we submitted a proposal to the Department of Defense
        to bundle our file security software with 50,000 units of Zenith
        183 lap top computers. We have now received a reply from the
        Office of Contracts stating that the Army and Navy must justify
        their need for security software. It is very important that we
        follow up on our proposal immediately.

        Once source of justification can come from the end users
        themselves, and I want you to contact all of your major accounts
        during the next week to make certain they understand why file
 · · · · · · · · · · · · · · · ■ · · · · · · · · · · · · ■ · · · · · · · · · · · · ■ · · · · · · · · · ·
 |         ^         |         ^         |         ^         |         ^         |         ^         |         ^
 |0"         1"         2"         3"         4"         5"         6"
Delete EOL (clear tabs); Enter Number (set tab); Del (clear tab);
Left: Center: Right: Decimal: .= Dot Leader
```

Figure 2.21 *Tabs Set at Irregular Intervals*

2.7.1   Centering Existing Text

You can center one line of existing text by positioning the cursor at the left margin, pressing **Shift-F6** and the **Down Arrow** key, which reformats the text.

To center more than one line of existing text, use the **Block** feature:

Position the cursor and turn on **Block (Alt-F4)**
Define the Block
Press **Shift-F6 (Center)**
Change the N to Y to the prompt [Ctr]Y/N?Y
Press **Down Arrow**

2.7.2   Deleting Center Codes

Because of its position on the function keyboard, it is too easy to mistaken-ly enter center marker codes. **Bold (F6)** and **Print (Shift-F7)** are frequent-ly used keys that can easily be misentered as **center**. When you mistakenly enter a center code, strange things can happen to your text, including its disappearance from the screen. To remove center codes, whether they are there by mistake or you just want to reformat your text, refer to Section 3.2 for directions.

2.8   Flush Right Text

Setting text flush to the right margin is the same procedure as centering it. For new text, position the cursor at the left margin, press **Alt-F6**, and begin typing. Text is entered from right to left.
To set one line of existing text flush right:

Position the cursor at the left margin
Press **Alt-F6**
Press **Down Arrow** to reformat the text

To set more than one line of existing text flush right, use the **Block** feature:

Position the cursor and turn on **Block (Alt-F4)**
Define the Block
Press **Alt-F6 (Flush Right)**
Change the N to Y to the prompt [Flsr]Y/N?Y
Press **Down Arrow**

2.9   Automatic Indent

You can easily indent all the lines of a body of text with the **F4 (Indent)** function key. Position the cursor at the left margin and press **F4**. Any text that you enter will be positioned one tab stop in from the left margin. If you press **F4** twice, text will be entered two tab stops in. The automatic word wrap feature will honor the indent command until you press **Enter** to turn it off.
Existing text can also be reformatted with the Indent key:

Position the cursor and turn on **Block (Alt-F4)**
Define the Block
Press **F4 (Indent)** one or more times
Change the N to Y to the prompt (Indent)Y?Y
Press **Down Arrow** to reformat text

If you want both the left and right margins to be equally indented, follow the same procedure, but use **Shift-F4 (Double Indent)** instead of F4.

2.10 Line Spacing

You can change the amount of space between lines at any point in the document; this means that you can single-space one portion and double-space or triple-space others. WordPerfect uses the height of the current line to determine the actual space between lines on the printed copy.

To change line spacing, position the cursor on the line where you want the spacing to change, then press **Shift-F8 (Format)** to produce the menu (see Figure 2.22). Select item **1-Line**, which produces the menu in Figure 2.23. Select item **6-Line Spacing**.

You may enter any number and decimal, such as 1.5 or 2.2. Press **F7(Exit)** to record the change. If you want to change the space later in the document, follow the same procedure.

2.11 Justification

Setting the Justification is performed from the same Format Menu (see Figure 2.22). WordPerfect is preset to print a document with the lines justified on the right margin. If you want to make your document look less formal, you might want to create a "ragged" right edge. Select item **1-Line** from the Format menu (**Shift-F8**), then item **3-Justification** from the Line

```
Format

    1 - Line
               Hyphenation                Line Spacing
               Justification              Margins Left/Right
               Line Height                Tab Set
               Line Numbering             Widow/Orphan Protection

    2 - Page
               Center Page (top to bottom)   New Page Number
               Force Odd/Even Page           Page Number Position
               Headers and Footers           Paper Size/Type
               Margins Top/Bottom            Suppress

    3 - Document
               Display Pitch              Redline Method
               Initial Settings           Summary

    4 - Other
               Advance                    Overstrike
               Conditional End of Page    Printer Functions
               Decimal Characters         Underline Spaces/Tabs
               Language

Selection: 0
```

Figure 2.22 *Format Menu (Shift-F8)*

```
Format: Line

     1 - Hyphenation                            Off

     2 - Hyphenation Zone - Left                10%
                            Right               4%

     3 - Justification                          Yes

     4 - Line Height                            Auto

     5 - Line Numbering                         No

     6 - Line Spacing                           1

     7 - Margins - Left                         1"
                   Right                        1"

     8 - Tab Set                                0", every 0.5"

     9 - Widow/Orphan Protection                No


Selection: 0
```

Figure 2.23 *Line Format Menu (Shift-F8, 1-Line)*

Format menu. Change the Yes to **N** to turn off justification. Press **Enter** twice to return to the typing area. The keystrokes to turn off right justification are:

> Press **Shift-F8**
> Select **1-Line**
> Select **3-Justification**
> Change No to **Y**
> Press **Enter** twice

Note: When you turn off Justification, it is for the entire document. Therefore, it doesn't matter where the cursor is positioned when you bring up the menu.

2.12 Page Numbering

Page numbering is also selected from the Format Menu (Shift-F8) (see Figure 2.22). WordPerfect is preset not to number pages. To turn page numbering on:

> Press **Shift-F8**
> Select **2-Page**

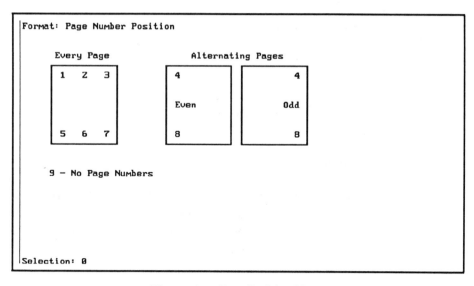

```
Format: Page

    1 - Center Page (top to bottom)        No

    2 - Force Odd/Even Page

    3 - Headers

    4 - Footers

    5 - Margins - Top                      1"
                  Bottom                   1"

    6 - New Page Number                    1
        (example: 3 or iii)

    7 - Page Numbering                     No page numbering

    8 - Paper Size                         *8.5" x 3.42"
        Type                               *Standard
                                           (*requested form is unavailable)
    9 - Suppress (this page only)

Selection: 0
```

Figure 2.24 *Page Format Menu (Shift-F8, 2-Page)*

```
Format: Page Number Position

    Every Page                Alternating Pages

    ┌───────────┐       ┌───────────┐ ┌───────────┐
    │ 1   2   3 │       │ 4         │ │         4 │
    │           │       │           │ │           │
    │           │       │ Even      │ │       Odd │
    │           │       │           │ │           │
    │ 5   6   7 │       │ 8         │ │         8 │
    └───────────┘       └───────────┘ └───────────┘

    9 - No Page Numbers




Selection: 0
```

Figure 2.25 *Page Position Menu*
(Shift-F8, 2-Page, 7-Page Number Position)

This produces the Page Format menu (see Figure 2.24). Select **7-Page
Numbering**. This produces the Page Position menu (see Figure 2.25).

As you can see, WordPerfect permits you to place page numbers in a
variety of positions. Enter the number corresponding to the position you

wish. Press **Exit (F7)** to return to the typing area. The summary of keystrokes to number pages is:

> Press **Shift-F8**
> Select **2-Page**
> Select **7-Page number position**
> Enter **Corresponding number**
> Press **Exit (F7)**

2.12.1 *Page Numbers Not Beginning with 1*

There may be times when you want to begin numbering your pages with a number other than 1. *Position the cursor anywhere on the page where the new numbering system is to begin.*Then:

> Press **Shift-F8**
> Select **2-Page**
> Select **6-New page number**
> Enter **New page number**
> Press **Exit (F7)**

The new number is displayed on the status line of the typing area.

2.12.2 *Changing Arabic Numbers to Roman*

For the front and end matter of longer documents, you might want to use Roman numerals instead of the default Arabic numbers. Move the cursor to the first page of the introduction and follow the steps outlined above. When you enter the new page number, type it as a lowercase *i* or an uppercase *I*. WordPerfect will now produce consecutive numbering in Roman numerals. Then move the cursor to the first page of the document body and start the new page numbering with the Arabic number 1.

CHAPTER 3

Backing Up Files, Correcting Mistakes, and Using the Thesaurus

3.1 Backing Up Files

WordPerfect provides several methods for backing up files. If you're a new computer user, heed all of the warnings and horror stories people tell about losing weeks of work because they did not take the time to duplicate their files. You want to protect yourself from power failure by Saving your work frequently, which WordPerfect helps you do with an automatic backup feature. And you want to protect your files on disk against disk damage. Most power failures do not occur because of lightening or brown outs but because of human mistakes, such as kicking the power cord loose. Files stored on a hard disk are often lost when the disk wears out or the computer is stolen. Files stored on floppy disks are particularly vulnerable because floppy disks themselves are fragile. Any kind of bend, coffee stains, cigarete ashes, or magnetic force can annihilate the data. All important files should be copied and stored in a separate place.

3.1.1   *Copying Files from a Hard Disk*

If your computer is equipped with a hard disk, you should make a back-up copy of important files on a floppy disk. There are two easy ways to do this:

1. When you have finished working on a document, Save it once to the hard disk in the usual way (F10). Then Save the same document to a floppy on the A: drive. When the message center prompts:

    ```
    Document to be saved:C:\WP\STAFFMEM
    ```

    just enter

    ```
    Document to be saved: A:staffmem
    ```

    Press **Enter** to Save the file on the floppy disk

2. Copy the file through DOS. At the C:, with a floppy disk in the A: drive, type:

    ```
    C:copy c:\wp\staffmem a:
    ```

    This tells DOS to copy a file named STAFFMEM, located in the WP directory onto the floppy disk in drive A:.

3.1.2   *Saving Your Work with Timed Document Backup*

You can set WordPerfect to protect your data automatically against power failure by Saving text to a temporary file at timed intervals. You set the number of minutes. Then, every 15 (or whatever you set) minutes WordPerfect interrupts you to Save the document. To turn on this automatic Save feature, go to the Setup menu (see Figures 3.1 and 3.2):

> Press **Shift-F1 (Setup)**
> Select **2-Backup**
> Select **1-Timed Document Backup**
> Change No to **Y**
> Enter the number of minutes between Saving
> Press **Enter** three times

```
Setup

     1 - Backup

     2 - Cursor Speed                    30 cps

     3 - Display

     4 - Fast Save (unformatted)         Yes

     5 - Initial Settings

     6 - Keyboard Layout

     7 - Location of Files

     8 - Units of Measure




Selection: 0
```

Figure 3.1 *Setup Menu (Shift-F1)*

```
Setup: Backup

     Timed backup files are deleted when you exit WP normally.  If you
     have a power or machine failure, you will find the backup file in the
     backup directory indicated in Setup: Location of Files.

        Backup Directory

     1 - Timed Document Backup            No
         Minutes Between Backups          30

     Original backup will save the original document with a .BK! extension
     whenever you replace it during a Save or Exit.

     2 - Original Document Backup         No




Selection: 0
```

Figure 3.2 *Timed Document Menu*
(Shift-F1, 1-Backup)

When WordPerfect Saves text through the **Timed Document** feature, it stores the text in a special file on the disk. It does not replace your original file. Before Exiting WordPerfect you *MUST Save your work* using the F-10 (Save Text) key. When you Exit WordPerfect properly, the temporary file is destroyed.

In the case of a power failure or software failure, however, all the work that was Saved in the temporary file is preserved. Using **List Files (F5)**, you can find your document under the file name {WP}Back.1 or {WP}Back.2. You then rename this file (see Section 6.1.4) and Retrieve it. It will contain all the text through the last time the timer Saved it.

3.1.3 *Original Document Backup*

Although you set this feature from the same menu (see Figure 3.2) as Timed Document, they should not be confused. They have nothing to do with each other.

When you save your work through the **F10 (Save Text)** key, you replace the file on disk with the revised text on the screen. Once you replace it, the file on disk can never be recovered. Sometimes this can cause a problem. WordPerfect's **Original Document Backup** keeps both files, the one on the disk as well as the revised file. Here's what happens each time you Save your document.

File Name	Backup File Name
Staffmem	Staffmem.BK
Staffmem1	Staffmem.BK
Staffmem2	Staffmem1.BK

As you can see, WordPerfect keeps the last *two* versions of any file. So, if you've made a drastic mistake and want to find valuable lost text, the backup file may have it.

To retrieve any file with a .BK extension, you must first Rename it through the List Files feature (see Section 6.1.4). The only disadvantage in turning on this backup feature is that it takes up double the space on your disk.

3.2 Reveal Codes and Deleting Code Markers

WordPerfect responds to your commands by embedding codes within the text. For example, when you tell WordPerfect to **Bold** a word, it places a Bold command marker on each side of the Bold zone, such as:

```
[B]Zenith 183[b]
```

This is a simple concept but an important one for serious WordPerfect users. Whenever something goes wrong with the way your document looks, it is usually because you've entered an improper code. You have to find the unwanted code marker and delete it.

WordPerfect makes it possible for you to see the embedded command code markers. When you press **Reveal Codes (Alt-F3 or F11 on IBM-AT keyboard),** the upper portion of the screen shows the text and the lower half shows the same text with the code markers (see Figure 3.3). Using the **Arrow** keys, begin moving the cursor. You'll see that the cursor passes across code markers just as it does text.

3.2.1 *Deleting Codes*

If you press the **Del** or **Backspace keys,** you will delete both text and codes. To delete the Bold attribute, move the Reveal Code cursor until it rests on either the [b] or [B] (see Figure 3.4). When you press **Del,** both code brackets are erased and the text returns to normal (see Figure 3.5).

3.2.2 *Working in the Reveal Codes Screen*

Reveal Codes does not switch you from the original document; it only shows you what is happening behind the scene. Therefore, you can con-

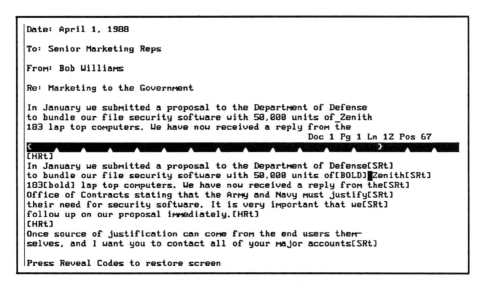

Figure 3.3 *Text with Reveal Codes Activated (Alt-F3)*

```
Date: April 1, 1988

To: Senior Marketing Reps

From: Bob Williams

Re: Marketing to the Government

In January we submitted a proposal to the Department of Defense
to bundle our file security software with 50,000 units of_Zenith
                                        Doc 1 Pg 1 Ln 12 Pos 67
{                                                              }
[HRt]
In January we submitted a proposal to the Department of Defense[SRt]
to bundle our file security software with 50,000 units of[BOLD] Zenith[SRt]
183[bold] lap top computers. We have now received a reply from the[SRt]
Office of Contracts stating that the Army and Navy must justify[SRt]
their need for security software. It is very important that we[SRt]
follow up on our proposal immediately.[HRt]
[HRt]
Once source of justification can come from the end users them-
selves, and I want you to contact all of your major accounts[SRt]

Press Reveal Codes to restore screen
```

Figure 3.4 *Cursor Position to Delete a Code*
(Alt-F4, Position Cursor)

```
Date: April 1, 1988

To: Senior Marketing Reps

From: Bob Williams

Re: Marketing to the Government

In January we submitted a proposal to the Department of Defense
to bundle our file security software with 50,000 units of Zenith
183_lap top computers. We have now received a reply from the
                                        Doc 1 Pg 1 Ln 13 Pos 13
{                                                              }
In January we submitted a proposal to the Department of Defense[SRt]
to bundle our file security software with 50,000 units of Zenith[SRt]
183 lap top computers. We have now received a reply from the[SRt]
Office of Contracts stating that the Army and Navy must justify[SRt]
their need for security software. It is very important that we[SRt]
follow up on our proposal immediately.[HRt]
[HRt]
Once source of justification can come from the end users them-
selves, and I want you to contact all of your major accounts[SRt]
during the next week to make certain they understand why file[SRt]

Press Reveal Codes to restore screen
```

Figure 3.5 *Deleted Codes*
(Alt-F4, Position Cursor, Del)

tinue to work on your document in any way you wish. You could, in fact,
work with **Reveal Codes** turned on all the time. The cursor in the **Reveal
Codes** screen corresponds to the cursor in the text screen, so you know
where you are at all times.

Occasionally, when a haywire command code is entered by mistake, text will disappear from the text screen and cannot be restored by **Rewrite Screen (Ctrl-F3)**. Usually this lost text will appear on the **Reveal Codes** screen and you can begin looking for the troublesome codes.

3.2.3 *Finding Troublesome Code Markers*

Turning on **Reveal Codes** is a start toward locating bad markers, but unless you know the cause of a formatting problem, you might not know where to look for the bad code or which one to look for, especially in long documents. For example, if you enter a Flush Right (Alt-F6) code by mistake, your text will align itself as shown in Figures 3.6, 3.7, and 3.8.

Looking at Figure 3.7, it is not immediately obvious that some of the original text has disappeared and you might not discover the error until you print the document. When you discover the error, you'll obviously begin looking for the unwanted code near the misaligned text. If you can't find it but know that the problem is being caused by a certain type of code, such as [Flsh Rt] in this example, you can use WordPerfect's **Search** function to find it.

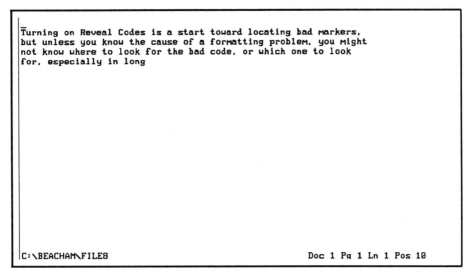

Figure 3.6 *Text Before the Wrong Marker was Inserted*

```
                 Turning on Reveal Codes is a start toward locating bad markers,
        cause of a formatting problem, you might not know where to look for the bad co
                 or which one to look for, especially in long documents. For
                 example, if you




C:\BEACHAM\FILE7                                           Doc 1 Pg 1 Ln 1 Pos 10
```

Figure 3.7 *Misaligned Text*

```
                 Turning on Reveal Codes is a start toward locating bad markers,
        cause of a formatting problem, you might not know where to look for the bad co
                 or which one to look for, especially in long documents. For
                 example, if you



C:\BEACHAM\FILE7                                           Doc 1 Pg 1 Ln 1 Pos 10
                   {
Turning on Reveal Codes is a start toward locating bad markers,[SRt]
but unless you know the        cause of a formatting problem, you might not kn
ow where to look for the bad code,
or which one to look for, especially in long documents. For[SRt]
example, if you



Press Reveal Codes to restore screen
```

Figure 3.8 *Misaligned Text Seen Through Reveal Codes*

3.3   Search

WordPerfect allows you to search for words, strings, and codes either forward or backward through the document, *beginning at the position of the cursor.* To begin a search, press either **F2 (forward Search)** or **Shift-F2 (backward Search).** The message center will prompt:

```
-->Srch:
```

The arrow indicates the direction of the search. You can use the **Up and Down Arrow** keys to change the direction. If you **press F2**, then **Up Arrow**, the prompt will show that the direction has been reversed.

```
<--Srch:
```

If you want to Search the entire document, it is best to begin at the top or bottom of the document. Press **Home-Home-Up Arrow** to move the cursor to the document's beginning.

Enter the word, string, or codes at the prompt. WordPerfect searches for the exact combination of letters, so if you tell it to search for:

```
-->Srch:sort
```

it will find "sorted," "sorting," and "resort" as well as "sort." If you want WordPerfect to search only for sort, leave a space on either side of the word.

```
<--Srch: _sort_
```

If you enter the search word in lowercase letters, WordPerfect will find both upper- and lowercase occurrence, but if you enter uppercase as the search word, WordPerfect finds only those uppercase occurrences.

Once you have entered the search word, press **F2** or **Esc** to begin the search. WordPerfect will stop on the first occurrence. To continue looking for other occurrences, press F2 again. The message center will indicate that WordPerfect is still looking for the same word. Press F2 a second time and the search continues. When WordPerfect has found the last occurrence or decides that there is no such word in your document, it will prompt:

```
String not found
```

When WordPerfect has finished searching, it positions the cursor at the last occurrence. If you want to return the cursor to its position before the search began, press **Ctrl-Home**. The message center prompt will say:

```
Go to
```

Press **Ctrl-Home** again and the cursor will return to its presearch position.

Normally, WordPerfect searches only through the document body. If you want to search the headers, footers, footnotes, and endnotes as well, press **Home** before you begin the search with **F2**. The extended search keystrokes are:

Press **Home**
Press **F2** or **Shift-F2**
Enter the search word
Press **F2** or **Esc**

3.4   Replace

You can search for any words, strings, or codes and replace them with others. Or you can search for them and simply delete them altogether. You can search and replace only *one* string at a time.

When you press **Alt-F2**, the message center asks:

```
w/Confirm (Y/N)?No
```

WordPerfect wants to know if you want it to stop at each occurrence or if it should replace all occurrences. If you want it to stop at each occurrence, which gives you the option of replacing the word or not, then change the No to **Y**.

A word of caution. Before you begin a **Replace** operation, be sure to Save your work. Sometimes WordPerfect finds occurrences you didn't expect and you want the option of being able to retrieve your original document and trying it again.

Once you have entered your w/Confirm choice, WordPerfect then asks what you want to search for.

```
-->Srch:
```

The same conditions apply here as for a simple **Search** (see Section 3.3 above). Enter your word, string, or code and press either **F2** or **Esc**. The prompt then asks:

```
Replace with:
```

There are several things you can do with Replace:

1. Replace one word with another word.

2. Replace a word with a string of words (or vice versa).

3. Replace codes.

4. Add codes, such as Bold, to words.

5. Delete words or codes.

Here are examples of each.

1. -->Srch:bear

    ```
    Replace with:bare
    ```

2. -->Srch:Dow

    ```
    Replace with:Dow Chemical Corporation
    ```

3. -->Srch:[Hrt]

    ```
    Replace with:[Hrt][Hrt]
    ```

4. -->Srch:House and Garden

    ```
    Replace with:House and Garden
    ```

5. -->Srch:[Ctr]

    ```
    Replace with:
    ```

To delete a word or code, as in example 5, enter the word or code to be deleted, then press **F2** or **Esc**.

3.4.1   Block Search and Replace

If you do not want to search the entire document or if there is only a section that requires a replacement, you can **Block** the section you want to search. The keystrokes for **Block Searches** are:

Press **Alt-F4**
Block text
Press **Alt-F2**
Enter word/string to be replaced
Press **F2**
Enter replacement word/string
Press **F2**

3.5   Thesaurus

You can use the Thesaurus in conjunction with a document or by itself. As with a dictionary, it breaks words into their parts of speech (e.g., verbs, nouns, adjectives) and also provides antonyms. The Thesaurus does not give definitions of words. Therefore, the Thesaurus is useful for jogging your memory but is not a substitute for a dictionary.

3.5.1   Using the Thesaurus

If your computer is equipped with a hard disk and you have installed all the WordPerfect disks on it, you need only press the **Alt-F6 (Thesaurus)** key to start this feature. If you are running WordPerfect from floppy disks, remove the WordPerfect system disk from drive A: and insert your backup disk labeled **Thesaurus Backup**.

3.5.2   Looking Up Words Not in the Document

You can start the Thesaurus from a blank screen or from anywhere within a document. If the cursor is positioned on a word, WordPerfect assumes you want to research that word. If the cursor is on a blank space, Word-Perfect asks you what word you want to look up. When you press **Alt-F1** from a blank space, the screen in Figure 3.9 appears. Notice that the top four lines are reserved to display your document. The message center asks for the Word: you want to look up. Type it in (see Figure 3.10). Press **Enter** (see Figure 3.11).

Figure 3.9 *Thesaurus Screen (Alt-F1)*

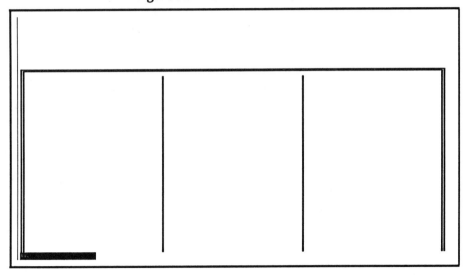

Figure 3.10 *Entering a Word to Look Up*
(Alt-F1, Type in Word)

Let's examine the results to better understand how the Thesaurus thinks. First, you should note that the Thesaurus is very literal. If you misspell the word when you type it in, the Thesaurus cannot find it. There is no "guess" feature as there is in the Speller. Second, "argument" is a noun; "argue" is the verb. We asked for the noun and that's what we got.

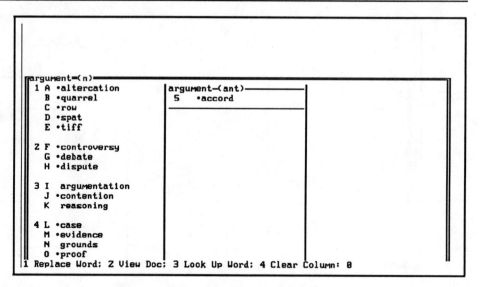

Figure 3.11 *Researching the Word "Argument"*
(Alt-F1, Type in Word, Enter)

If we had asked for a word that functions as both a noun and verb, such as "research," the Thesaurus would list both. Third, for the word "argument" the Thesaurus has produced five categories of words: the first four categories give words with similar definitions and the fifth category gives opposites. The first four categories represent subtle but important differences in the uses of the word "argument:" (1) disagreement on a personal basis, (2) nonpersonal disagreement, (3) logical or reasoned disagreement, (4) legal argument. The preferred word in each category is listed first.

Many of the words have bullets beside them, which indicate that they have their own synonyms. To look at those, press the corresponding alphabet letter. To cross-reference "altercation" press **A**. To look at "controversy" press **F** (see Figure 3.12). Notice that the corresponding alphabetical characters have switched to column 2. Using the **Arrow** keys, you can toggle these characters from one column to another. Looking up "controversy" we get what is shown in Figure 3.13.

3.5.3. *Looking Up Words Contained in Your Document*

When the cursor is positioned on any character within a word and you select **Alt-F1 (Thesaurus)**, that is the word that WordPerfect searches for alternative choices. In Figure 3.14 the cursor is positioned on "examine."

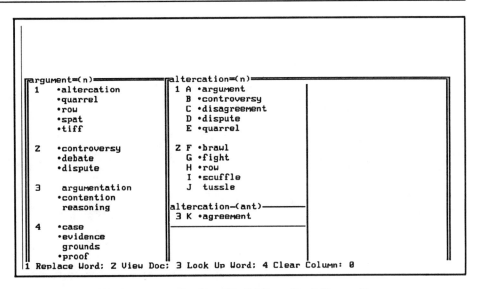

Figure 3.12 *Looking Up "Altercation" (Press A)*

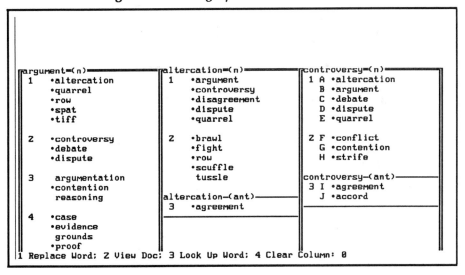

Figure 3.13 *Looking Up "Controversy"*
(Left Arrow, F)

Press **Alt-F1** and the Thesaurus produces the choices shown in Figure 3.15.

Notice that the Thesaurus produces only "examine" in its verb form and does not indicate that "examination" is the noun form. The Thesaurus believes there are two general categories of the way "examine" is used.

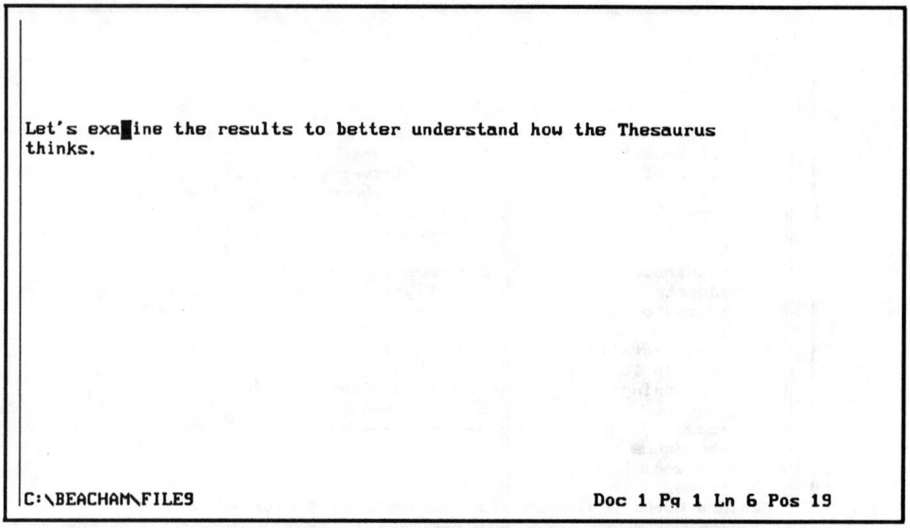

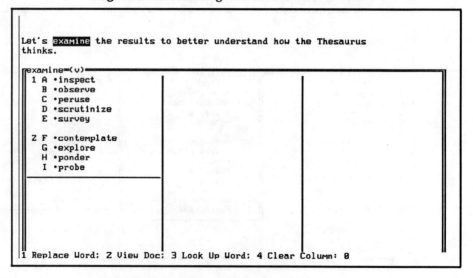

Figure 3.14 *Positioning the Cursor to Use Thesaurus*

Figure 3.15 *Thesaurus Choices for "Examine"*
(Alt-F1)

The first use is to "look at" something, such as "Let's examine this tissue under the microscope." The second use is to "think about" something, as in "We will examine his idea and give you an answer tomorrow."

If you want to look at alternative definitions for any of the words that have bullets beside them, enter the corresponding alphabetical letter.

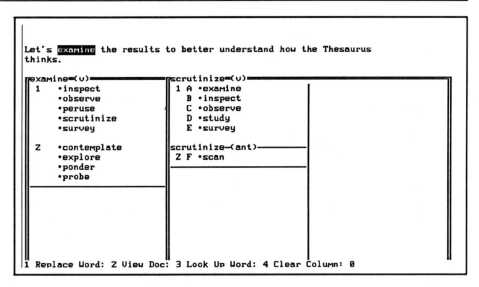

```
Let's examine the results to better understand how the Thesaurus
thinks.

examine=(v)                  scrutinize=(v)
  1    •inspect                1 A •examine
       •observe                  B •inspect
       •peruse                   C •observe
       •scrutinize               D •study
       •survey                   E •survey

  Z    •contemplate          scrutinize-(ant)
       •explore                Z F •scan
       •ponder
       •probe




1 Replace Word: Z View Doc: 3 Look Up Word: 4 Clear Column: 0
```

Figure 3.16 *Looking Up "Scrutinize"*
(File9, Alt-F1, D)

Selecting **D** for **scrutinize**, WordPerfect presents us with the word's choices shown in Figure 3.16.

3.5.4 Look Up

Item **3-Look Up** permits you to call up a word not on the list. As long as a column is empty, you can press **3** and enter any word (see Section 3.5.2).

3.5.5 Clearing Columns

The Thesaurus has three columns and about 30 lines in a column. When there are more words than the length of a column, WordPerfect wraps the remaining words to the next column. If you ask the Thesaurus to find a second or third word, it places them in the next empty column.

If all three columns are occupied, you must clear one before you can search another word. To clear a column, position the cursor anywhere within the column and select **4-Clear column**. All remaining columns will move to the left, clearing the furthermost right column.

3.5.6 Replacing Words in the Document

If you find a word you like on the list provided by the Thesaurus, you can replace the existing word with any word on the list (see Figure 3.17):

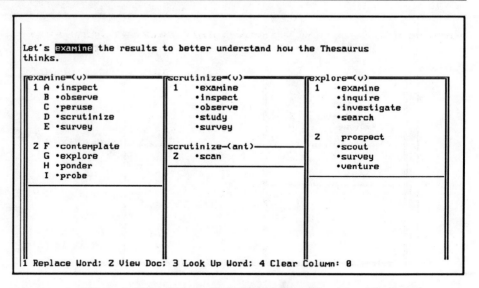

Figure 3.17 *Replacing a Text Word with a Thesaurus Word*
(Alt-F1, 1-Replace Word)

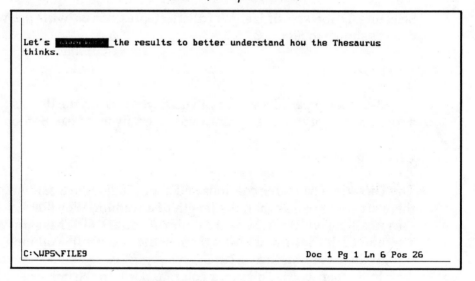

Figure 3.18 *"Examine" Replaced with*
"Scrutinize" (Alt-F1, 1-Replace Word, G)

Select **1-Replace word**
Press letter for Word: **G**

When you enter a letter, the new word replaces the former word (see Figure 3.18).

CHAPTER 4

Spell Checking

WordPerfect's Speller not only identifies words that you might have misspelled but also helps find the correct spelling of the word that you intended to use. The Speller dictionary does not interface with the Thesaurus and you must Exit one to enter the other. During a Spell Check, WordPerfect attempts to match words in your document against the words in its dictionary. In order to speed up this process, WordPerfect first seaches a short list of the most commonly used words before switching to the remaining words in the full dictionary.

4.1 The Dictionaries

WordPerfect's default dictionary is a 115,000 word version of *Webster's Collegiate Dictionary*. It includes many proper names, such as months, states, and some surnames. Words that you use frequently that are not in the default dictionary can easily be added. You can also purchase other, specialized dictionaries, such as legal, medical, or foreign language, which enhance your spell-checking capabilities.

4.2   Beginning the Spell Check from Floppy Disks

Operating the Speller is the same for both hard disk and floppy drive computers. However, starting Spell Check from floppies requires an extra step. With the document on the screen, remove your **data disk** from drive **B:** and insert the disk labeled **Speller Backup**. Do not remove either the System disk or Speller disk during the Spell Check. When you have completed the Spell Check, remove the Speller disk from drive B:, insert your data disk, and **Save** the revised document that is on the screen.

4.3   Operating the Speller

If you want to check the spelling of a particular word, position the cursor on that word before starting the Speller. Similarly, you can Spell Check a block or page or the entire document.

When you press **Ctrl-F2 (Spell)**, WordPerfect offers a menu with options (see Figure 4.1). Select items 1, 2, or 3. WordPerfect begins searching for matches. When it comes to a word it doesn't recognize or to a word containing a number, it stops (see Figure 4.2).

The Speller can't locate the word "submited," but it does have a similar word, "submitted." You have five options for dealing with the mismatched word. They are:

```
STAFF MEMO

Date: April 1, 1988

To: Senior Marketing Reps

From: Bob Williams

Re: Marketing to the Government

In January we submited a proposal to the Department of Defense
to bundle our file security software with 50,000 units of Zenith
183 lap top computers. We have now received a reply from the
Office of Contracts stating that the Army and Navy must justify
their need for security software. It is very important that we
follow up on our proposal immediately.

Once source of justification can come from the end users
themselves, and I want you to contact all of your major accounts
during the next week to make certain they understand why file
security is particularly important for lap top computers which
are more vulnerable to loss and theft..

Check: 1 Word: 2 Page: 3 Document: 4 New Sup. Dictionary: 5 Look Up: 6 Count: 0
```

Figure 4.1 *Beginning a Spell Check (Ctrl-F2)*

```
From: Bob Williams

Re: Marketing to the Government

In January we [submited] a proposal to the Department of Defense to
bundle our file securety software with 50,000 units of Zenith
183 lap top computers. We have now received a reply from the
Office of Contracts stating that the Army and Navy must justify
their need for security software. It is very important that we
follow up on our proposal immediately for for of the requirements


=============================================================================

   A. submitted








Not Found: 1 Skip Once; 2 Skip; 3 Add Word; 4 Edit; 5 Look Up:   0
```

Figure 4.2 *Locating a Misspelled Word*
(Ctrl-F1, 2-Page)

1. **Skip Once.** WordPerfect ignores the mismatched word this time but continues looking for it. This is useful for deliberate misspellings.

2. **Skip.** WordPerfect forgets about this word altogether for the duration of this Spell Check. WordPerfect will not stop on this word again.

3. **Add Word.** The word is added to the dictionary permanently as a valid word. If at some future time you do not want it as part of the default dictionary, you must remove it (see Section 4.3.7) through the utility menu.

4. **Edit.** When you select this item, you can then move the cursor within the mismatched word and make necessary corrections. When you've finished, press **Enter** and the corrected word replaces the misspelled one.

5. **Look Up.** This feature helps you find words that match a similar pattern or that sound like your word (see Section 4.3.5).

6. **Replace.** You can replace the mismatched word with one of the suggested words by typing the corresponding letter. In Figure 4.2, there is only one word, so type A.

You must select one of these options or press **F1 (Cancel)** to stop the Spell Check altogether.

Once we change "submitted" to "submitted" by pressing **A**, the Speller continues its search and finds "securety" and suggests two alternatives (see Figure 4.3). This time we'll press B to select the correct word.

4.3.1 Spell Checking Blocks

There will be times when you want to Spell Check units other than a page or the entire document. You can **Block** any amount of text, then turn on the Speller:

Position cursor
Press **Alt-F4**
Define Block
Press **Ctrl-F2**

4.3.2 Words that Appear as Doubles

Because it is a common error to type the same word twice, WordPerfect spots these double words. A double word appears in Figure 4.4. The menu choices for correcting the double are a little different from correct-

```
From: Bob Williams

Re: Marketing to the Government

In January we submitted a proposal to the Department of Defense
to bundle our file securety software with 50,000 units of Zenith
183 lap top computers. We have now received a reply from the
Office of Contracts stating that the Army and Navy must justify
their need for security software. It is very important that we
follow up on our proposal immediately for for of the requirements
listed.

================================================================================

    A. securely              B. security




Not Found: 1 Skip Once; 2 Skip; 3 Add Word; 4 Edit; 5 Look Up:  0
```

Figure 4.3 *Finding Mismatched Words*
(Ctrl-F2, 2-Page, A)

```
In January we submitted a proposal to the Department of Defense
to bundle our file security software with 50,000 units of Zenith
183 lap top computers. We have now received a reply from the
Office of Contracts stating that the Army and Navy must justify
their need for security software. It is very important that we
follow up on our proposal immediately [for] [for] of the requirements
listed.

Once source of justification can come from the end users
themselves, and I want you to contact all of your major accounts
during the next week to make certain they understand why file




Double Word: 1 2 Skip: 3 Delete 2nd: 4 Edit: 5 Disable Double Word Checking
```

Figure 4.4 *Finding Double Words*

ing mismatched words. Item **3-Delete 2nd** eliminates one occurrence of the double when it is a straight duplication. Item **4-Edit** gives you a chance to correct a misspelling. For example, the memo should have read "for *four* of the requirements listed." The double "for" was not the mistake. To turn off Double Word checking for this pass of the Spell Check, select item **5**.

4.3.3   Words with Numbers

WordPerfect does not attempt to check numbers, but it will stop at all occasions in which letters and numbers are mixed. This feature has limited use but can be of value for checking formulas or for spaces that have been inadvertently dropped between words and numbers, such as "122Elm Street."

4.3.4   Counting Words

At the end of every Spell Check, WordPerfect gives you a word count for that portion of the document it checked. If you simply want to count words in the *entire* document without Spell Checking:

Press **Ctrl-F2**
Select **6-Count**

4.3.5 *Looking Up Words*

WordPerfect guesses at possible alternatives for mismatched words, but its guess might not be good enough. Or, at times, you might want to use the **Look Up** feature by itself without having a particular word in mind. You can Look Up words by designating some pattern of letters. For example, you aren't sure how to spell "rhinoceros" and WordPerfect isn't able to guess that's what you want. So you select **5-Look Up** from the Speller menu and enter.

```
Word or word pattern:r*n*os
```

This tells WordPerfect that you know the word begins with an "r," has an "n" somewhere in the middle, and ends with "os." It doesn't matter how many letters come between when you use the "*" method. WordPerfect finds two words which qualify (see Figure 4.5). Needless to say, this is a very useful feature for finding difficult-to-spell words; it's more useful even than a dictionary. You can place the * before, within, or after any letters.

With * it doesn't matter how many characters fall between the letters you stipulate. If you want to be more specific, you can use a ?, which allows only one character to fall between your letters. If you enter:

```
To: Senior Marketing Reps

From: Bob Williams

Re: Marketing to the Government

In January we submitted a proposal to the Department of Defense
to bundle our file security software with 50,000 units of Zenith
183 lap top computers. We have now received a reply from the
Office of Contracts stating that the Army and Navy must justify
their need for security software. It is very important that we

=============================================================================

   A. rhinoceros          B. rhinos




Word or word pattern: r*n*os
```

Figure 4.5 *Looking for Words by Their Patterns*
(Ctrl-F2, 5-Look Up, r*n*os, Enter)

```
|
|
|
|
|
|===================================================================
|
| A. min            B. minable         C. minaret
| D. minarets       E. minatory        F. mince
| G. minced         H. mincemeat       I. mincer
| J. mincers        K. minces          L. mincing
| M. mind           N. minded          O. mindedly
| P. mindedness     Q. mindful         R. mindfully
| S. mindfulness    T. minding         U. mindless
| V. mindlessly     W. mindlessness    X. minds
|
|Press any key to continue
```

Figure 4.6 *Search for All Words Beginning with
"Min" (Ctrl-F2, 5-Look Up, Word Pattern:min*, Enter)*

```
Word or word patterns:min*
```

Your screen will look like Figure 4.6. However, if you place a question mark at the end:

```
Word or word patterns:min?
```

WordPerfect gives you only 11 letter words beginning with "min" (see Figure 4.7).

4.3.6 *Dictionary Full?*

Whenever you select **3-Add word**, WordPerfect stores the added word in a temporary file and, when the Spell Check has finished, it stores those words in the dictionary. It also places skipped words in the temporary file but does not add those to the dictionary. The amount of temporary storage is limited and if you add or skip more words than the storage area can handle then WordPerfect will tell you that the "Dictionary is full." What this means is that the temporary storage is full. There is no practical limit to the size of the dictionary.

When this happens, simply stop the Spell Check program by pressing **F1**. WordPerfect will permanently store the added words and clear the temporary storage area. You can run the Spell Check again. This time

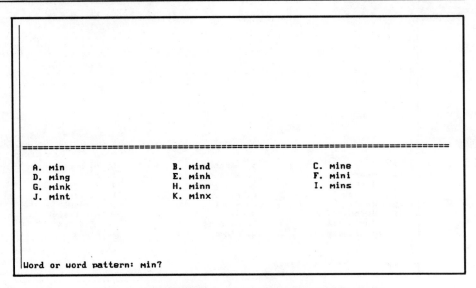

Figure 4.7 *Search for Four Letter Words Beginning with "Min" (Ctrl-F2, 5-Look Up, Word Pattern:min?, Enter)*

WordPerfect will recognize the added words. Or, you can start the Spell Check from the position you stopped by using the **Block Spell Check** method (see Section 4.3.1)

4.3.7   Editing Words in the Dictionary

WordPerfect's permanent storage dictionary, which contains added words, is a file named WP{WP}EN.SUP. You can Retrieve this file like any data file with **Shift-F10**. Each word appears on a separate line. If this has become a large dictionary, you can search for particular words with **Shift-F2 (Search)**. You'll notice, however, that WordPerfect alphabetizes its word list, so finding the words you want to edit is easy.

Work on this file as you would any data file, then Save it under the same file name. WordPerfect automatically checks this file whenever the Spell Check is in progress.

4.3.8   Making Your Own Word List

If you frequently use words that are not in the default dictionary, you might want to add them to the dictionary supplement before you run the Spell Check. Simply Create (or Retrieve) a file named WP{WP}EN.SUP and begin adding words. Each word is placed on a separate line. When you've added all the words you wish, Save it to disk.

A supplemental dictionary can have any name; therefore you can take any list of words and call it a dictionary using any file name you wish. The only difference is that WordPerfect automatically checks the file whose name is WP{WP}EN.SUP, whereas you must tell WordPerfect if another list should also be used.

This is accomplished when you begin the Spell Check. When you press **Ctrl-F2**, select item **4-New Sup. Dictionary**, the message center will ask you to give the dictionary's name. Just enter the name of the file containing your list of words.

4.3.9 *Using Other Dictionaries*

Many software vendors have produced specialized dictionaries, and many of them are compatible with WordPerfect. Check with your computer dealer before purchasing one; chances are you can find all kinds of dictionaries. WordPerfect Corporation itself produces dictionaries for 14 languages, as well as legal and medical terminology.

To use any of these compatible dictionaries, start the Speller with **Ctrl-F2**, then select item **4-New Sup. Dictionary**. Type in the file name of the dictionary and WordPerfect will check it along with its default and own supplemental dictionary.

Although WordPerfect can use only one New Supplemental Dictionary at a time, you can bypass having to name the supplemental dictionary by giving it the name WP{WP}EN.SUP.

4.3.10 *Spell Checking Foreign Language Words and Documents*

WordPerfect has built-in a simple but unique feature for Spell Checking documents using WordPerfect's foreign language dictionaries. By placing a "Language" marker within the text, just as if it were an ordinary code, WordPerfect will automatically switch to the special dictionary to Spell Check.

This feature is especially useful if multilingual dictionaries are being used. You might work frequently with documents that contain passages in German, French, Italian, and Spanish. Rather than running the Spell Check four times for each language, you can run it once by coding which sections contain which languages.

To enter the language codes, position the cursor at the beginning of the section containing a particular language and then:

Press **Shift-F8**
Select **4-Other**
Select **5-Language**
Enter Language code
Press **F7**

At the end of the section, proceed through the same steps to switch back to English or to another language.

The foreign language dictionaries (and thesauruses) currently available through WordPerfect and their codes are as follows:

Canadian French	CA
Danish	DA
German	DE
English	EN
Spanish	ES
French	FR
Icelandic	IC
Italian	IT
Dutch	NE
Norwegian	NO
Portuguese	PO
Finnish	SU
Swedish	SV
British English	UK

CHAPTER 5

Printing

Printing has typically been the most troublesome aspect of word processing. Part of the reason is that a second piece of hardware is involved that must interface properly with the software. Most of the problems, however, result from the complexity of operations that you can perform with sophisticated software like WordPerfect. Placing the right codes at the right place in the document seems easy enough, but it is also easy to give WordPerfect conflicting commands, which will cause it to stop altogether or produce haywire results. For a simple example, if you change the top margin to 1.5 inches, then change it again later to 1.6 inches, two codes exist. Unless you delete the 1.5-inch code, WordPerfect must decide between the two. It doesn't always make the same choice twice, and sometimes it decides not to choose at all, depending on the kind of conflicting codes it encounters (see Figure 5.1).

This explanation is meant to be more encouraging than a warning. Usually you can analyze why the printer is misbehaving and fix it, knowing that the source of trouble is either printer compatibility for the operations you want to print or from the unwanted codes you've embedded in the text.

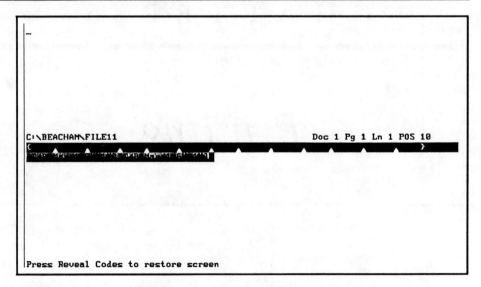

```
C:\BEACHAM\FILE11                              Doc 1 Pg 1 Ln 1 POS 10
```

Press Reveal Codes to restore screen

Figure 5.1 *Conflicting Codes (Alt-F3)*

5.1   Setting Up the Printer

WordPerfect 5.0 supports the full features of over 150 printers, and it is capable of running others for basic features. If your printer is on the list of officially supported printers (see Chapter 16 for the complete list), you can specify it and compatibility shouldn't be a problem. However, you *must specify your printer* before you can begin. You need do this only one time. WordPerfect remembers your printer and assumes you want to use it every time you print. If you're new to computers, you might be interested in knowing that every printer is "driven" by a set of unique specifications. When you specify your printer, you are activating the "printer driver," which is the mediator between WordPerfect's language and the printer's.

Printer selection and setup are accessed through the **Print (Shift-F7)** menu from the **typing area** (see Figure 5.2).

5.1.1   *Selecting Your Printer Make and Model*

Looking at item **S-Select Printer** under Options, notice that the default printer selection is Standard Printer. This is a generic printer selection that will drive some of the features in many dot-matrix printers. If your printer is not on the list of WordPerfect supported printers, use the Standard Printer default. However, this is a last resort choice.

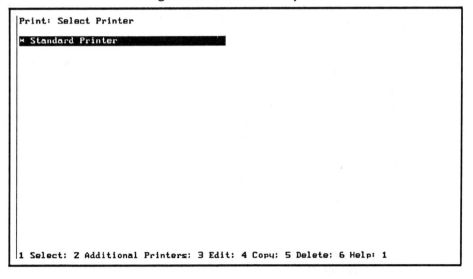

```
Print

        1 - Full Document
        2 - Page
        3 - Document on Disk
        4 - Control Printer
        5 - Type Through
        6 - View Document
        7 - Initialize Printer

Options

        S - Select Printer            Standard Printer
        B - Binding                   0"
        N - Number of Copies          1
        G - Graphics Quality          Medium
        T - Text Quality              High




Selection: 0
```

Figure 5.2 *Print Menu (Shift-F7)*

```
Print: Select Printer
⊠ Standard Printer













1 Select; 2 Additional Printers; 3 Edit; 4 Copy; 5 Delete; 6 Help: 1
```

Figure 5.3 *Printer Selection Menu (Shift-F7, S)*

To select your printer, press **S**, which brings up the menu shown in Figure 5.3.

To install your printer model, follow instructions for installing **Additional Printers**. A list of printers will appear on the screen (see Figure 5.4). In Figure 5.5 we have selected an Epson FX-86e/286e.

If it is not listed here, insert the second printer diskette into the **A:** drive and select **2-Other Disks.** When you have found your printer, move the cursor until the name is highlighted, then press **1-Select.** The message center displays the printer model. Press **Enter.**

5.1.2   *Choosing Ports and Sheet Feeders*

This menu has named the printer we selected and now wants some information about the printer itself. Knowing some things about Epson FX-86e/286e printers, WordPerfect makes assumptions. For example, the Epson FX-86e/286e cannot be equipped with a sheet feeder, and if you try to change item 3, the message center will tell you that the Epson does not come with a sheet feeder.

WordPerfect also assumes that you have attached your printer to the parallel port. This is the large, 25-pin plug called the LPT port. If there is only one LPT port on your computer, the default setting of **LPT1** is correct and you need not change it. If there are two LPT ports and you're plugged into the second one, you'll change the default by pressing **2-Port,** then selecting **2-LPT 2.** *Do not change the port unless you need to* (see Figure 5.7).

```
Select Printer: Additional Printers

  ALPS PZ400C
  AST TurboLaser
  Alps PZ000/PZ100
  Brother HR-15XL/20/35
  C.ITOH 8510 Prowriter
  C.ITOH C-310 CP
  C.ITOH C-310 EP/CXP
  C.ITOH C-715F
  C.ITOH ProWriter jr. Plus
  Canon LBP-8 A1/A2
  Canon LBP-8II
  Centronics 351
  Centronics GLP II
  Citizen MSP-15
  Citizen MSP-25
  Citizen Premiere 35
  Cordata LP300X
  Daisy Systems M45-Q
  Daisywriter 2000
  Data General 6321
  Dataproducts LZR-1230

1 Select: 2 Other Disk: 3 Help: 4 List Printer Files: 1
```

Figure 5.4 *Additional Printers List*
(Shift-F7, S, 2-Additional Printers)

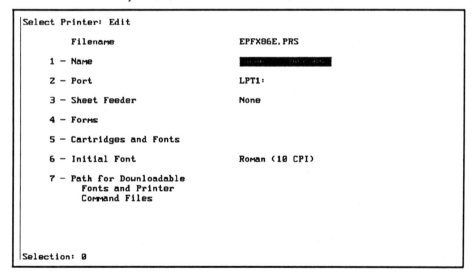

Figure 5.5 *Selecting Your Printer and Model*
(Shift-F7, S, 2-Additional Printers, Down Arrow)

```
Select Printer: Edit

        Filename                EPFX86E.PRS

    1 - Name

    2 - Port                    LPT1:

    3 - Sheet Feeder            None

    4 - Forms

    5 - Cartridges and Fonts

    6 - Initial Font            Roman (10 CPI)

    7 - Path for Downloadable
        Fonts and Printer
        Command Files



Selection: 0
```

Figure 5.6 *Printer Edit Menu*
(Shift-F7, S, 2-Additional Printers, Down Arrow, Enter)

If you are running your printer from a serial port, which is the smaller 9-pin plug, you'll designate a **Com** port. If there's only one serial port on your computer, select **4-Com 1**. Many laser printers run from the serial (COM) port.

```
Select Printer: Edit

        Filename                       EPFX86E.PRS

    1 - Name                           Epson FX-86e/286e

    2 - Port                           LPT1:

    3 - Sheet Feeder                   None

    4 - Forms

    5 - Cartridges and Fonts

    6 - Initial Font                   Roman (10 CPI)

    7 - Path for Downloadable
        Fonts and Printer
        Command Files




Port: 1 LPT 1: 2 LPT 2: 3 LPT 3: 4 COM 1: 5 COM 2: 6 COM 3: 7 COM 4: 8 Other: 0
```

Figure 5.7 *Changing the Port*
(Shift-F7, S, 2-Additional Printers, Down Arrow, Enter, 2-Port)

5.1.3   *Completing the Printer Selection Process*

For the time being, this is all that's necessary to define your printer. If you want to select type fonts, see Section 5.1.5. To complete the printer definition process and return to the typing area, press **Enter**. The screen will then look like the one in Figure 5.8.

Now there are two printers on the list: WordPerfect's Standard Printer and the Epson we've chosen. The bullet is still positioned by the Standard Printer. To change it to the Epson, press **1-Select** (see Figure 5.9). Press **F7 (Exit)** to return to the typing area.

You have now defined your printer and completed the process. If you want to learn how to switch printers or select different type fonts, continue reading. If you want to begin printing, skip to Section 5.2.

5.1.4   *Switching Between Selected Printers*

As you've guessed by now, you can fill your working printer list with different printers. If you have an occasion to use different printers — perhaps your dot matrix printer is attached to the PRT 1 port and your laser printer is attached to the COM 1 port — then you can easily switch back and forth once you've defined the printers and placed them on the working list. To switch printers:

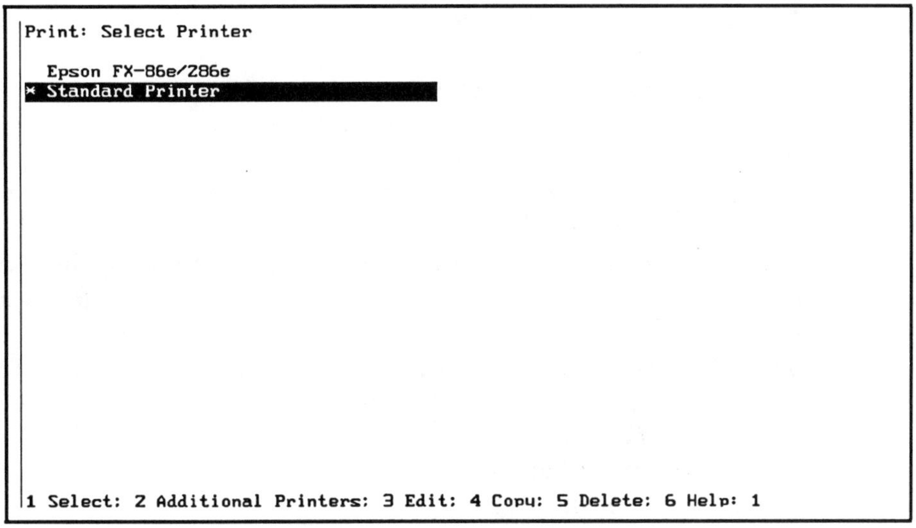

```
Print: Select Printer

   Epson FX-86e/286e
 ⊠ Standard Printer



1 Select: 2 Additional Printers: 3 Edit: 4 Copy: 5 Delete: 6 Help: 1
```

Figure 5.8 *List of Printers Selected*

Press **Shift-F7**
Select **S-Select Printer**
Use **Arrow Keys** to highlight printer choice
Press **1-Select**
Press **F7 (Exit)** to return to typing area

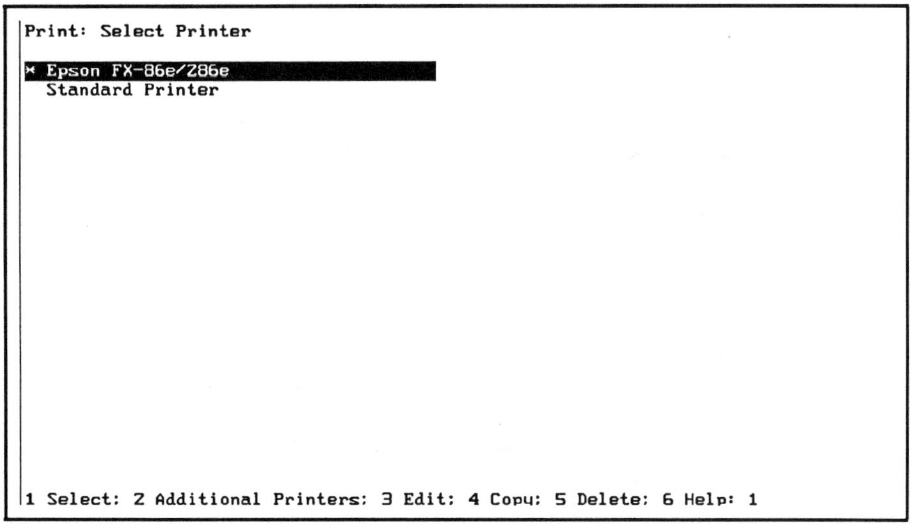

```
Print: Select Printer

 ⊠ Epson FX-86e/286e
   Standard Printer



1 Select: 2 Additional Printers: 3 Edit: 4 Copy: 5 Delete: 6 Help: 1
```

Figure 5.9 *Changing the Default to the Selected Printer*

5.1.5   *Changing Typefaces (Fonts)*

The only other item to check for the initial print run are the typeface selections that are available with your printer. Looking at item 6 in Figure 5.7, we see that for our Epson FX-86e/286e WordPerfect has selected Roman (10 CPI), a standard typeface. There is no need to change it. However, one of the exceptional features of WordPerfect 5.0 is the ease with which you can change typefaces, either as a default for the printer or within the document itself. The ease and options are so appealing that you might want to start using them right away.

From the Printer Selection: Edit menu (see Figure 5.6), press **6-Initial Font** to bring up the type font choices available with your printer. For the Epson FX-86e/286e there are 36 (see Figure 5.10).

The bullet is positioned by the default type font, Roman (10 CPI). Using the **Dn Arrow** key, move the cursor to **Roman Italic**, then press **1-Select** (or **Enter**). Press **1-Select** again, then **Enter** again to return to the typing area. You have now specified Roman Italic as the type font. When printed on the Epson, it looks like Figure 5.11. If you specify sans serif (10 CPI), when printed it looks like Figure 5.12.

```
Select Printer: Initial Font

  Roman (10 CPI)
  Roman (12 CPI)
  Roman (17 CPI)
  Roman (20 CPI)
  Roman (5 CPI)
  Roman (6 CPI)
  Roman (8.5 CPI)
  Roman (PS)
  Roman Dbl-High (10 CPI)
  Roman Dbl-High (12 CPI)
  Roman Dbl-High (17 CPI)
  Roman Dbl-High (20 CPI)
  Roman Dbl-High (5 CPI)
  Roman Dbl-High (6 CPI)
  Roman Dbl-High,Wide (PS)
  Roman Dbl-Wide (PS)
  Roman Italic (PS)
  Roman Subscript (10 CPI)
  Roman Subscript (12 CPI)
✕ San Serif (10 CPI)
  San Serif (12 CPI)

1 Select: N Name search: 1
```

Figure 5.10 *Type Fonts for the Epson FX-86e/286e*
(Shift-F7, S, 2-Additional Printers, Down Arrow, Enter, 6-Initial Font)

STAFF MEMO

Date: April 1, 1988

To: Senior Marketing Reps

From: Bob Williams

Re: Marketing to the Government

In January we submitted a proposal to the Department of Defense to bundle our file security software with 50,000 units of **Zenith 183** *lap top computers. We have now received a reply from the Office of Contracts stating that the Army and Navy must justify their need for security software. It is very important that we follow up on our proposal immediately.*

Once source of justification can come from the end users themselves, and I want you to contact all of your major accounts during the next week to make certain they understand why file security is particularly important for lap top computers which are more vulnerable to loss and theft..

Figure 5.11 *Roman Italic Type*
(Shift-F7, S, 2-Additional Printers, Down Arrow, Enter, 6-Font,
Cursor to Roman Italic, Enter, 1-Select, Enter)

5.1.6   *Editing Type Font Selections*

Once you have defined your printer, you can change the type font easily and as often as you wish. The keystrokes to change type fonts are:

Press **Shift-F7**
Select **S-Select Printer**
Select **3-Edit**
Select **6-Initial Font**

This brings up the font choices (see Figure 5.8). Now:

Move Cursor with **Arrow Keys** to your font choice
Press **Enter** or **1-Select**
Press **1-Select**
Press **Enter**

Figure 5.12 shows sans serif (10 CPI).

```
STAFF MEMO

Date: April 1, 1988

To: Senior Marketing Reps

From: Bob Williams

Re: Marketing to the Government

In January we submitted a proposal to the Department of Defense to
bundle our file security software with 50,000 units of Zenith 183
lap top computers. We have now received a reply from the Office of
Contracts stating that the Army and Navy must justify their need
for security software. It is very important that we follow up on
our proposal immediately.

Once source of justification can come from the end users
themselves, and I want you to contact all of your major accounts
during the next week to make certain they understand why file
security is particularly important for lap top computers which are
more vulnerable to loss and theft..
```

Figure 5.12 *Type Font Changed to Sans Serif (10 CPI)*

5.2   Starting a Print Job

All standard print jobs are initiated through the **Shift-F7 (Print)** key.
WordPerfect assumes that you will normally print the document that is
on the screen. (To print from disk, see Section 5.2.3). So, with the document on the screen, press **Shift-F7** to bring up the Print menu (see Figure
5.13).

5.2.1 *Printing a Page or an Entire Document*

If you want to print either the full document or the page on which the
cursor is positioned, select item **1-Full Document** or **2-Page**. As soon as
you enter one of the numbers, printing begins. You have no control over
this type of print job except to stop it (see Section 5.2.5). If you want to
print multiple copies or change the print quality, you must enter them
into the Options menu (see Figure 5.13) *before* pressing 1 or 2.

5.2.2 *Printing Specific Pages*

WordPerfect allows you to print any combination of specific pages. With
the document on the screen, select item **3-Document on Disk** (see Figure
5.14) from the Print menu (Shift-F7). You are not actually printing from

```
Print

     1 — Full Document
     2 — Page
     3 — Document on Disk
     4 — Control Printer
     5 — Type Through
     6 — View Document
     7 — Initialize Printer

Options

     S — Select Printer          Epson FX-86e/286e
     B — Binding                 0"
     N — Number of Copies        1
     G — Graphics Quality        Medium
     T — Text Quality            High




Selection: 0
```

Figure 5.13 *Print Menu (Shift-F7)*

```
Print

     1 — Full Document
     2 — Page
     3 — Document on Disk
     4 — Control Printer
     5 — Type Through
     6 — View Document
     7 — Initialize Printer

Options

     S — Select Printer          Epson FX-86e/286e
     B — Binding                 0"
     N — Number of Copies        1
     G — Graphics Quality        Medium
     T — Text Quality            High
```

Figure 5.14 *Specifying Page Numbers*
(Shift-F7, 3-Document on Disk, Type the Document Name, Enter,
Type Page Numbers)

the disk but the steps are the same. The prompt in the message center will ask for

```
Document name:
```

Type the document name and press **Enter**. The prompt will then say:

```
Page(s): (All)
```

Enter the page numbers or combination of page numbers you want to print. They are separated by commas with no spaces between them (see Figure 5.14).

There are several options for entering numbers:

1. One page number or a series of individual page numbers, such as **4,7,14**

2. A string of contiguous page numbers, such as **6-23**

3. A combination of individual pages and strings, such as **4,9,12-19,25**

4. From any page through the end of the document, as **19-**

5. From the beginning of the document through any page, as **-12**

6. With New Page Number options, such as **i-ix**

If you have assigned chapter numbers, any combination of chapters and pages can be used. Chapter numbers and page numbers are separated by a colon, as 2:13. This would print Chapter 2, page 13. You can combine Chapter combinations using the same method in item #3 above. 2:13-3:9,4:6-24 prints Chapter 2, page 13 through page 9 of Chapter 3 and Chapter 4, pages 6-24.

When you have specified your page numbers, press **Enter** to begin printing. You can also print text which you Block. See Section 5.4 for instructions.

5.2.3 *Printing from the Disk/Fast Save*

In order to speed up Saving documents, WordPerfect has included an option called **Fast Save**. This causes a document to be stored to the disk in an unformatted condition, unsuitable for printing. In other words, if you Fast Save a document, you can't print it from disk. The default is to "Slow" Save so you can print from disk.

Printing from disk is a useful feature if you want to print without supervising the computer. WordPerfect allows you to enter a list of print jobs (see Section 5.2.6) and then walk away from the computer but this can be done only if the documents can be printed from the disk. (Otherwise you would have to Retrieve each document each time a new print job started.)

You can print a document on disk by selecting item **3-Document on Disk, giving the document name,** and any specific **page numbers** you want. If you want to print the entire document, just press **Enter** when the prompt asks:

```
Page(s):(All).
```

5.2.4 *Turning On Fast Save*

Press **Shift-F1** (see Figure 5.15), then:

Select **4-Fast Save**
Change No to **Y**

5.2.5 *Printer Control: Stopping a Job*

The only way to correctly stop a print job is through **4-Control Printer**. When you select this from the **F-7 (Print)** menu, the status report sheet shown in Figure 5.16 comes up.

This is really a reporting sheet, not a selection menu, that gives the status of the job currently being printed and the list of jobs waiting to be printed. The five items at the bottom of the page permit you to stop or cancel a print job in progress.

If you want to interrupt (stop) a job in progress, press **5-Stop**. This temporarily causes the printer to stop. When you are ready to begin printing the same job again, just press **4-Go (start printer)**. To Cancel a print job altogether, see Section 5.2.7.

```
Setup

    1 - Backup

    2 - Cursor Speed                   30 cps

    3 - Display

    4 - Fast Save (unformatted)        Yes

    5 - Initial Settings

    6 - Keyboard Layout

    7 - Location of Files

    8 - Units of Measure




Selection: 0
```

Figure 5.15 *Setup Menu (Shift-F1)*

```
Print: Control Printer

Current Job

Job Number: n/a                        Page Number:  n/a
Job Status: n/a                        Current Copy: n/a
Paper:      n/a
Location:   n/a
Message:    No print jobs


Job List

Job  Document              Destination        Print Options




Additional Jobs Not Shown: 0



1 Cancel Job(s); 2 Rush Job; 3 Display Jobs; 4 Go (start printer); 5 Stop: 0
```

Figure 5.16 *Printer Status Report*
(Shift-F7, 4-Control Printer)

Note: Many printers are equipped with memory of their own and they store signals from the computer. When you select 5-Stop or 1-Cancel, the computer stops sending signals, but because the printer has stored signals, it will continue printing for a short time until it clears its memory. If there's an emergency, such as jammed paper, you can turn off the printer itself *after* you have stopped the job through WordPerfect.

5.2.6 *Entering Multiple Print Jobs*

You can enter print orders for multiple jobs, then keep track of them through the Printer Control report sheet. To enter multiple print orders, follow the same steps as entering a single Print from Disk order (see Section 5.2.3). When you have entered the first job, the printer begins. Enter the second print job following the same steps, then the third and fourth. Each job is recorded on the Printer Control status sheet (see Figure 5.17).

5.2.7 *Listing and Canceling Print Jobs*

Any of the print jobs listed on the Status Report can be canceled or can be given priority. Item **1-Cancel** permanently removes a print job from the list of print jobs, including the one currently in progress. WordPerfect assigns each print job a number and when you press 1-Cancel, WordPerfect asks you to enter the number of the print job(s) you want to cancel. You can cancel as many or all of the jobs as you wish. To cancel them all, enter an asterisk (*) instead of a job number. When WordPerfect asks if you want to cancel them all, press **Y**. Then press **F7 (Exit)** to leave the Print menu.

You can enter more print jobs than WordPerfect can show on the Status Report sheet. To see the entire list, press **3-Display Jobs.**

```
Print: Control Printer

Current Job

Job Number: # 1                          Page Number:  2
Job Status: Printing                     Current Copy: 1 of 1
Paper:      Standard 8.5"x11"
Location:   Continuous Feed
Message:


Job List

Job  Document            Destination      Print Options
1 C:\WP\Chpt5            LPT1             Continuous
2 C:\WP\Matthews         LPT1             Continuous
3 C:\WP\Staffmem         LPT1             8.5"x11"


Additional Jobs Not Shown: 0



1 Cancel Job(s); 2 Rush Job; 3 Display Jobs; 4 Go (start printer); 5 Stop: 0
```

Figure 5.17 *Printer Control Status Sheet Showing*
Multiple Print Jobs

5.2.8 *Rush Jobs*

If you want to change the priority of certain jobs — that is, change the order in which they will be printed — press **2-Rush Job**. WordPerfect will ask which job number you want to rush. Enter the number. You have the option of interrupting the current job in favor of the rush job, or you can allow the current job to finish, and then print the rush job:

```
Interrupt current job?:
```

Press **N** if you want the current job to finish before beginning the rush job. Press **Y** to interrupt the current job, then press **F7 (Exit)**. If you interrupt a job that is printing, it continues printing as soon as the rush job has finished.

If you interrupt a job, allow WordPerfect to continue printing that job until it comes to a natural stopping point. *Do not turn off the printer.* Depending on how much of a page has been printed, WordPerfect will either stop at the bottom of the current page or it will print one more page. In any case, WordPerfect stops at the end of a page so that when the job is picked up again after the rush job, printing can proceed from the top of a new page. If your printer has a large buffer (memory), printing could continue for a while before the job is interrupted.

WordPerfect offers many more print options and formatting capabilities for advanced printing, including graphics. See Chapter 12 for instructions.

5.3   Text Quality and Fast Print

The speed with which WordPerfect prints your document depends on the quality of printing you select. The choices are Draft, Medium, and High. You can also elect to print only text, only graphics, or both. Graphics usually takes much longer to print than text. Selecting text quality affects the speed of dot matrix printers more than it does laser printers.

To change the print quality, press **Shift-F7 (Print)**, then **T-Text Quality**. The menu choices list at the bottom of the page offer:

```
1-Do not print  2-Draft  3-Medium  4-High
```

Selecting **2-Draft** tells the printer to ignore special attributes, such as Bold face and Underlining. Press **F7 (Exit)** to continue. Depending on your printer, there might not be a difference between Medium and High text quality.

With dot-matrix printers, print quality is achieved by striking over letters in a different pattern. This fills in the gaps between the dots and gives the type a solid look. For letter quality printing, all text receives at least one more strike over. Bold text will receive at least two strike overs. Striking over slows the printer down, of course, and can cut the printer's draft quality speed by as much as 75 percent. So for working copies in the editing phase, you'll probably select Draft quality printing.

If your document contains graphics, you might not want to print them for draft quality work. To stop graphics printing, press **G-Graphics Quality**, then **1-Do not print** and **F7 (Exit)**.

When you select some printers, WordPerfect will offer advice about the text quality choices you should make. Figure 5.18 shows WordPerfect's advice for the Epson FX-80.

5.4   Printing Blocks

There are frequent occasions when you might not want to print an entire page. Using WordPerfect's standard Print features, you can print only the entire document or specified pages. Using **Block**, you can print any por-

```
Printer Helps and Hints:  Epson FX-80

High Quality print is extremely slow but will micro-space and right justify
up to 1/120th of an inch.  If you do not require this high quality we
suggest that you set your default quality to be medium or draft. Both of
these qualities will be much quicker.
In the medium or draft modes there will be a slight round off error in
spacing when using Pica Compressed and Pica Compressed Dbl-Wide.  This is
because no micro-spacing is available to accomadate 17.14 or 8.57 pitch.
There will also be a problem right justifying in medium or draft modes.
The horizontal movement of these modes is 1/10ths which creates an "all or
nothing" situation (either there is a space between words or there is not).
Graphics in medium or draft assumes 10 CPI.




Press Exit to quit. Cursor Keys for More Text. Switch for Sheet Feeder Help
```

Figure 5.18 *WordPerfect's Advice for the Epson FX-80*

tion of a page or from the middle of one page to the middle of the next. Follow these steps:

> Position the cursor and turn on **Block (Alt-F7)**
> Define the Block
> Press **Shift-F7 (Print)**

The message center will prompt:

```
Print block (Y/N)?No
```

Change the No to **Y** to print the Block (see Figure 5.19).

5.5   Printing from the Screen

Working through DOS rather than WordPerfect, you can quickly print one entire screen by pressing **Shift-PrtSc (Print Screen)**. The advantages to Print Screen are that it's very fast, requiring only one keystroke, and that it prints everything on the screen, including the status line and message center. You can also print Menus and Help screens, which cannot be printed through WordPerfect.

```
STAFF MEMO

Date: April 1, 1988

To: Senior Marketing Reps

From: Bob Williams

Re: Marketing to the Government

In January we submitted a proposal to the Department of Defense
to bundle our file security software with 50,000 units of Zenith
183 lap top computers. We have now received a reply from the
Office of Contracts stating that the Army and Navy must justify
their need for security software.

Once source of justification can come from the end users
themselves, and I want you to contact all of your major accounts
during the next week to make certain they understand why file
security is particularly important for lap top computers which
are more vulnerable to loss and theft..

It is very important that we follow up on our proposal
immediately.
```

Figure 5.19 *Printing a Block of Text*
(Alt-F4, Block Text, Shift-F7)

If your printer isn't printing, the quickest way to discover whether you have a hardware problem or a WordPerfect problem is to use **Print Screen**. If you can print a screen through DOS, WordPerfect is the problem. If you cannot print a screen, the problem lies with your printer or the cables connecting the printer and computer.

5.6 Type Through

This is not the same feature as Typeover (see Section 1.11) but rather turns your computer into a typewriter. This feature has limited use because (1) many printers are not designed for it, and (2) it negates the advantages that computers have over typewriters.

When you turn on Type Through, every character or line that you strike is immediately printed. This allows you to move the print head up or down, left or right just as the space bar and backspace keys work on a typewriter. You can move the print head in any direction at any time. The advantage is that you can fill out forms and work with formatting a page as you would on a typewriter. Use the Arrow keys to change the position of the print head.

To turn on Type Through, press **Shift-F7 (Print)** and select **5-Type Through**. WordPerfect will ask if you want to print **1-By line** or **2-By Character**. The difference is important. If you select **Character**, every time you strike a key the text goes immediately to the printer. **Line Type Through** enters one entire line on the computer screen and allows you to edit it before sending it to the printer. When you are ready to print, press **Enter**.

Remember, with **Type Through** you have to make decisions about carriage returns just as with a typewriter. WordPerfect does not ring a bell when you've exceeded the right margin but continues accepting characters. There is no Word Wrap with Type Through. The status line, of course, indicates the position of the cursor.

5.7 Printing with Macros

You can create a macro (keystroke chain) to carry out frequently used printing instructions, such as selecting a printer, specifying paper length, or choosing type fonts. You might, for example, print a bulletin board notice every Monday announcing the week's activities. The notice is on 14-inch paper and printed with large bold type. There are a number of keystrokes required to specify all this. By creating a macro with the name "Bulletin," you can enter all your specifications and start printing with two keystrokes. Macros are very useful. See Chapter 15 for instructions to create macros.

5.8 Ordering Print Jobs with List Files

There are a number of procedures you can perform with **List Files** (see Section 6.1), but one of the most useful is sending print orders to the Printer Control. This is convenient if you have many jobs to enter or if you want to review your file names. For example, you might want to print all the letters sent to John Matthews. Through **List Files** you can search for them all and enter the print order from the same screen. You can even perform a Word Search of all documents to look for key words or dates (see Section 6.1).

Press F5 (**List Files**) to produce a screen of file names (see Figure 5.20). Move the cursor to highlight the name of the document you want to print. When you select item **4-Print**, WordPerfect asks you whether you want to print all the pages or selected ones (see Section 5.2.2 and Figure 5.21).

Enter the page numbers of the pages you want to print or press **Enter** to print the entire document. [If you are using the Fast Save feature (see

```
03/21/88  17:11              Directory C:\WP5\*.*
Document size:        0   Free: 11171840   Used:   3165700      Files:  83

.  <CURRENT>      <DIR>             .. <PARENT>       <DIR>
ALPSPZ40. PRS     4193   03/18/88 10:09    AND      .WPG    1466   02/06/88 07:17
APPLAUSE. WPG     1774   02/06/88 07:17    ARROW1   .WPG     342   02/06/88 07:17
ARROW2   . WPG     352   02/06/88 07:17    ARROW3   .WPG     340   02/06/88 07:17
ARROW4   . WPG     404   02/06/88 07:17    ARROW5   .WPG     698   02/06/88 07:17
AWARD    . WPG    1746   02/06/88 07:17    BADNEWS  .WPG    4167   02/06/88 07:17
BOMB     . WPG     950   02/06/88 07:17    BOOK     .WPG    1904   02/06/88 07:17
BORDER   . WPG   13662   02/06/88 07:17    CHARACTR.DOC   52559   02/24/88 15:38
CHECK    . WPG    1070   02/06/88 07:17    CLOCK    .WPG    6038   02/06/88 07:17
COMPASS  . WPG    2126   02/06/88 07:17    CONFID   .WPG    2242   02/06/88 07:17
EGA512   . FNT    7168   02/06/88 07:16    EGAITAL  .FNT    3584   02/06/88 07:16
EGASMC   . FNT    3584   02/06/88 07:16    EGAUND   .FNT    3584   02/06/88 07:16
EPFX80   . PRS    5524   03/21/88 17:08    EPFX86E  .PRS    7188   03/18/88 10:23
FACTORY  . WPG     972   02/06/88 07:17    FATARROW.WPG     342   02/06/88 07:17
FC       . DOC    1906   02/06/88 07:17    FC       .EXE   23552   02/06/88 07:17
FEET     . WPG    1384   02/06/88 07:17    FLAG     .WPG     554   02/06/88 07:17
GAVEL    . WPG     912   02/06/88 07:16    GLOBE    .WPG    2542   02/06/88 07:16
GOODNEWS. WPG     4494   02/06/88 07:16    GRAB     .COM   12747   02/06/88 07:16
HEARYE   . WPG    5400   02/06/88 07:16    HOURGLAS.WPG    1830   02/06/88 07:16

1 Retrieve: 2 Delete: 3 Rename: 4 Print: 5 Text In: 6 Look:
7 Change Directory: 8 Copy: 9 Word Search: N Name Search: 6
```

Figure 5.20 *List Files (F5)*

```
03/21/88  17:11              Directory C:\WP5\*.*
Document size:          0   Free: 11171840   Used:  3165700        Files:  83

. <CURRENT>      <DIR>                  .. <PARENT>      <DIR>
ALPSPZ40.PRS      4193  03/18/88 10:09  AND       .WPG      1466  02/06/88 07:17
APPLAUSE.WPG      1774  02/06/88 07:17  ARROW1    .WPG       342  02/06/88 07:17
ARROW2  .WPG       352  02/06/88 07:17  ARROW3    .WPG       340  02/06/88 07:17
ARROW4  .WPG       404  02/06/88 07:17  ARROW5    .WPG       698  02/06/88 07:17
AWARD   .WPG      1746  02/06/88 07:17  BADNEWS   .WPG      4167  02/06/88 07:17
BOMB    .WPG       950  02/06/88 07:17  BOOK      .WPG      1904  02/06/88 07:17
BORDER  .WPG     13662  02/06/88 07:17  CHARACTR  .DOC     52559  02/24/88 15:38
CHECK   .WPG      1070  02/06/88 07:17  CLOCK     .WPG      6038  02/06/88 07:17
COMPASS .WPG      2126  02/06/88 07:17  CONFID    .WPG      2242  02/06/88 07:17
EGA512  .FNT      7168  02/06/88 07:16  EGAITAL   .FNT      3584  02/06/88 07:16
EGASMC  .FNT      3584  02/06/88 07:16  EGAUND    .FNT      3584  02/06/88 07:16
EPFX80  .PRS      5524  03/21/88 17:08  EPFX86E   .PRS      7188  03/18/88 10:23
FACTORY .WPG       972  02/06/88 07:17  FC        .EXE     23552  02/06/88 07:17
FC      .DOC      1906  02/06/88 07:17  FLAG      .WPG       554  02/06/88 07:17
FEET    .WPG      1384  02/06/88 07:17  GLOBE     .WPG      2542  02/06/88 07:16
GAVEL   .WPG       912  02/06/88 07:16  GRAB      .COM     12747  02/06/88 07:16
GOODNEWS.WPG      4494  02/06/88 07:16  HOURGLAS  .WPG      1830  02/06/88 07:16
HEARYE  .WPG      5400  02/06/88 07:16

Page(s): (All)
```

Figure 5.21 *Entering Pages to Print Through List Files*
(F5, 4-Print)

Section 5.2.4), WordPerfect will tell you "Error — Document was fast saved—must be retrieved to print."]

WordPerfect will begin printing the first document, but you can continue to order print jobs through **List Files**. Be sure to refer to Section 6.1 for important ways to look for files you might want to print.

5.9 Troubleshooting Printing Problems

If you have just gotten your system up and running or just switched to WordPerfect from another word processor, and your printer doesn't work, the problem is probably caused by insufficient setup. If you've been printing from WordPerfect and the printer stops, you might have a hardware problem. And, if the printer is printing but the text is printing incorrectly, you probably have embedded unwanted codes into the document.

5.9.1 *Printer Problems with New Computers and Software*

If you have never printed with your new system and can't get it started, try printing through DOS. Press **Shift-PrtSc (Print Screen)**. If the printer doesn't respond try the following:

1. Double check the cable and power cord connections.

2. See if the printer is getting power. A power-on indicator light should be lit.

3. Exit WordPerfect properly and reboot the system by pressing **Ctrl-Alt-Del**. As DOS reboots, the printer should respond by positioning the print head.

4. Most printers have a button or switch which takes them on- and off-line. The printer could be getting power but not be online with the computer. Usually, the on- and offline buttons are located on the front of dot-matrix printers. Try pushing them. If the printer is off-line and you press the online button, the print head will position itself.

5. Try a Print Screen again. If nothing happens and you're absolutely sure that the cabling and power are all right, you might have a hardware problem and you should contact your computer dealer.

6. If your dealer has installed DOS on your new computer, it is almost certain that there is no problem with that software. However, as a last resort check your DOS directory to make certain there is a Print file listed. If there's not a PRINT.EXE or PRINT.COM file or if your software has not been installed by a knowledgeable computer person, that could be the problem.

To check the DOS directory:

Return to the C:
Enter C:**CD ** (change to the root directory)
Enter C:**dir/p**

File names will be listed. However, the root directory might or might not contain DOS files. If you don't see any of the files shown in Figure 5.22, DOS resides in its own directory, which you can see in the root directory on your screen. Looking at Figure 5.23, you'll see that there are several files that say <DIR>. One of them says DOS. We'll change to the DOS directory to look for the PRINT.EXE file:

```
Strike a key when ready . . .
5Z0Z     CPI      459    3-17-87  12:00p
APPEND   EXE     5825    3-17-87  12:00p
ASSIGN   COM     1561    3-17-87  12:00p
ATTRIB   EXE     9529    3-17-87  12:00p
BACKUP   COM    31961    7-24-87   9:40a
CHKDSK   COM     9850    3-18-87  12:00p
COMP     COM     4214    3-17-87  12:00p
CPANEL   COM    19858    8-24-87  12:00p
DEBUG    COM    15897    3-17-87  12:00p
DISKCOMP COM     5879    3-17-87  12:00p
DISKCOPY COM     6Z95    3-17-87  12:00p
DRAWTREE COM    12159    1-01-80  12:39a
EDLIN    COM     7526    3-17-87  12:00p
FIND     EXE     6434    3-17-87  12:00p
GRAFTABL COM     6128    3-17-87  12:00p
GRAPHICS COM     3300    3-17-87  12:00p
JOIN     EXE     8969    3-17-87  12:00p
LABEL    COM     2377    3-17-87  12:00p
MORE     COM      313    3-17-87  12:00p
NUMLCKFX COM       15    1-28-88  10:44a
ODDPRMPT BAT       77   11-12-87  11:08a
RECOUER  COM     4299    3-18-87  12:00p
Strike a key when ready . . .
```

Figure 5.22 *Checking DOS for a PRINT.EXE File*

```
123            <DIR>      1-12-88   3:52p
AUTOEXEC BAT      5Z      3-15-88  10:18a
NORTON         <DIR>      1-14-88   3:09p
WORDPERF       <DIR>      2-10-88   9:40a
WS4            <DIR>      1-19-88   4:57p
WS5            <DIR>      3-04-88  11:48a
WINDOWS        <DIR>      1-22-88   4:19p
QUATTRO        <DIR>      1-25-88   3:11p
RAPID          <DIR>      1-25-88   2:57p
MOUSE    SYS   14301      8-25-87   3:16p
VENTURA        <DIR>      1-27-88   3:17p
TYPESET        <DIR>      1-27-88   3:18p
VP       BAT      5Z      1-27-88   3:23p
WORD           <DIR>      2-03-88   3:15p
Q&A            <DIR>      2-03-88   3:32p
CONFIG   SYS      46      3-15-88  10:17a
WP5            <DIR>      2-18-88  11:22a
BEACHAM        <DIR>      2-23-88   4:17p
PM             <DIR>      3-15-88  10:12a
PMTUTOR  BAT      76      3-15-88  10:17a
       26 File(s)   11171840 bytes free

Enter 'EXIT' to return to WordPerfect
C>
```

Figure 5.23 *Looking for the DOS Directory*

```
C:CD DOS
C:dir/p
```

Now look for the **PRINT.EXE** file.

5.9.2   *Print Screen Works but WordPerfect Doesn't*

This situation probably results from improper installation of WordPerfect's software or improperly designating your printer. Here are some things to try.

1. Go to the Print menu (**Shift-F7**) and double check to see if the model of your computer is the same as the model WordPerfect shows. If it isn't, go through the printer selection process again (see Section 5.1.1). Remember, it is important that you not only specify the correct manufacturer, such as Epson, but also the correct model, FX-86e/286e. If you specify a dot-matrix model and you're running a laser printer, WordPerfect can't drive it.

2. If the model has been correctly specified, the port selection can be the only other setup problem. On some computers, such as the Toshiba 3100 laptop model, there's a switch that controls signal output to the PRT and COM ports. Check the manual that came with your computer for any directions concerning port switches or DIP switches.

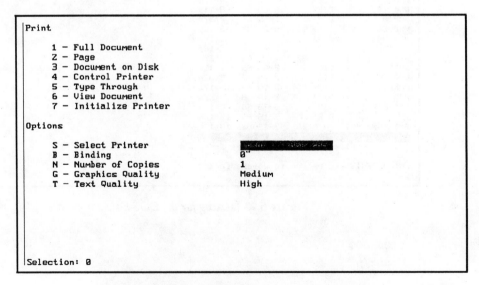

Figure 5.24 *Checking the Printer Model Specified*
(Shift-F7)

5.9.3 *The Printer Prints but the Text Looks Crazy*

There are two obvious reasons why the text does not appear on the page as you intended it: (1) the form of the paper or the format is incorrectly specified, and (2) unwanted codes have been embedded in the text.

1. To check the paper size, press **Shift-F8** and select **2-Page**. Item **8-Paper Size** will tell you if you're printing on correctly specified paper.

2. Check item **5-Margins Top/Bottom** from this same settings sheet. Also check left and right margins by selecting item **1-Line**.

3. Most probably, misaligned text is caused by codes that you've inadvertently embedded in the document. See Section 3.2.3 for instructions.

C H A P T E R 6

Working with Files

As with any filing system, the more files it contains the more organized you have to be with it. You'll want to rename, rearrange, and discard your electronic files from time to time. You'll also want to copy them, and sophisticated users will want to convert them into ASCII characters. You can work through DOS to accomplish these tasks, but WordPerfect provides more convenient ways of dealing with your filing system.

6.1 Using List Files

When you press **F5 (List Files)**, the message center displays the name of the WordPerfect directory. You can use List Files to work in this or any other directory. For the time being, we'll work in the WP directory. Press **Enter** to bring up the list of files (see Figure 6.1).

There are several things to notice about this list. First, it is alphabetized. If you look at the same directory in DOS, the files are listed by the date they were created. As with DOS, WordPerfect records the date and time when the file was created or last changed. The column between the file name and the date gives the size of the file in bytes. 20,940 means there are that many characters and spaces in Chpt3.

Knowing the size and date of your files is helpful in deciding which ones to delete or store elsewhere. Even if your computer is equipped with

```
03/22/88  09:48              Directory C:\WP5\*.*
Document size:      225    Free: 11171840   Used:  3165700        Files:   84

PC       .WPG      2578  02/06/88 07:16  ↑ PENCIL   .WPG      3510  02/06/88 07:16
PHONE    .WPG      4180  02/06/88 07:17    POINT    .WPG      1790  02/06/88 07:17
PRESENT  .WPG      1414  02/06/88 07:17    PRINTER  .TST     10863  02/22/88 13:17
PTR      .EXE    199680  03/07/88 11:50    PTR      .HLP    126414  03/07/88 11:50
RPTCARD  .WPG      6054  02/06/88 07:17    SCISSORS.WPG       568  02/06/88 07:17
SNEAKER  .WPG      1212  02/06/88 07:17    SPELL    .EXE     34816  02/05/88 17:34
STANDARD.PRS       1005  03/09/88 13:03    THINKER  .WPG      4626  02/06/88 07:17
TOSHP321.PRS       2773  03/21/88 14:29    USMAP    .WPG      9098  02/06/88 07:17
WE'RE#1  .WPG      3234  02/06/88 07:17    WP       .DRS     72784  02/06/88 07:16
WP       .EXE    242176  03/09/88 13:03    WP       .FIL    296760  03/09/88 13:03
WP       .MRS      3660  03/09/88 13:03    WPHELP   .FIL     57139  03/09/88 13:03
WPHELP2  .FIL     19535  03/09/88 13:03    WPRINTA  .ALL    209644  03/07/88 12:06
WPRINTB  .ALL    207986  03/07/88 12:08    WPRINTC  .ALL    228410  03/07/88 12:08
WPSMALL  .DRS     13822  03/09/88 13:03    WPTEXT   .PRS       994  03/09/88 13:03
WP{WP}   .SET       688  03/21/88 16:39    WP{WP}EN.HYC     45200  03/07/88 12:10
WP{WP}EN.HYL    362265  03/07/88 12:10    WP{WP}EN.LEX    292143  02/05/88 17:34
WP{WP}EN.THS    361421  02/05/88 17:35    WP}WP{   .BV1         0  03/22/88 09:44
WP}WP{   .CHK         0  03/22/88 09:33    WP}WP{   .GF1         0  03/22/88 09:47
WP}WP{   .SPC      4096  03/22/88 09:33    WP}WP{   .TV1         0  03/22/88 09:44

1 Retrieve; 2 Delete; 3 Rename; 4 Print; 5 Text In; 6 Look;
7 Change Directory; 8 Copy; 9 Word Search; N Name Search: 6
```

Figure 6.1 *List of Files in the WP Directory (F5)*

a hard disk, you'll eventually want to transfer or delete files. The size and date will also help you identify files you want to retrieve.

At the top of the page you'll see the amount of free space remaining on the disk as well as the number of bytes you've used. If you're using floppy disks, WordPerfect reads them and gives the same information. This information tells you whether your disk contains enough space to store the document on the screen.

When WordPerfect Saves a file, it temporarily requires double the space of the file being stored. That is, if you want to Save a file that is 20,000 bytes and you have only 35,000 free bytes, WordPerfect cannot Save it and will tell you that the disk is full.

Also notice that the list of files contains WordPerfect system files as well as the data files you've created. *Never* try to Retrieve a WordPerfect file except for the supplementary dictionary (see Section 4.3.8).

The following sections describe the function of the menu items at the bottom of the screen.

6.1.1 Marking Files

There are several operations, such as Print, Delete, and Search, that you can perform on the files in List Files, but you might not want to work on the entire list of files, especially if it's long. You can single out particular files by marking them. Move the cursor to the file name and enter an

asterisk (*). Any operation that you request will be performed only on the marked files.

To remove the * mark from a file, position the cursor on the marked file name and press * again. If you want to "unmark" all the marked files, press **Home *** (see Figure 6.2).

6.1.2 Retrieving Files

The advantage to retrieving files through **1-Retrieve** is that you can look at the file names and decide which file you're really looking for. You can also **Look** at any document on disk before retrieving it. A third advantage is that you can search for files in another directory.

Using the **Arrow** keys, move the cursor to the file you want to Retrieve. Press **1** and the file is brought up. When you Retrieve a file it is combined with whatever text is on the screen (see Section 6.4), so you should begin List Files from an empty typing area if you plan to Retrieve.

6.1.3 Deleting Files

If you want to throw away a file, use **2-Delete**. Move the cursor to the file name and press **2**. WordPerfect will ask:

```
03/22/88  09:57            Directory C:\WP5\*.*
Document size:        0   Free: 10876928   Used:    209098      Marked: 8

. <CURRENT>    <DIR>                  .. <PARENT>    <DIR>
ALPSP240.PRS     4193  03/18/88 10:09   AND      .WPG     1466  02/06/88 07:17
APPLAUSE.WPG     1774  02/06/88 07:17   ARROW1   .WPG      342  02/06/88 07:17
ARROW2   .WPG     352  02/06/88 07:17   ARROW3   .WPG      340  02/06/88 07:17
ARROW4   .WPG     404  02/06/88 07:17   ARROW5   .WPG      698  02/06/88 07:17
AWARD    .WPG    1746  02/06/88 07:17   BADNEWS  .WPG     4167  02/06/88 07:17
BOMB     .WPG     950  02/06/88 07:17   BOOK     .WPG     1904  02/06/88 07:17
BORDER   .WPG   13662  02/06/88 07:17   CHARACTR.DOC    52559  02/24/88 15:38
CHECK    .WPG    1070  02/06/88 07:17   CHPT1    .        28926  03/18/88 14:29
CHPTZ    .       29141  03/18/88 15:02   CHPT3    .        20940  03/18/88 16:30
CHPT4A   .       13195  03/21/88 09:56   CHPT5    .        29998  03/21/88 11:33
CHPT6    .       26983  03/21/88 12:12   CHPT7    .        34083  03/21/88 12:49
CHPT8    .       25832  03/21/88 13:55   CLOCK    .WPG     6038  02/06/88 07:17
COMPASS  .WPG    2126  02/06/88 07:17   CONFID   .WPG     2242  02/06/88 07:17
EGA51Z   .FNT    7168  02/06/88 07:16   EGAITAL  .FNT     3584  02/06/88 07:16
EGASMC   .FNT    3584  02/06/88 07:16   EGAUND   .FNT     3584  02/06/88 07:16
EPFX80   .PRS    5524  03/21/88 17:08   EPFX86E  .PRS     7188  03/18/88 10:23
FACTORY  .WPG     972  02/06/88 07:17   FATARROW.WPG      342  02/06/88 07:17
FC       .DOC    1906  02/06/88 07:17   FC       .EXE    23552  02/06/88 07:17

1 Retrieve: 2 Delete: 3 Rename: 4 Print: 5 Text In: 6 Look:
7 Change Directory: 8 Copy: 9 Word Search: N Name Search: 6
```

Figure 6.2 *Examples of Marked Files*
(F5, Position Cursor, *)

```
Delete \WP\file name (Y/N?):No
```

As soon as you press **Y**, the file is deleted. There are no second chances, so be certain the file is the one you want. To Delete several files, **mark** them (see Section 6.1.1). A blank will appear in the position of the file(s) you deleted. The next time you call up List Files, there will be no blank (see Figure 6.3).

6.1.4   *Renaming Files*

Once you have set up your electronic filing system, you might find that some files require different names. Move the cursor to the file you want to rename and press **3-Rename**. The prompt will ask:

```
New name:
```

Type the new name and press **Enter**. The old name in the list of files will immediately change to the new name. You can change the name of a file as often as you wish, but WordPerfect will not allow you to select the name of a file that already exists.

```
03/22/88  10:36            Directory C:\WP5\*.*
Document size:        0   Free: 10876928   Used:  3409413        Files:  127

COMPASS .WPG    2126 02/06/88 07:17    CONFID  .WPG    2242 02/06/88 07:17
EGA512  .FNT    7168 02/06/88 07:16    EGAITAL .FNT    3584 02/06/88 07:16
EGASMC  .FNT    3584 02/06/88 07:16    EGAUND  .FNT    3584 02/06/88 07:16
EPFX80  .PRS    5524 03/21/88 17:08    EPFX86E .PRS    7188 03/18/88 10:23
FACTORY .WPG     972 02/06/88 07:17    FATARROW.WPG     342 02/06/88 07:17
FC      .DOC    1906 02/06/88 07:17    FC      .EXE   23552 02/06/88 07:17
FEET    .WPG    1384 02/06/88 07:17    FILE1           737 02/20/88 18:12
FILE10  .       1312 03/17/88 16:41    FILE103 .       1277 03/17/88 16:30
FILE11  .        447 03/04/88 10:15    FILE14  .        467 03/09/88 14:38
FILE15  .        981 03/09/88 15:06    FILE2   .       1510 02/21/88 19:04
FILE20  .        745 03/13/88 09:36    FILE21  .       1118 03/14/88 17:59
FILE22  .       1133 03/14/88 18:00    FILE23  .       1168 03/14/88 18:02
FILE24  .        699 03/14/88 16:21    FILE26  .       1959 03/14/88 16:50
FILE27  .        566 03/15/88 15:23    FILE28  .        571 03/15/88 15:28
FILE29  .        571 03/15/88 15:34    FILE3   .       1132 03/15/88 12:58
FILE30  .        988 03/16/88 13:22    FILE31  .        988 03/16/88 13:23
FILE32  .        993 03/16/88 15:01    FILE33  .        993 03/16/88 13:21
FILE35  .        993 03/17/88 17:03    FILE36  .        993 03/16/88 15:27
FILE37  .        993 03/16/88 15:31    FILE38  .        993 03/16/88 15:32
```

Figure 6.3 *Last Chance Prompt for Deleting Files*
(F5, 2-Delete)

6.1.5 Printing

You can add the names of files you want to Print to the Printer Control by positioning the cursor on the file name and selecting **4-Print** (see Section 5.2.6).

You can also **Mark** (see Section 6.1.1) several files with an asterisk and select **4. Print**. WordPerfect will ask:

```
Print marked files? (Y/N) No
```

Change No to **Y** and WordPerfect prints all the files marked by an asterisk in alphabetical order of the file names (see Figure 6.4).

If the files were Fast Saved (see Section 5.2.3), an error message will appear (see Figure 6.5).

6.1.6 Text In

This feature allows you to convert WordPerfect files to ASCII characters and to use WordPerfect as a text editor. See Section 6.8 for instructions.

```
03/22/88   10:40                Directory C:\WP5\*.*
Document size:          0   Free: 10876928   Used:    209098        Marked: 8

. <CURRENT>     <DIR>                      .. <PARENT>     <DIR>
ALPSP240.PRS    4193  03/18/88 10:09       AND      .WPG    1466  02/06/88 07:17
APPLAUSE.WPG    1774  02/06/88 07:17       ARROW1   .WPG     342  02/06/88 07:17
ARROW2  .WPG     352  02/06/88 07:17       ARROW3   .WPG     340  02/06/88 07:17
ARROW4  .WPG     404  02/06/88 07:17       ARROW5   .WPG     698  02/06/88 07:17
AWARD   .WPG    1746  02/06/88 07:17       BADNEWS  .WPG    4167  02/06/88 07:17
BOMB    .WPG     950  02/06/88 07:17       BOOK     .WPG    1904  02/06/88 07:17
BORDER  .WPG   13662  02/06/88 07:17       CHARACTR.DOC   52559  02/24/88 15:38
CHECK   .WPG    1070  02/06/88 07:17       CHPT1    .      28926  03/18/88 14:29
CHPT2   .      29141  03/18/88 15:02       CHPT3    .      20940  03/18/88 16:30
CHPT4A  .      13195  03/21/88 09:56       CHPT5    .      29998  03/21/88 11:33
CHPT6   .      26983  03/21/88 12:12       CHPT7    .      34083  03/21/88 12:49
CHPT8   .      25832  03/21/88 13:55       CLOCK    .WPG    6038  02/06/88 07:17
COMPASS .WPG    2126  02/06/88 07:17       CONFID   .WPG    2242  02/06/88 07:17
EGA512  .FNT    7168  02/06/88 07:16       EGAITAL  .FNT    3584  02/06/88 07:16
EGASMC  .FNT    3584  02/06/88 07:16       EGAUND   .FNT    3584  02/06/88 07:16
EPFX80  .PRS    5524  03/21/88 17:08       EPFX86E  .PRS    7188  03/18/88 10:23
FACTORY .WPG     972  02/06/88 07:17       FATARROW.WPG     342  02/06/88 07:17
FC      .DOC    1906  02/06/88 07:17       FC       .EXE   23552  02/06/88 07:17

Print marked files? (Y/N) No
```

Figure 6.4 *Printing Marked Files*
(F5, Mark Files, 4-Print)

```
03/22/88  10:40            Directory C:\WP5\*.*
Document size:        0   Free: 10876928   Used:   209098        Marked: 8

. <CURRENT>      <DIR>                  .. <PARENT>     <DIR>
ALPSPZ40.PRS      4193  03/18/88 10:09  AND       .WPG    1466  02/06/88 07:17
APPLAUSE.WPG      1774  02/06/88 07:17  ARROW1    .WPG     342  02/06/88 07:17
ARROW2  .WPG       352  02/06/88 07:17  ARROW3    .WPG     340  02/06/88 07:17
ARROW4  .WPG       404  02/06/88 07:17  ARROW5    .WPG     698  02/06/88 07:17
AWARD   .WPG      1746  02/06/88 07:17  BADNEWS   .WPG    4167  02/06/88 07:17
BOMB    .WPG       950  02/06/88 07:17  BOOK      .WPG    1904  02/06/88 07:17
BORDER  .WPG     13662  02/06/88 07:17  CHARACTR  .DOC   52559  02/24/88 15:38
CHECK   .WPG      1070  02/06/88 07:17  CHPT1     .      28926* 03/18/88 14:29
CHPT2   .        29141* 03/18/88 15:02  CHPT3     .      20940* 03/18/88 16:30
CHPT4A  .        13195* 03/21/88 09:56  CHPT5     .      29998* 03/21/88 11:33
CHPT6   .        26983* 03/21/88 12:12  CHPT7     .      34083* 03/21/88 12:49
CHPT8   .        25832* 03/21/88 13:55  CLOCK     .WPG    6038  02/06/88 07:17
COMPASS .WPG      2126  02/06/88 07:17  CONFID    .WPG    2242  02/06/88 07:17
EGA51Z  .FNT      7168  02/06/88 07:16  EGAITAL   .FNT    3584  02/06/88 07:16
EGASMC  .FNT      3584  02/06/88 07:16  EGAUND    .FNT    3584  02/06/88 07:16
EPFX80  .PRS      5524  03/21/88 17:08  EPFX86E   .PRS    7188  03/18/88 10:23
FACTORY .WPG       972  02/06/88 07:17  FATARROW  .WPG     342  02/06/88 07:17
FC      .DOC      1906  02/06/88 07:17  FC        .EXE   23552  02/06/88 07:17
```

Figure 6.5 *Attempting to Retrieve "Fast Saved"*
Files (F5, Mark Files, 4-Print, Y)

6.1.7 Look

This very useful feature allows you to enter a document and Search it without having to Retrieve it. You can also Look at other directories.

If you want to Look at a file in the default directory, move the cursor to the file name and select **6-Look**. If you've created a Document Summary (see Section 6.3), the file opens there. Otherwise it opens with the first line of the document. A full screen comes up. Using any of the cursor movements, you can scroll through the document. You can also **Search (F2)** the document for key words or phrases. When you've finished looking, press **F7 (Exit)** to return to the List Files menu. If you want to Retrieve this file, press **1-Retrieve**.

If your directory contains many files, you might want to isolate particular ones by their file extensions (see Section 6.4). After pressing **5-List Files**, (the directory name appears in the message center), enter ***.** and the file extension. In Figure 6.6 we entered ***.prs** to produce a selected list of files.

6.1.8 Creating and Changing Directories

When you first press F5, the message center shows the WordPerfect directory. If you want to view another directory, you can enter it here. You can

```
03/22/88  10:53               Directory C:\WP5\*.PRS
Document size:          0  Free: 10876928  Used:    21677      Files:  6

. <CURRENT>    <DIR>                  .. <PARENT>    <DIR>
ALPSP240.PRS      4193  03/18/88 10:09  EPFX80   .PRS    5524  03/21/88 17:08
EPFX86E .PRS      7188  03/18/88 10:23  STANDARD.PRS    1005  03/09/88 13:03
TOSHP321.PRS      2773  03/21/88 14:29  UPTEXT   .PRS     994  03/09/88 13:03












1 Retrieve: 2 Delete: 3 Rename: 4 Print: 5 Text In: 6 Look:
7 Change Directory: 8 Copy: 9 Word Search: N Name Search: 6
```

Figure 6.6 *Selecting Files by Their Extension*
(*F5, *.prs*)

also select item **7-Change Directory** from the List Files menu. In either
case enter:

```
c:\directory name
```

If you select item 7 and no directory exists by that name, WordPerfect
will ask if you want to **create** a directory. Answer Y to make a new directory.

6.1.9 Copying Files

It is easier to copy files through WordPerfect than through DOS. Position
the cursor on the name of the file you want to copy. When you select **8-
Copy**, WordPerfect asks:

```
Copy the file to:
```

Enter the directory and file name, such as:

```
Copy the file to:c:\sym\travel
```

where sym is the directory and travel is the file name.

You have several options for naming the path and file. You can copy the file to the same directory under another file name. If you select a file name that already exists, WordPerfect *copies over* that file. Be careful not to destroy good files this way. You can also copy into another directory or you can copy into another disk drive, such as B:travel. This is a convenient way to back up files from a hard disk to floppies.

6.1.10 *Searching Files*

This is one of the jazziest features in WordPerfect 5.0. WordPerfect will search any or all files for words or word combinations and mark them with an asterisk. For example, over a period of time you might have 100 files, some of which contain references to zoning regulations. You're not sure which files those are, so you ask WordPerfect to search the files for you.

When you select item **9-Search** from the List Files menu, WordPerfect offers four options for searching (see Figure 6.7). The difference, of course, between searching document summaries, only the first page, and the entire document is simply the amount of time it takes to complete the search. WordPerfect can search 100 document summaries quickly but could take a long time to search 100 long documents. However, unlike the F2 (Search) feature, when WordPerfect finds the first occurrence of the pattern it marks the file. Since there is no need to continue searching the

```
03/22/88  10:55              Directory C:\WP5\*.*
Document size:         0   Free: 10876928   Used:   3409413        Files:   127

.  <CURRENT>     <DIR>                      ..  <PARENT>    <DIR>
ALPSPZ40.PRS        4193   03/18/88 10:09   AND       .WP6      1466   02/06/88 07:17
APPLAUSE.WP6        1774   02/06/88 07:17   ARROW1    .WP6       342   02/06/88 07:17
ARROW2  .WP6         352   02/06/88 07:17   ARROW3    .WP6       340   02/06/88 07:17
ARROW4  .WP6         404   02/06/88 07:17   ARROW5    .WP6       698   02/06/88 07:17
AWARD   .WP6        1746   02/06/88 07:17   BADNEWS   .WP6      4167   02/06/88 07:17
BOMB    .WP6         950   02/06/88 07:17   BOOK      .WP6      1904   02/06/88 07:17
BORDER  .WP6       13662   02/06/88 07:17   CHARACTR. DOC     52559   02/24/88 15:38
CHECK   .WP6        1070   02/06/88 07:17   CHPT1     .        28926   03/18/88 14:29
CHPT2   .          29141   03/18/88 15:02   CHPT3     .        20940   03/18/88 16:30
CHPT4A  .          13195   03/21/88 09:56   CHPT5     .        29998   03/21/88 11:33
CHPT6   .          26983   03/21/88 12:12   CHPT7     .        34083   03/21/88 12:49
CHPT8   .          25832   03/21/88 13:55   CLOCK     .WP6      6038   02/06/88 07:17
COMPASS .WP6        2126   02/06/88 07:17   CONFID    .WP6      2242   02/06/88 07:17
EGA51Z  .FNT        7168   02/06/88 07:16   EGAITAL   .FNT      3584   02/06/88 07:16
EGASMC  .FNT        3584   02/06/88 07:16   EGAUND    .FNT      3584   02/06/88 07:16
EPFX80  .PRS        5524   03/21/88 17:08   EPFX86E   .PRS      7188   03/18/88 10:23
FACTORY .WP6         972   02/06/88 07:17   FATARROW. WP6       342   02/06/88 07:17
FC      .DOC        1906   02/06/88 07:17   FC        .EXE     23552   02/06/88 07:17
```

Figure 6.7 *Search Options (F5, 9-Search)*

marked file, it goes to the next file in the list. This speeds up searching time.

If you select **1, 2,** or **3** the prompt will ask for the **Word Pattern:**. As soon as you type in the pattern and press **Enter,** WordPerfect begins its search. It tells you which file it is currently searching, such as **17 of 92.** When it finishes, all the files that contain the specified word pattern will be marked with an asterisk on the List Files screen.

Item **4-Conditions** provides the opportunity to enter more criteria for searching. It brings up the settings sheet in Figure 6.8.

Item **4-File Date** lets you specify a time range. So, in addition to searching for "zoning ordinance 4237-B," you can search for all references to it in the files created between 1/1/84 and 7/1/87. You may leave any part of the date blank; e.g., type 8//84 if you want to search only the month of August.

You can also search any element in the Document Summaries with item 7. See Section 6.3 for instructions about creating a Document Summary.

6.1.10.1 Unmarking Files

Item 2 in the Conditions Settings Sheet (see Figure 6.8) will remove all the asterisks from the files. You can also remove them by returning to the List

```
Word Search

   1 - Perform Search on              All 127 File(s)

   2 - Undo Last Search

   3 - Reset Search Conditions

   4 - File Date                      No
         From (MM/DD/YY):             (All)
         To   (MM/DD/YY):             (All)

                  Word Pattern(s)

   5 - First Page
   6 - Entire Doc
   7 - Document Summary
         Creation Date (e.g. Nov)
         Descriptive Name
         Subject/Account
         Author
         Typist
         Comments

Selection: 1
```

Figure 6.8 *Conditions Settings Sheet*
(F5, (9-Search, 4-Conditions)

Files screen and pressing **Home ***. If you want to unmark specific files rather than all of them, move the cursor to the file name and press *****.

6.1.11 *Word Patterns and Logical Operators*

You are limited to 40 characters when entering your word pattern. However, you can ask for combinations of words or for parts of words. For example, there might be several zoning ordinances that begin with "42." You can enter your word pattern as **zoning ordinance 42*-B**. The ***** tells WordPerfect to look for any number beginning with 42 and ending with -B, such as 42RS4-B. An asterisk tells WordPerfect to look for any number of characters; a question mark is used for only one character.

You can include two logical operators in a pattern. A semicolon or space represents **And** while a comma represents **Or**. To look for zoning ordinances A and B you would enter **4237-B;4237-A**. Unless WordPerfect found both in a single document, it would not mark the file. With a comma, **4237-B,4237-A**, WordPerfect would mark a file that contained either number.

6.2 Setting Up Your Filing System Using File Extensions

In addition to the eight-character file name you can assign to any data file, you can also assign three more characters past the decimal. In the List Files screen (see Figure 6.9) you'll notice that the WordPerfect files contain a three-character "extension," such as .PRS or .EXE. The data files have not been given extensions.

If there is a logical reason to assigning file extensions, you can use the search functions to locate files. Correspondence, for example, might have a file extension of .ltr while staff memos might have .mem. You can now use the **6-Look** feature to locate files with specified extensions. All letters tagged Matthews.ltr can be selected from the list:

Press F5 (List Files)
Select **6-Look**
Enter in the message center **C:\directory\file name.extension**

such as C:\WP\Matthews.ltr.

```
03/22/88  09:48           Directory C:\WP5\*.*
Document size:        225  Free: 11171840   Used:  3165700          Files:  84

PC       .WPG     2578  02/06/88 07:16  ▲  PENCIL   .WPG     3510  02/06/88 07:16
PHONE    .WPG     4180  02/06/88 07:17  │  POINT    .WPG     1790  02/06/88 07:17
PRESENT  .WPG     1414  02/06/88 07:17  │  PRINTER  .TST    10863  02/22/88 13:17
PTR      ▓▓▓▓   199680  03/07/88 11:50     PTR      .HLP   126414  03/07/88 11:50
RPTCARD  .WPG     6054  02/06/88 07:17     SCISSORS.WPG      568  02/06/88 07:17
SNEAKER  .WPG     1212  02/06/88 07:17     SPELL    ▓▓▓▓   34816  02/05/88 17:34
STANDARD ▓▓▓      1005  03/09/88 13:03     THINKER  .WPG     4626  02/06/88 07:17
TOSHP321 ▓▓       2773  03/21/88 14:29     USMAP    .WPG     9098  02/06/88 07:17
WE'RE#1  .WPG     3234  02/06/88 07:17     WP       .DRS    72784  02/06/88 07:16
WP       ▓▓▓▓   242176  03/09/88 13:03     WP       .FIL   296760  03/09/88 13:03
WP       .MRS     3660  03/09/88 13:03     WPHELP   .FIL    57139  03/09/88 13:03
WPHELP2  .FIL    19535  03/09/88 13:03     WPRINTA  .ALL   209644  03/07/88 12:06
WPRINTB  .ALL   207986  03/07/88 12:08     WPRINTC  .ALL   228410  03/07/88 12:08
WPSMALL  .DRS    13022  03/09/88 13:03     WPTEXT   ▓▓▓▓     994  03/09/88 13:03
WP{WP}   .SET      688  03/21/88 16:39     WP{WP}EN.HYC    45200  03/07/88 12:10
WP{WP}EN.HYL    362265  03/07/88 12:10     WP{WP}EN.LEX   292143  03/05/88 17:34
WP{WP}EN.THS    361421  02/05/88 17:35     WP}WP{   .BV1        0  03/22/88 09:44
WP}WP{   .CHK        0  03/22/88 09:33     WP}WP{   .GF1        0  03/22/88 09:47
WP}WP{   .SPC     4096  03/22/88 09:33     WP}WP{   .TV1        0  03/22/88 09:44

1 Retrieve: 2 Delete: 3 Rename: 4 Print: 5 Text In: 6 Look:
7 Change Directory: 8 Copy: 9 Word Search: N Name Search: 6
```

Figure 6.9 *List Files Screen (F5)*

6.3. Document Summary

To help you keep track of a complicated filing system, WordPerfect gives you the opportunity to make notes to yourself in a special summary format. The Document Summary is attached to a specific file and includes:

Descriptive file name
Subject of the text
Author
Typist
Comments

The comments section displays the first 400 characters of the file or up to 780 characters of your own comments. Basically, the document summary is a way of writing yourself notes that you can browse while looking for particular files and that WordPerfect can use to quickly identify search criteria.

To bring up the Document Summary feature press **Ctrl-F5 (Text In/Out)**, **Comment**, then **Create** (see Figure 6.10). Fill in data for any of the categories by selecting their corresponding number. You are limited to 40 characters per category except comments, which can contain 780.

```
Document Summary

        System Filename        (Not named yet)

        Date of Creation       May 4, 1988

    1 - Descriptive Filename

    2 - Subject/Account

    3 - Author

    4 - Typist

    5 - Comments

  ┌──────────────────────────────────────────────────────────────┐
  │ Chapter 6  Working with Files; As with any filing system, the more the │
  │ files it contains the more organized you have to be with it. You'll want │
  │ to rename, rearrange, and discard your electronic files from time to time. │
  │ You'll also want to copy them, and sophisticated users will want to │
  │ convert them into ASCII characters. │
  └──────────────────────────────────────────────────────────────┘

Selection: 0
```

Figure 6.10 *Document Summary Settings Sheet*
(Ctrl-F5, 5-Comment, 1-Create)

To Save your summary, press **F7 (Exit)**. To cancel your summary press **F1**.

6.3.1   *Automatic Document Summary*

If you want to make Document Summary a standard feature of your record keeping, you can change the default to automatically create a summary anytime you Save or Exit a file. This feature not only saves keystrokes but also serves as a reminder to fill in the summary. To turn on the automatic summary:

> Press **Shift-F1 (Setup)** (see Figure 6.11)
> Select **5-Initial Settings** (see Figure 6.12)
> Select **3-Document Summary** (see Figure 6.13)
> Select **1-Create on Save/Exit**
> Change No to **Yes**

6.3.2   *Subject Search*

Item **3-Subject/Account** is used to tag the file in the same way a memorandum or letter would use RE:. In fact, if WordPerfect finds "RE:" in the first 400 characters of the document, it automatically inserts the associated text into the Document Summary.

```
Setup

    1 - Backup

    2 - Cursor Speed              30 cps

    3 - Display

    4 - Fast Save (unformatted)   Yes

    5 - Initial Settings

    6 - Keyboard Layout

    7 - Location of Files

    8 - Units of Measure




Selection: 0
```

Figure 6.11 *Setup Menu (Shift-F1)*

```
Setup: Initial Settings

    1 - Beep Options

    2 - Date Format              3 1, 4

    3 - Document Summary

    4 - Initial Codes

    5 - Repeat Value             8

    6 - Table of Authorities






Selection: 0
```

Figure 6.12 *Initial Settings Menu*
(Shift-F1, 5-Initial Settings)

If "RE:" isn't the term you use to tag your documents, you can change WordPerfect to honor your tag. In the **Setup: Document Summary** menu (see Figure 6.13), change item 2 from RE: to your own tag.

```
Setup: Document Summary

    1 - Create on Save/Exit        No

    2 - Subject Search Text        RE:

















Selection: 0
```

Figure 6.13 *Document Summary Setup Menu*
(Shift-F1, 5-Initial Settings, 1-Create)

6.4   Combining Files

WordPerfect allows you to combine any number of files. The only limitation is the memory capacity of your computer. This is a useful feature in several circumstances. You might, for example, have several people working on different sections of a report. When everyone has finished, you can take their disks and put the report together. Or, you might want to combine stock sections of the zoning ordinances into letters or reports. If these stock sections are in WordPerfect files, you can pull them into your report anywhere you want.

Combining files is simply a matter of retrieving them. Wherever you position the cursor is the point at which the first character of the retrieved file will begin. If that is in the middle of a document, all the text beyond the cursor will be moved down and the retrieved text is inserted. You can retrieve either with **Shift-F10 (Retrieve Text)** or through F5 (List Files).

When you combine files, you are bringing a file stored on disk into a file that is on the screen, which probably has its own file name. If you attempt to Save or Exit, the combined file will be Saved under the name of the first file unless you change it. If you do not want to replace the original file with the combined file, enter a new file name.

6.5 Master Documents

Similar in concept to combining files, WordPerfect allows you to insert a code anywhere in a document that identifies the name of a file on disk. When you tell WordPerfect to **Expand** the document, it brings in the file associated with the marker. You can then **Condense** the same document and send the marked files back to the disk.

This is a useful feature when you're working with long documents or when you don't need to see certain sections very often. Condensing parts of the document just makes it easier to deal with. WordPerfect refers to **Subdocuments** as the documents on disk that will be brought into the Master Document. To create a Master Document:

Retrieve the document that will serve as the shell
Position the cursor where you want the filed document to appear
Press **Alt-F5 (Mark Text)** (see Figure 6.14)
Select **2-SubDoc**
Enter the file name of the document on disk
Press **Enter**

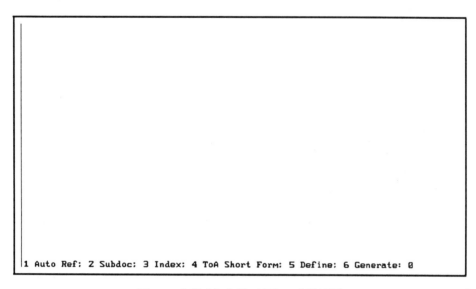

1 Auto Ref: 2 Subdoc: 3 Index: 4 ToA Short Form: 5 Define: 6 Generate: 0

Figure 6.14 *Mark Text Menu (Alt-F5)*

When you press Enter, WordPerfect draws a box on the screen with the name of the file that will be retrieved when you Expand the Master Document.

You can also see through Reveal Codes that the marker has been placed (see Figure 6.15).

6.5.1 Expanding Master Documents

If you want to look at or print a Master Document, you must Expand it. The keystrokes are:

Press **Alt-F5 (Mark Text)**
Select **6-Generate** (see Figure 6.16)
Select **3-Expand Master Document**

WordPerfect tells you that it is "Expanding master document." Depending on the speed of your microprocessor, this could take some time. When the document has been expanded, it places another box at the end of the inserted file (see Figure 6.17). Notice that the new margin settings and text for this particular document appear between the Subdoc Start and Subdoc End markers.

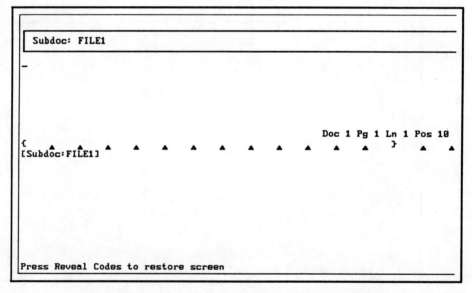

Figure 6.15 *Looking at a Subdocument Marker (Alt-F3)*

```
Mark Text: Generate

    1 - Remove Redline Markings and Strikeout Text from Document

    2 - Compare Screen and Disk Documents and Add Redline and Strikeout

    3 - Expand Master Document

    4 - Condense Master Document

    5 - Generate Tables, Indexes, Automatic References, etc.












Selection: 0
```

Figure 6.16 *"Generate" Menu*
(Alt-F5, 6-Generate, 3-Expand)

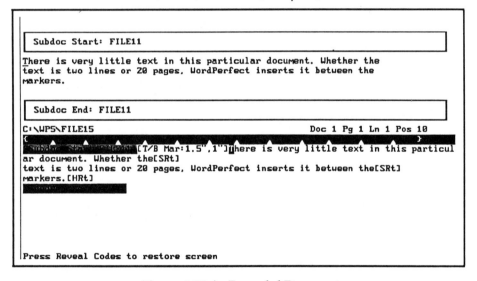

Figure 6.17 *An Expanded Document*

These boxed notations *do not print* but are included only to remind you of the condensed documents. They also do not affect work on the screen. Notice that when you move the cursor down the screen using the Arrow key, the boxes do not occupy lines.

6.5.2   *Condensing Master Documents*

Follow the same steps to Condense the document to its Shell form:

Press **Alt-F5**
Select **2-Generate**
Select **4-Condense Master Document**

WordPerfect will ask if you want to **Save Subdocs? (Y/N)Y**. If you've made any changes to the Subdocuments, Save them by pressing **Y** or **Enter**.

6.5.3   *Deleting or Moving Subdocument Markers*

Deleting a Subdocument code is the same as deleting any WordPerfect marker. You must first **Condense** the document. If you fail to Condense it, WordPerfect removes the marker but does not remove the text in the Subdocument file. Then move the cursor just past the box marker that says **Subdoc** and turn on **Reveal Codes (Alt-F3)**.

Press the **Left Arrow** key one time. The cursor will jump to the top side of the **Subdoc** box and its corresponding code is highlighted in Reveal Codes (see Figure 6.18).

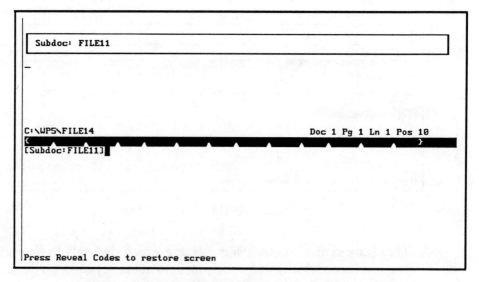

Figure 6.18 *Positioning the Cursor On the Subdoc Marker*
(Move the Cursor Just Past the Block, Alt-F3, then Press Left Arrow
to Highlight Marker)

Press **Del**. Both the beginning and ending Subdocument markers are deleted and the box disappears from the screen.

If you want to Move a Subdocument, you must first delete the markers, then reposition the cursor and go through the creation steps described in Section 6.5.

6.6	**Locked Files**

You can secure any file so that it can be retrieved only with the assigned password. Not only is the data file locked but so are any Backup files, Undelete, Move, virtual, or temporary files. Although the file name continues to appear in the directory, there is no way anyone can retrieve the file without the password.

Because of the seriousness of locking a document and forgetting the password or losing the paper on which you wrote the password, we suggest that you create a locked file that contains only the passwords. Give this locked file a name which you can't possibly forget, such as your mother's first name or your home town. Be sure to maintain this directory of locked files.

If you don't want to lock your files, you can copy them onto floppy disks and store them in a safe, but WordPerfect's locked file feature is a lot more convenient.

To lock files:

Retrieve the document
Press **Ctrl-F5 (Text In/Out)**
Select **2-Password**
Select **1-Add**

The message center will ask you to enter the password. You cannot see the word that you type in (to prevent passersby from looking over your shoulder). Press **Enter**. The message center will again ask you to enter the password. The purpose of this double entry is to ensure that you entered it correctly the first time. Type it in again and press **Enter**. If you typed it the same way both times, WordPerfect accepts this as the password.

Save the document before you Exit.

The next time you Retrieve the document, the message center will ask you to enter the password. An incorrect password produces a message "File is Locked." The correct password brings the document to the screen.

6.6.1   *Removing the Password*

With the locked document on the screen, press **Ctrl-F5 (Text In/Out)**. Select **2-Password**, then **2-Remove**. Press **F7** to return to the screen.

6.7   Using DOS through the Shell

WordPerfect permits you to temporarily leave the WordPerfect system and return to DOS (the C: prompt). You can get to DOS by exiting the system, but there are times you might want to perform a DOS command, such as formatting a disk, or to run another software system. For example, you might want to check numbers in your spreadsheet before writing a section in a WordPerfect document.

This is good theory, but in practice you are limited by the computer's memory. WordPerfect remains loaded in memory when you use the DOS shell, and certain files from DOS are also loaded into memory. You can certainly format a disk or backup files, but you probably can't load a spreadsheet. You can, however, load the WordPerfect Library. While using the DOS shell, *do not* use the DOS files CHKDSK (Check disk) or DELETE.

Exiting to DOS is easy. Press **Ctrl-F1** and press **1-Go to DOS**. To reenter WordPerfect, type the word **Exit** at the C:. Do not use the F7 (Exit) function key. WordPerfect returns you to your document.

6.8   Text In/Out: Converting Files to ASCII or from One Software Program to Another

You can use WordPerfect to convert text to and from ASCII characters. This is useful if you want to use WordPerfect files with other software. You might, for example, want to work with files that you created with your old word processor or give your current files to another department that has standardized on WordStar rather than WordPerfect. Through the Text In/Out feature you can also edit DOS files and other program files.

6.8.1   *Converting WordPerfect 5.0 Files to WP 4.2 Files*

Although WordPerfect 5.0 can read WP 4.2 files, documents created under WP 5.0 are not readable with the WP 4.2 system disk. If files are being shared between departments using different versions of the software, you must convert 5.0 files to 4.2 as follows:

Press **Ctrl-F5** (see Figure 6.19)
Select **4-Save WP 4.2**
Type name of Document to be saved

If you select the same name as the current 5.0 document, WordPerfect will ask if you want to **Replace** it. There's no harm in replacing a 5.0 document with a 4.2 format, but you might want to save the 4.2 document under a different name.

6.8.2 *DOS Text Files*

When you convert text to DOS Text files, you preserve special formatting instructions, such as tabs, margins, centering, indent, and carriage returns. Other software that has this same conversion feature can interpret these special instructions and bring a file into their program that closely resembles the WordPerfect file.

To convert a WordPerfect file to DOS Text, press **Ctrl-F5** and select **1-DOS** Text. Press **Enter** to Save the file under the current name, or type a new name (see Figure 6.20).

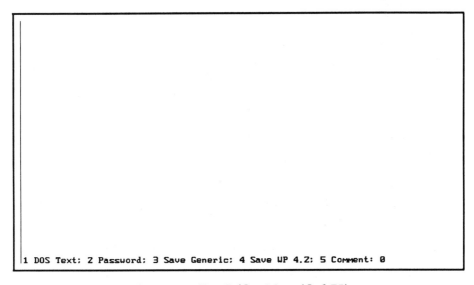

1 DOS Text: 2 Password: 3 Save Generic: 4 Save WP 4.2: 5 Comment: 0

Figure 6.19 *Text In/Out Menu (Ctrl-F5)*

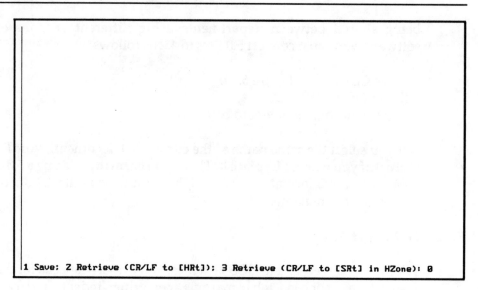

1 Save: 2 Retrieve (CR/LF to [HRt]): 3 Retrieve (CR/LF to [SRt] in HZone): 0

Figure 6.20 *Save/Retrieve DOS Text Menu*
(Ctrl-F5, 1-DOS Text)

If you Save the DOS Text file under the same name, you will not be able to Retrieve it with the **Shift-F10** function key. Rather, you have to Retrieve it through **Text In** conversion or through **List Files**.

6.8.3   *Retrieving DOS Text Files*

Normally, to retrieve files of ordinary text you'll press **Ctrl-F5**, and select **1-DOS Text** and **3-Retrieve (CR/LF to [SRt] in HZone)**. This retrieval method eliminates hard returns which would cause the text to format incorrectly. However, if you want to import files as they were created, which means maintaining the hard carriage returns and line feed codes, select item **2-Retrieve (CR/LF to [HRt])**. The HZone, by the way, is "Hyphenation Zone," setting that changes where a word is hyphenated (see Section 11.8.2).

6.8.4   *Generic Text Files*

If you are converting files and do not want to include special formatting instructions, use item **3-Save Generic**. Practically, the only time selecting the Save and Retrieval method becomes an issue is for documents that contain charts, long indents, and special alignments.

Mail Merge and Database Management

While WordPerfect is not a full-blown database manager, there are many database functions that you can perform with it. You can, for example, set up and manage a large database of customers that includes not only their address information but a profile of who they are and their purchasing record. You can query your database to select customers who meet criteria that you enter. You could ask WordPerfect to select all customers in certain states whose hobby is gardening (see Chapter 8 for instructions for Sorting). The trick is to set up the database with foresight.

Merging, which includes mail merge, is simply the process of combining information from one data file into another. While mail merge is one of the most common uses for merges, there are other sophisticated uses, such as combining macros or printing long documents.

All mail merges begin with understanding your database. It is sometimes possible to convert a database produced through other software into WordPerfect (see Section 7.3). WordPerfect Corporation also produces a product which is designed as a database manager that is, of course, compatible with WordPerfect.

7.1   The Structure of WordPerfect's Database

The database is broken down into **fields** and **records**. Using customers as an example of one use for a database, you can think of all the data about one customer as a complete record. If there are 100 different customers in the database, there would be 100 records. Within each record are fields, and understanding fields is the trick to creating a successful WordPerfect database.

Every merge operation requires a database file, such as names and addresses, and a document file, such as a letter. Information in the database is divided into fields, such as the name in field 1, the street in field 2, and the city/state/zip in field 3. When you merge, you pull information from a field and place it in the letter. For example, if we wanted the person's name to appear on the first line of the heading, we place the code ^F^ where the name should appear.

```
April 15, 1988
^F1^
```

The ^F1^ is WordPerfect's code that tells it to look in Field No. 1 (thus, F1) in the database and pull all the data it finds there into the ^F1^ position in the letter. Now, let's look at a hypothetical customer database. Here's one record:

```
John M. Matthews
410 Cherry Street
Oxen Hill, MD 21865
phone 301-368-3596
36 years old
spouse: Suzanne Matthews
2 children: boys 3, 9
```

Right now there are no codes in the record to separate the data; so we could not merge the name and address. To create a **field**, WordPerfect requires the code ^R to be placed in the database. To enter this code press either **Ctrl-R** or **F9 (Merge R)**. You cannot use Shift-6, which is the caret. Placing the first field marker in our database:

```
John M. Matthews
410 Cherry Street
```

```
Oxen Hill, MD 21865^R
phone 301-368-3596
36 years old
spouse: Suzanne Matthews
2 children: boys 3, 9
```

We have designated one field that contains three lines. The ^R, which WordPerfect understands is ^R1, corresponds to the ^F1^ marker in the letter. So, when you start the merge, WordPerfect looks for ^R1 in the first record and merges the data into the letter. If all you were doing is merging names and addresses, WordPerfect would go to the next record, that is the next customer in the database, and merge that name and address from ^R. It would continue through the entire database until all the names and addresses had been merged.

So that WordPerfect knows where one record has ended and the next begins, you must place a ^E (Ctrl-E) at the end of the customer data. *Do not skip a line between the ^E of one record and the first line of the next:*

```
John M. Matthews
410 Cherry Street
Oxen Hill, MD 21865^R
phone 301-368-3596
36 years old
spouse: Suzanne Matthews
2 children: boys 3, 9
^E
```

The relationship between the ^F^ codes that you placed in the letter and the ^R codes that are in the database form the entire mechanism for merging. It is essential that you understand how this works before proceeding. WordPerfect calls the letter the **primary file** and calls the database the **secondary file**.

7.1.1 How to Merge

Once you've set up your database, merging is quite easy. This simple example illustrates how all merges work. Bring up an empty screen and enter **Dear ^F1^**. To enter the ^F1^ code, position the cursor and press **Shift-F9**. This produces a string of codes along the bottom of the screen (see Figure 7.1).

Press the letter F and WordPerfect asks:

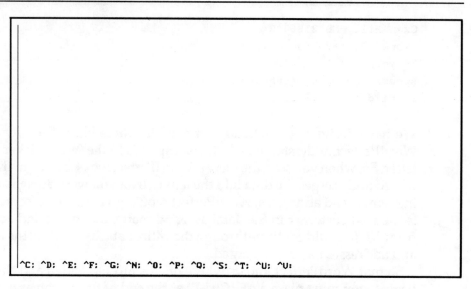

```
^C: ^D: ^E: ^F: ^G: ^N: ^O: ^P: ^Q: ^S: ^T: ^U: ^U:
```

Figure 7.1 *WordPerfect's Merge Codes (Shift-F9)*

```
Field:
```

Type the number **1** and press **Enter**. Save this file under the name **letter**. This is the primary file. Exit this file. Bring up a second empty screen and type your name, followed by **^R**. Use **Ctrl-R** or **F9** to place the markers. Do not use Shift-6. Just below your name place a **^E** code, using either **Ctrl-E** or **Shift-F9**. Save this file as **names**. This is the database, or the **secondary file**:

```
Deborah Beacham^R
^E
```

Now you are ready to merge:

Press **Ctrl-F9**
Select **1-Merge**
Primary file:**letter**
Secondary file:**names**

Remember, the primary file is the shell document that contains the ^F^ codes. The secondary file is the database. *See Section 7.2.3 for important instructions about the ^F^ function.*

7.2 Refining Your Database

Look at our one-record database again:

```
John M. Matthews
410 Cherry Street
Oxen Hill, MD 21865^R
phone 301-368-3596
36 years old
spouse: Suzanne Matthews
2 children: boys 3, 9
^E
```

If we wanted to send a merged letter to Dr. Matthews, we could bring in his full name and address for the heading, but we could not say "Dear Dr. Matthews:" The ^F1^ code picks out the first ^R field, which in this example is comprised of three lines; so all three lines will be merged. We need to divide the one field into several fields so we can merge with more flexibility. We'll separate each piece of data with an ^R code. Each ^R corresponds to the ^F codes in the primary file:

```
Dr.^R (F1)
John ^R(F2)
M.^R (F3)
Matthews ^R(F4)
410 Cherry Street ^R(F5)
Oxen Hill ^R(F6)
MD 21865 ^R(F7)
```

There is no limit to the number of fields you can have in a WordPerfect record, so you are free to create as many fields as you think will be useful in the future. The fields are easy to combine but cannot be separated during a merge. With the seven address fields we can enter the address codes as shown in Figure 7.2. When this primary file is merged with our database, we get what is shown in Figure 7.3.

There are several important principles to notice here:

1. You can combine fields in any combination that you wish. By setting up the database so that Dr. John M. Matthews' name occupies four fields instead of one, we can write the salutation as "Dr. Mat-

```
April 15, 1988

^F1 ^F2 ^F3 ^F4
^F5
^F6, ^F7

Dear ^F1 ^F4 :

We are writing to everyone in ^F6 about the zoning ordinances
proposed for our area.




C:\WP5\FILE20                                    Doc 1 Pg 1 Ln 1 Pos 10
```

Figure 7.2 *Entering Field Codes for a Merge*

```
April 15, 1988

Dr. John R. Matthews
410 Cherry Street
Oxen Hill, MD 21865

Dear Dr. Matthews:

We are writing to everyone in Oxen Hill about the zoning ordinances
proposed for our area.




C:\WP5\FILE21                                    Doc 1 Pg 1 Ln 1 Pos 10
```

Figure 7.3 *The Merged Document*

thews." If we create yet another field with his wife's name, we can combine the fields to say "Dear Suzanne and John." You can add punctuation between fields, as we did with the city and state.

2. You can use a field as many times as you wish. In the example we used ^F4^ (Matthews) twice and ^F7^ (Oxen Hill) twice. Whenever

WordPerfect comes to a ^F4^, it will always pull out "Matthews" from the database.

3. It doesn't matter how long the data is in a field. WordPerfect fits it into the text and makes any necessary line adjustments.

4. Although a field can occupy as many lines as you wish, only one ^R code can be placed on a line. In other words, you could not have:

```
Dr.^R John^R M.^R Matthews^R
```

5. WordPerfect brings data into the primary document at the exact position of the ^F code. This permits you to set up forms or insert data any way you want.

6. The ^R codes in the database do not indicate field numbers, such as ^R1, ^R3, ^R7, but they are there nonetheless. WordPerfect simply counts the number of ^R codes and numbers them consecutively. If you add a field between two existing fields, WordPerfect renumbers them.

This last item is the most important principle to remember when setting up your data base. *Every field in every record must contain corresponding data.* That is, if the last name is in the fourth field in the first record, every record must contain a ^R field that is dedicated to last names. It is fine with WordPerfect to leave a field blank, but you *must* have that field in *all* the other records. For example, not everyone will have a middle initial, but you will not eliminate the middle initial field. Just leave it blank. The second record in our database is:

```
Mrs. ^R
Helen ^R
^R
Jacobson ^R
```

The last name is still in ^R4 just as it is in Dr. Matthews' record. If we had eliminated the middle initial field:

```
Mrs. ^R
Helen ^R
Jacobson ^R
```

the last name would be in ^R3. If we merged letters to both Dr. Matthews and Mrs. Jacobson, WordPerfect would pull inconsistent data from each record.

7.2.1 *Assigning Field Codes for Complex Data*

Let's look at the rest of the information in our Dr. Matthews' record:

```
Dr. ^R
John ^R
M. ^R
Matthews ^R
410 Cherry Street ^R
Oxen Hill ^R
MD 21865 ^R
phone 301-368-3596
36 years old
spouse: Suzanne Matthews
2 children: boys 3, 9
^E
```

Because the phone number will always appear in ^R(8) and the person's age in ^R(9), there's no reason to enter any words other than the raw data. Extraneous words will hinder WordPerfect's ability to sort certain records from the database (see Chapter 8). We might also want to create separate fields for Mrs. Matthews. In this record she uses her husband's name, but other records might contain spouses who use different names:

```
Dr.^R
John^R
M.^R
Matthews^R
410 Cherry Street^R
Oxen Hill^R
MD 21865^R
301-368-3596^R
36^R
Mrs.^R
Suzanne^R
^R
```

```
Matthews^R
2 children: boys 3, 9^R
^E
```

Suppose we want to set up a database that will allow us to target records by the gender and age of the children. For example, we might send letters to all parents in Oxen Hill announcing the formation of new troops of Cub Scouts and Girl Scouts. The database might be devised to list the gender and age in one field and the child's name in another:

```
Dr.^R
John^R
M. ^R
Matthews^R
410 Cherry Street^R
Oxen Hill^R
MD 21865^R
301-368-3596^R
36^R
Mrs.^R
Suzanne^R
^R
Matthews^R
boy 1980^R
Kevin^R
boy 1985^R
Bruce^R
^E
```

With this setup, we can ask WordPerfect to sort all the records that contain boys born between September 1981 and September 1978 who live in Oxen Hill. The Matthews' son, Kevin, meets the criteria. His record would be sorted out along with the other qualifying boys. That subdatabase then becomes the secondary file that we'll use for the merge.

Just to make it easier to see how we might construct a letter to parents, we'll show the hidden field numbers that WordPerfect recognizes.

```
Dr.^R(1)
John^R(2)
M.^R(3)
Matthews^R(4)
```

```
410 Cherry Street^R(5)
Oxen Hill^R(6)
MD 21865^R(7)
301-368-3596^R(8)
36^R(9)
Mrs.^R(10)
Suzanne^R(11)
^R(12)
Matthews^R(13)
boy 1980^R(14)
Kevin^R(15)
boy 1985^R(16)
Bruce^R(17)
^E
```

Now, when we enter the **^F^** codes in the **primary** file, we assign **^F#s^** to correspond with the **^R#s** (see Figure 7.4). When the letter and database are merged, the **^F#s^** and **^R#s** are matched up, so the first record will produce the merged letter shown in Figure 7.5.

When the first record has been merged, WordPerfect automatically looks for a second record and continues merging as long as there are additional records, or until you tell it to stop (see Section 7.4.5).

```
April 15, 1988

^F1 and ^F10 ^F2 ^F3 ^F4
^F5
^F6, ^F7

Dear ^F1 and ^F10 ^F4 :

I am writing to invite your son, ^F15, to join the new cub scout
den being formed in the Oxen Hill area.




C:\WP5\FILE22                              Doc 1 Pg 1 Ln 1 Pos 10
```

Figure 7.4 *Entering Codes in the Primary File*

```
April 15, 1988

Dr. and Mrs. John R. Matthews
410 Cherry Street
Oxen Hill, MD 21865

Dear Dr. and Mrs. Matthews:

I am writing to invite your son, Kevin, to join the new cub scout
den being formed in the Oxen Hill area.




C:\WP5\FILE23                              Doc 1 Pa 1 Ln 1 Pos 10
```

Figure 7.5 *Merging the Primary and Secondary Files*

7.2.2   *Some Tips for Setting Up Your Database*

As you can see from the discussion above, the single most important
aspect of establishing your database is consistency in fields from one
record to the next. If you think that your database will be extensive, or if
several different people are entering data, you might want to "boilerplate"
your fields and give them names so there will no mistake about what data
to enter into which field.

You can enter reminders into the fields after you've entered the ^R as
long as there is at least one space between the ^R and the reminder note.
In our example database we might add some tags, such as:

```
Dr.^R (1)Title
John^R (2)First name
M.^R (3)Middle initial
Matthews^R (4)Last name
410 Cherry Street^R (5)Street
Oxen Hill^R (6)City
MD 21865^R (7)State/zip
301-368-3596^R (8)Phone
36^R (9)Age
Mrs.^R (10)Spouse
```

```
Suzanne^R (11)First name
^R (12)Middle initial
Matthews^R (13)Spouse's last name
boy 1980^R (14)Child's gender/birth date
Kevin^R (15)Child's first name
boy 1985^R (16)Second child's gender/birth date
Bruce^R (17)Second child's name
^E
```

Any text that comes after the ^R will not be included in the merge. If we make a separate file of only the merge codes and tags, we have an empty record ready to be filled in:

```
^R (1)Title
^R (2)First name
^R (3)Middle initial
^R (4)Last name
^R (5)Street
^R (6)City
^R (7)State/zip
^R (8)Phone
^R (9)Age
^R (10)Spouse
^R (11)First name
^R (12)Middle initial
^R (13)Spouse's last name
^R (14)Child's gender/birth date
^R (15)Child's first name
^R (16)Second child's gender/birth date
^R (17)Second child's name
^E
```

This boilerplate is Saved in a separate file under any file name. We've named this one **rec** (for "record"). When you are ready to enter a new record, retrieve the boilerplate file and fill in the data. Then, with the cursor positioned beneath the **^E** of the last record, retrieve **rec** again. This assures that data will always be entered into the correct field. It also facilitates selecting the correct field when you're entering the ^F^ codes in the primary file.

7.2.2.1 *Planning Ahead*

As you can imagine, a database can become complicated very fast. While WordPerfect doesn't care how many fields you create, the more fields you have the longer it takes to fill in a record. At the same time, you don't want to restrict your sorting capabilities by limiting the fields.

You will spend your time well if you carefully plan what you want your database to do and how you might expand its uses in the future. Analyze your data to determine which items are seldom changed, such as names and addresses, and which are constantly changing, such as outstanding monthly balances. If you want to use your database to send out monthly statements, place the "balance" field just beneath the person's name so that you can **Search** for the name and enter the monthly balance without having to scroll down the record. If all you do with your database is bill your customers, you might not want to break the name into four fields as we did above. The first field could contain the entire name, the second field the balance, and the third field all the address information:

```
Dr. John M. Matthews^R (1) Name
$487.85^R (2) Balance
410 Cherry Street
Oxen Hill, MD 21865^R (3) Address
```

With this field layout you can use **F2 (Search)** to find the name of the person to bill, then enter the balance. Once you have entered all the balances, you can ask WordPerfect to send a bill to everyone who has an outstanding balance.

Here's where planning ahead counts. At the present time your company sells a limited product line and you do not need to itemize. Creating field 2 as the "balance" field is convenient because it's near the name of the customer. But for multiple products you might want to itemize in the future, you should set up the database so you can add fields at the end of the record. It's better to "boilerplate" more capacity than you currently need.

```
^R (1) Name
^R (2) Address
^R (3) Phone
^R (4) Balance
```

```
^R (5)Item #1
^R (6)Amount
^R (7)Item #2
^R (8)Amount
^R (9)Item #3
^R (10)Amount
^R (11)Item #4
^R (12)Amount
```

With this boilerplate you can enter only the balance, or you can itemize up to four items. When you merge, you can tell WordPerfect to select only those fields that contain data (see Section 7.2.3). WordPerfect will even add up the total of the individual items (see Chapter 14).

Please note that this example is a fairly elaborate task for a word processor. You should not consider using WordPerfect to manage complicated customer accounts or to keep records that will track the history of an account. But you can use WordPerfect effectively to identify segments of the audience you want to reach and to produce many types of documents, from letters to monthly statements, for them. For example, if your database consists of military personnel, you might want to devise the fields so that you can identify branch, rank, post, duties, and current assignment. This type of setup would allow you to sort out all procurement officers in charge of approving purchases for the Military Airlift Command.

7.2.3 *More About the ^F^ Code*

If you place an ^F^ code in the primary document and there is no data in that field, WordPerfect inserts a blank, which isn't always what you want. Some people might have titles, others might not:

```
^R (1)Name
^R (2)Title
^R (3)Company
^R (4)Address
```

If you enter your ^F^ codes as:

```
^F1^
^F2^
```

```
^F3^
^F4^
```

and someone has neither a title nor company affiliation, WordPerfect leaves two blank lines between the name and address:

```
Dr. John M. Matthews


410 Cherry Street
Oxen Hill, MD 21865
```

To eliminate this problem, place a question mark after the field number:

```
^F1^
^F2?^
^F3?^
^F4^
```

If there is no data in that field, WordPerfect skips to the next field query without inserting a blank.

7.2.3.1   *Keys for Entering ^F^ Codes*

To review a moment, the ^F^ codes can be placed only with the **Shift-F9 (Merge Codes)** function key. If you are accustomed to the previous versions of WordPerfect, you might find this cumbersome. With older versions, you could use **Ctrl-F** and then enter the field number. Version 5.0 requires the ^ marker on both sides of the F. You can achieve this by pressing **Ctrl-F**, adding the field number, and pressing **Ctrl-F** again to produce **^F1^F** if you're determined to use the old method.

7.2.3.2   *Merging Punctuation Marks*

Punctuation marks are entered along with the ^F^ code. An example is:

```
Dear ^F1^:
```

To make a space between city and state, enter ^F3^, ^F4.

7.3   Converting Existing Third-Party Databases to WordPerfect

Many users will have no need for this, but it is possible, though not necessarily a good idea, to import data from other software into WordPerfect. The advisability depends on how data is laid out. If you can get it into WordPerfect using DOS Text files (see Section 6.8) in such a way that you can separate the data, you can add the ^R and ^E codes. Sometimes you can use **Search/Replace** to identify a code or character and replace it with the appropriate WordPerfect code. For example, the data that you import from a WordStar file comes into WordPerfect as a continuous line with commas separating the fields:

```
Dr. John M. Matthews,410 Cherry Street,Oxen Hill,Md,21865,301-
566-3782
```

At the end of the WordStar record is a hard return [HRt]. Our first step is to replace it with a more identifiable marker, whose use you'll see soon. Position the cursor at the first record, press **Alt-F2 (Replace)** and tell WordPerfect to Replace **[HRt]** with **?[HRt]** (see Figure 7.6).

Now we'll separate the data with **Search/Replace**. By searching for commas and replacing them with hard returns [HRt], we can rearrange the one-line WordStar record into separate lines for WordPerfect.

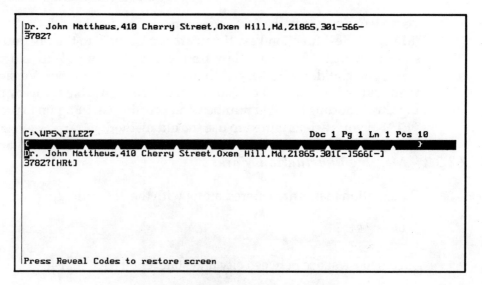

Figure 7.6 *Replace a [HRt] with ?[HRt]*

```
Press Alt-F2 (Replace)
W Confirm (Y/N?) N
Search:, (comma)
Press Esc
Replace with:^R (Ctrl-R)[HRt] (Enter)
Press Esc
```

This replaces all the commas with the ^R field code and a hard return, which moves the data onto separate lines (see Figure 7.7).

The final step of our record conversion from WordStar is to insert the ^E codes, which we can also perform with Replace:

```
Search:?[HRt]
Replace with:^R[HRt]^E
```

This replaces all the ?[HRt] with a ^R[HRt] at the end of the phone number and a ^E at the end of the record (see Figure 7.8). Without too many steps, we've converted a WordStar record to WordPerfect.

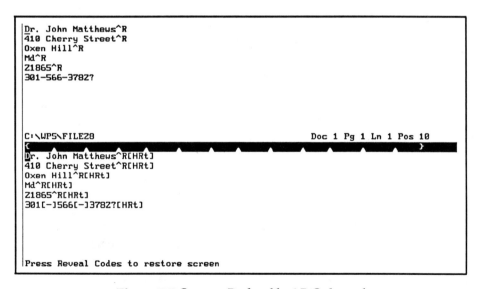

Figure 7.7 *Commas Replaced by ^R Codes and Hard Returns [HRt]*

```
Dr. John Matthews^R
410 Cherry Street^R
Oxen Hill^R
Md^R
21865^R
301-566-3782?




C:\WP5\FILE29                                      Doc 1 Pg 1 Ln 1 Pos 10
{                                                                        }
Dr. John Matthews^R[HRt]
410 Cherry Street^R[HRt]
Oxen Hill^R[HRt]
Md^R[HRt]
21865^R[HRt]
301[-]566[-]3782?[HRt]




Press Reveal Codes to restore screen
```

Figure 7.8 *Completed Record Conversion*

7.4   Other Merge Functions

Just as you place ^F codes in a primary document to bring in specified
fields, there are other merge codes that you can position in both primary
and secondary files.

7.4.1   *Merge Codes for the Primary File*

^D inserts the current date. If your computer is equipped with a clock or
if you fill in the date when DOS is booted, the date code assures that your
correspondence is correctly dated every time you merge. This feature is
especially useful for documents that have the current date distributed
throughout the text.

^C stops the merge, permitting you to enter text from the keyboard.
This is useful when your merge documents contain some similar data and
some variable data. For example, if you are mail merging monthly bill-
ings, the name and address fields will remain constant on your invoice,
but the amount of the bill will vary from customer to customer. By placing a ^C in the primary document at the position where the amount will
be filled in, you will stop the merge for each record. When you've filled
in the balance due, press **F9 (Merge R)** to continue to the next record.

^O is a hidden prompt that appears on the screen but does not print. Its function is to remind you of what type of data you should enter at this position. This is especially useful for filling out complicated forms, such as will and testaments. Normally the ^O code is used in conjunction with the ^C code. The ^O code is entered in pairs, and whatever text comes between the ^Os is the "hidden message." For example, in a will and testament the name of the beneficiary could be set up as an ^F^ merge field, but the amount that the beneficiary is to receive would change from one condition to the next. So, in the appropriate section, you might enter:

```
^OAmount beneficiary receives^O^C
```

The cursor will stop because of the ^C code; the message between the ^O codes tells you what to insert. Whatever you enter is positioned at the first ^O. Press **F9 (Merge code)**. The ^O and ^C codes are removed and the merge continues, either to the next record or to the next ^C code.

^G starts a macro (see Macro Building in Chapter 15). This code is useful in both the primary and secondary files. In a **primary** file you might use the ^G code to test a condition of the record, then insert special files for those records meeting the condition. In **secondary** files you might want to change paper stock with a macro. For example, you've printed all the letters and now you want to print mailing labels using the same database. At the end of the secondary file, you could enter:

^C, which temporarily stops the job while you change letter head stock to labels.

^GLabels^G, which is a macro you've built to specify margins and form size (see Section 7.5).

^GMerge^G, which is another macro you've built to start the merge again.

Notice that macro codes are entered in pairs with the name of the macro between the first and second code.

7.4.2 *Merge Codes for the Secondary File*

If you have subdivided your database or if you want to fully automate your merge system, you can use other merge codes to switch from one database or one operation to another. For example, you might subdivide your database into customers by their professions. One file contains doctors, one lawyers, one accountants, one teachers, one nurses. Today you want to target only lawyers and teachers. So, you bring up the secondary file named **Lawyers** and move the cursor to the end of the entire database. Then you enter:

```
^STeachers^S
```

When WordPerfect has merged all the records in the **Lawyers** database, it automatically switches to the **Teachers** file and merges all those records.

^S denotes a secondary file. If you wanted to send the teachers a different letter from the one you sent the lawyers, you could enter the name of the new **primary file** at the same time you specify the new secondary file. Just under the ^S codes enter:

```
^STeachers^S
^PTeachers.ltr^P
```

The ^S code tells WordPerfect to use the secondary file (database) named Teachers and the ^P code tells it to use the primary file containing the teachers' letter.

You can string together as many primary and secondary files as you wish with these codes. Another example would be if you wanted to stagger the dates of the letters sent from your database. Maybe you want to send a third of the letters this week, another third next week, and the final third the following week, but you want to print them all today. Move the cursor a third of the way into your database and enter the file name of the primary file (letter) containing next week's date, such as:

```
^PLawyers.512^P
```

This tells WordPerfect to switch the primary file to the letter that is dated May 12. Two-thirds into the database enter:

```
^PLawyers.517^P
```

to switch to the May 17 letter.

7.4.3 Printing Merged Documents

When WordPerfect merges files, it presents all the merged documents on the screen. Each merged record, say a letter, is separated from the next by a Page Break. If you want to print all of the letters or any one of them, you would use the **Shift-F7 (Print)** key and order a standard print job.

If you are merging many records, you might not want to wait until the end of the merge to begin printing. Or, if the merged documents require more memory than your computer contains, you might send the letters directly to the printer.

To start a print job during a merge, insert a ^T in the **secondary file**. You can place it after any record or at the end of the database. We could merge our lawyers, print their letters, and switch to our teachers with the following merge codes placed at the end of the **Lawyers** database:

```
^T
^STeachers^S
^PTeachers.ltr^P
```

The ^T merge code does not stop the merge; it only interrupts it to complete the print job.

7.4.4 Sending Merged Text Directly to the Printer

A more important use of the **^T** print code is printing each document as it is merged by using **^T^N** codes in the **primary** file. **^T** tells WordPerfect to print; **^N** tells WordPerfect to go to the next record. These codes are placed at the end of the primary file (letter). They tell WordPerfect to print the first merged record and when that printing is finished to proceed to the second record in the database, merge and print it. When WordPerfect has merged the last record, it stops.

7.4.5 Stopping a Merge

If you want to cancel a merge in progress, you can press **Shift-F9 (Merge Codes)** and press **e**. This is the only correct way to stop a merge. Don't turn off the computer.

You can also insert merge codes into the **secondary file** that will stop the merge at a predetermined point. For example, you might want to test letters on a third of your layer database. Going to the secondary file, you could move the cursor to the end of any record and insert ^Q. Word-

Perfect will merge to that point and stop. If you wanted to print those let-ters you could enter ^T^Q.

As you'll see, merging occurs rapidly and off screen. If you want to see a merge in progress, enter ^U in either the primary or secondary files.

7.5   Creating Mailing Labels and Envelopes

In the same way that we pulled name and address information from the database and inserted it in the heading of the letter, we want to pull the same information and insert it on a mailing label or an envelope. The first step is to create a **primary** file that specifies the ^F^ codes of the fields we want to include in the address. Start with an empty screen and enter the codes (see Figure 7.9).

Skip a line between the codes and press **Enter** after the last code in order to move the cursor beneath the last code. This keeps the lines from run-ning together during the merge.

Now we need to enter the formatting instructions at the top of the page. (You'll want to build a macro if you use labels often. See Chapter 15.) First, measure the label you're using and think about where you want the ad-dress information to be placed. If you're using the small 1- x 3.5-inch stock that has room for only five lines, the margins will be different from a 3- x 4-inch label with a return address. To set your form specifications:

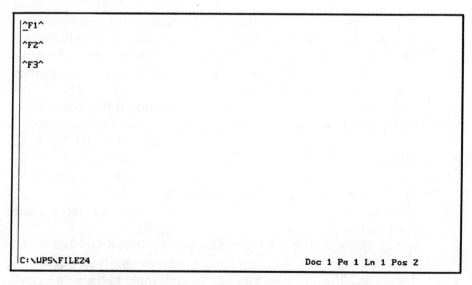

Figure 7.9 *Name and Address Merge Codes (Shift-F9, f)*

Press **Home-Home-Up Arrow** to move the cursor to the top of the page

Press **Shift-F8 (Format)**

Select **2-Page**

Select **5-Margins** and set the top to the appropriate number and the bottom margin to 0

Select **8-Paper Size**

Select **O-Other** (that's an "o" not a zero)

Enter **width,** press **Enter**

Enter **height,** press **Enter**

Select **4-Labels,** press **Enter twice**

Select **1-Line**

Select **7-Margins**

Set **Left/Right margins at 0.2 inches,** press **Enter**

Press **F7 (Exit)**

Save the file under the name **Labels**

Looking at the settings through reveal codes, we can see that the top/bottom margins have been set at 1.5",0"; the paper size is 3" x 4" and the L/R margins are 0.2" (see Figure 7.10).

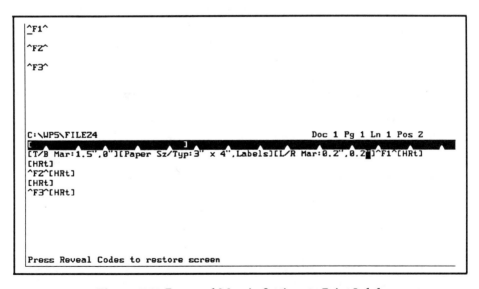

Figure 7.10 *Form and Margin Settings to Print Labels*
(Alt-F3)

```
Mr. David O.Whitten Editor
The Wall Street Review of
Books
Redgrave Publishing Company
380 Adams Street
Bedford Hills, NY  10507


================================================================================
Mr. Fred Danzig
Editor
Advertising Age
Crain Communications Inc.
740 N Rush Street
Chicago, IL  60611


================================================================================
Mr. Robert H. Albert
Editor
S & M Sales & Marketing
Management
Bill Communications
633 Third Avenue
New York, NY  10017

C:\WP5\FILE26                                        Doc 1 Pg 1 Ln 7 Pos 2
```

Figure 7.11 *Completed Merge for Mailing Labels*

This now becomes the primary file for merging the database into labels. Using the same secondary file, merge the documents. The merged results will look like Figure 7.11.

Notice two things. First, a double line is drawn between records signifying a page break. Second, the typing area of each page is only 9 lines long. In Figure 7.11, the cursor is positioned on line 9 just before the page break. Here's why. The height of the label is 3". Six lines of type can fit in 1", 18 lines in 3 inches. We set a top margin of 1.5" which takes up half of the label, or 9 lines. That leaves 9 lines for the typing area.

7.6   Merging Addresses on Envelopes

The process is the same for envelopes as for labels except that you will specify a different form size. You can either enter the size of the envelope when you select O-Other, or you can select item 5-Envelope. The major difference between printing labels and envelopes is that you must tell WordPerfect which paper bin contains the envelopes. This is accomplished by adding one step when you enter the margin settings in the primary file. Go through the printer selection process (see Section 5.1.2) and designate the envelope bin.

7.7 Printing Envelopes and Landscape Printing

When setting the envelope size for a laser printer, you might have to set it for "Landscape" printing, depending on whether the envelope is fed into the printer as a standard sheet of paper is, or whether it is turned 90 degrees.

To set a "Landscape" orientation, go to the printer selection menu:

Press Shift-F7
Select 5-Select printer
Select 3-Edit
Select 4-Forms
Enter Form Size
Press Enter

These keystrokes bring up the Forms setting sheet:

Press 2-Orientation
Select 2-Landscape
Press Enter
Select 1-Add (to record the new setting)
Press Enter

```
Select Printer: Forms

            Filename              EPFX86E.PRS

            Form Type             Standard

        1 - Form Size             8.5" x 11"

        2 - Orientation           Landscape

        3 - Initially Present     No

        4 - Location              Continuous

        5 - Page Offsets - Top    0"
                          Side    0"




Selection: 0
```

Figure 7.12 *Form Setting Sheet*

CHAPTER 8

Sorting

Sorting is one of WordPerfect's most powerful and useful features. Combined with the database and merge capabilities, sorting allows you to select and order complex data. This feature is so closely connected with database design that you should understand Chapter 7 before attempting to sort.

There are three types of sorting WordPerfect can perform.

1. **Line sort**: When you select Line sort, every hard return or soft return defines a record. In other words, every line of text is considered a separate record. If you were to start a phone book in WordPerfect, you would list a name and number, press **Enter** and list the second name and number. Each name and number becomes a record. You do not have to assign ^R codes if the entire record occupies only one line. When you want to sort, you can select any word or number in the record and reorder the list. Indexes, appendices, and table names are all good candidates for Line sorting.

2. **Paragraph sort**: Just as each line became a record in Line sort, every paragraph becomes a record. WordPerfect looks for a hard return and defines a paragraph as all text falling between two hard returns. You can sort paragraphs by any words or numbers contained within them. An example is a list of terms that have been defined and explained. You can alphabetize the dictionary by the term, or you can

select out of the list any terms you wish. You might ask WordPerfect to pull out all definitions dealing with "tax," such as "tax rate, tax code, taxable income, tax assessment." You can even add variations, such as "sliding tax" or, using Global sort (see Section 8.7), search the entire paragraph for any mention of "tax."

3. **Merge sort:** This is the selection you make when sorting a database that has been defined with merge codes. You can select records from the database based on as many as nine criteria. Merge sort is the most powerful of WordPerfect's sorting types.

You can sort an entire file or you can use Block (Alt-F4) to isolate only those records you want to sort. To use Block Sort, press **Alt-F4** and define the Block before proceeding with the sort procedure.

In order to demonstrate the simplicity of WordPerfect's sort, we'll begin with a personal phone book, which is an uncluttered example of a database. We'll then apply these principles to complicated sorting problems.

8.1   How Sorting Works

You select a file, either one on the screen or on disk and tell WordPerfect what criteria you want to use to order or to pull out records. You also tell WordPerfect whether to display the sorted file on the screen or store it to disk. The steps to sort are pretty easy, but the results of a sort gone wrong can be disastrous. No matter what, *before you start a sort, SAVE your document*. If the sort goes haywire, you can start over as long as it's on disk. A sort doesn't go wrong because the software is bad; rather, it's easy to specify a sort key that isn't consistent throughout the document.

8.1.1   Starting a Sort

Sorts are started with **Ctrl-F9 (Merge/Sort)**. Item **1-Merge** (see Chapter 7) is the selection if you want to merge a primary and secondary file. All sorting, including querying the database, is activated with **2-Sort**. When you select this item, WordPerfect asks:

```
Input file to sort:(Screen)
```

You may elect to sort the document on the screen or one on disk. Press **Enter** to select **screen**, or enter the name of a file on disk. If the document on screen is inappropriate for sorting, WordPerfect won't allow you to continue. Otherwise, WordPerfect asks:

```
Output file for sort:(Screen)
```

If you elect to output to disk, it is very wise to create a new file. If you name an existing file, WordPerfect will ask if you want to replace it. You don't. When you've specified an output file and pressed **Enter**, a complicated settings sheet appears (see Figure 8.1).

There are three basic divisions to this sheet and the first choice you make is the **Type** of sort. Press **7-Type**:

```
Type:1-Merge; 2-Line; 3-Paragraph:0
```

To query your database, select **1-Merge**. To sort single lines of text or numbers into ascending or descending order, select **2-Line**. To rearrange paragraphs by a key number, letter, word, or phrase, select **3-Paragraph**.

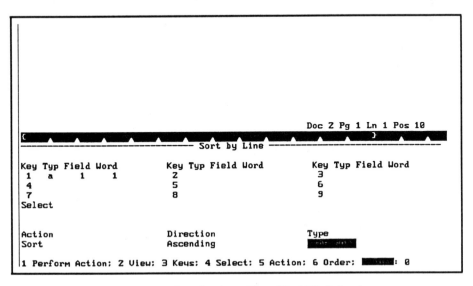

Figure 8.1 *Sort Settings Sheet (Ctrl-F9, 2-Sort)*

8.1.2 Line Sorts that Key On the First Word

For the first example, we'll select **Line** sort and work on our telephone book. As you can see from Figure 8.1, WordPerfect is preset for a Line sort, so all we need to do is tell WordPerfect what word we want to use to arrange the list.

In the short telephone book in Figure 8.2 the last names appear first. In order for WordPerfect to include the last name as a field, you *must place a hard return at the end of the last line in the list.*

To alphabetize the list by last name we simply press **1-Perform Action**. You'll see in the message center the number of records that WordPerfect is examining, as well as the number of records it actually *transferred.* If there's a discrepancy between the number "examined" and the number "transferred," there is something wrong with one of the fields in the database. The sorted list will appear on the screen if that is the output file you've selected (see Figure 8.3).

8.1.3 Sorting On Words Other than the First

Sorting on the first word is the simplest kind of sort. Chances are you'll want to sort your lists by words or numbers other than the first one. For example, our phone book might not list last names first (see Figure 8.4).

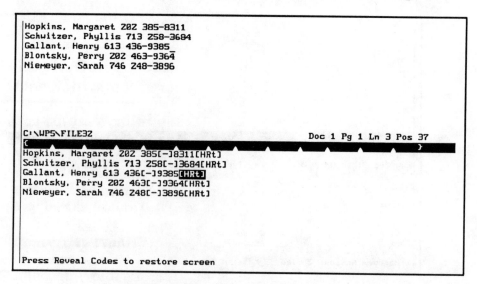

Figure 8.2 *Names to Alphabetize by the First Word*

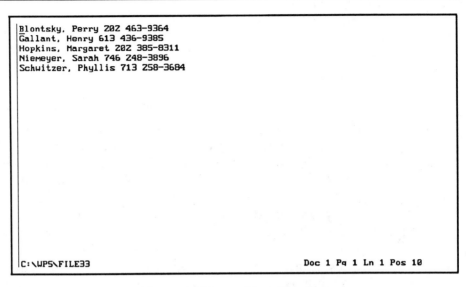

Figure 8.3 *Names After a Line Sort*
(Ctrl-F9, 2-Sort, Enter, Enter, 1-Perform Action)

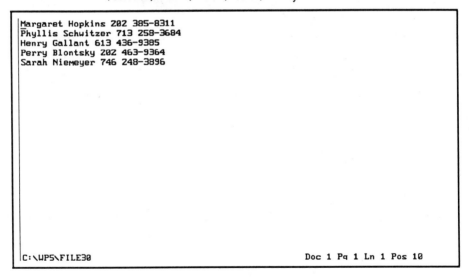

Figure 8.4 *Names to Alphabetize by the Second Word*

WordPerfect assumes that we want to sort by the first word. To change that to the second word we must enter the key word, which the nine keys at the top of the Merge/Sort settings sheet allow us to do. Bring up the settings sheet and select **3-Keys:**

Press **Ctrl-F9**
Select **2-Sort**
Press **Enter**
Press **Enter** again
Select **3-Keys**

The first key, or **Key1** (WordPerfect's designation), has been filled in by the default, which is how WordPerfect knew to sort our first phone list (see Figure 8.5). The first column tells WordPerfect the **Type** of character being sorted: alphabetical letters or numbers. The default is **a** (alphanumeric. See Section 8.1.5). The second column indicates the **Field** where the key word resides. With a Line sort, every line is a field, so this setting does not change. However, the third column, **Word**, is the key that will allow us to sort by the last name in the phone list. WordPerfect's default is to key on the first word. Using the **Arrow** key, move the cursor to the third column and enter a **2** (see Figure 8.6).

Now when WordPerfect sorts, it will look for the second word in the field. Press **F7 (Exit)** to record the change, then press **1-Perform Action** to begin the sort (see Figure 8.7).

You can sort on any word in the field as long as the key word is in the same position from one field to the next. WordPerfect defines a **word** as any contiguous string of characters or characters with numbers or

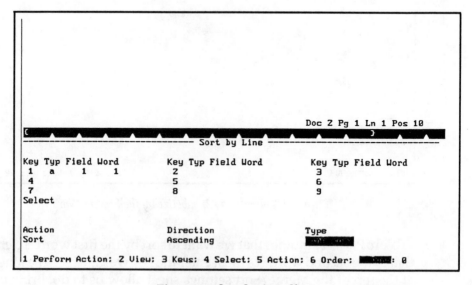

Figure 8.5 *Sort Settings Sheet*
(Ctrl-F9, 2-Sort, Enter, Enter)

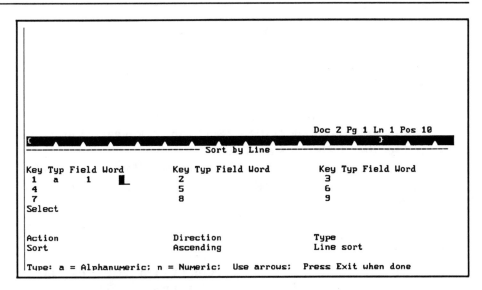

Figure 8.6 *Settings Sheet which Changes the Key Word*
(Ctrl-F9, 2-Sort, Enter, Enter, 3-Keys, Right Arrow, Type 2)

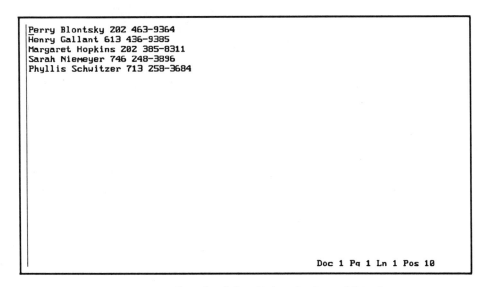

Figure 8.7 *Completed Sort Using the Second Word*

punctuation. When WordPerfect finds a space between two characters, it counts the second character as the beginning of a new word.

8.1.4   *Disappearing Text After Sorting*

If after a Sort there is no text on the screen, you can restore it with the **Arrow** keys. Looking at the screen through Reveal Codes (Alt-F3), you can see that the text is still there.

Warning: WordPerfect does not merge well when a "Split Screen" or "Switch Screen" is in memory. You should have only one file at a time in memory while merging.

8.1.5   *Numeric Searches*

If we wanted to sort our phone book by area code, we could designate the third "word" as the key. A word is any string of characters separated by a space. As long as the "numbers" are all the same length, WordPerfect treats them the same as text. In the example, we need only change the **Word** column to **3**, press **F7** and **1-Perform Action** (see Figure 8.8).

In our phone book we have not used parentheses or dashes to connect the area code with the phone number, but it wouldn't have mattered if they were since U.S. phone numbers are all the same length. In fact, notice

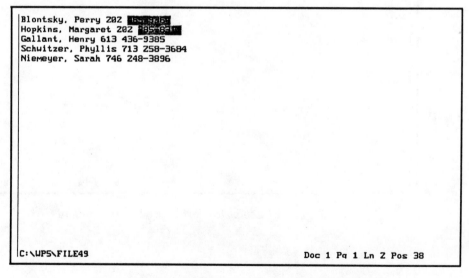

```
Blontsky, Perry 202 ▓▓▓▓▓
Hopkins, Margaret 202 ▓▓▓▓▓
Gallant, Henry 613 436-9385
Schwitzer, Phyllis 713 258-3684
Niemeyer, Sarah 746 248-3896
```

```
C:\WP5\FILE49                              Doc 1 Pg 1 Ln 2 Pos 38
```

Figure 8.8 *Completed Sort Using Area Code Numbers*

in Figure 8.8 that while the area code numbers are sorted in ascending order, the phone numbers are not. If the area codes were connected to the numbers by a dash or asterisk, WordPerfect would have recognized which was the lower of the two phone numbers (see Figure 8.9).

8.1.5.1 *Numeric Sorting with Strings of Uneven Length*

WordPerfect treats numbers of equal length just as it treats characters. That's why when we sorted the phone book by area code we did not have to change the *a* (alphanumeric) to an *n* (numeric). We could have changed it to an N, but it wasn't necessary. For all other numbers we must, as with the list in Figure 8.10.

Remember that you must place a **hard return** at the end of the last number. To sort, bring up the settings sheet, set the **Type** as **N**, the **Field** as **1** and the **Word** as **1**. Press **F7 (Exit)**, then **1-Perform Action** to start the sort (see Figure 8.11). As you can see, WordPerfect does not position the numbers around any alignment character that would make them line up beneath each other. See Chapter 14 for directions to align a column of numbers.

```
Hopkins, Margaret 202×▮▮▮▮▮▮
Blontsky, Perry 202×▮▮▮▮▮▮▮
Gallant, Henry 613×436-9385
Schuitzer, Phyllis 713×258-3684
Niemeyer, Sarah 746×248-3896




















C:\UPS\FILE38                          Doc 1 Pg 1 Ln 2 Pos 37
```

Figure 8.9 *Sorted Phone Numbers Connected to the Area Codes*

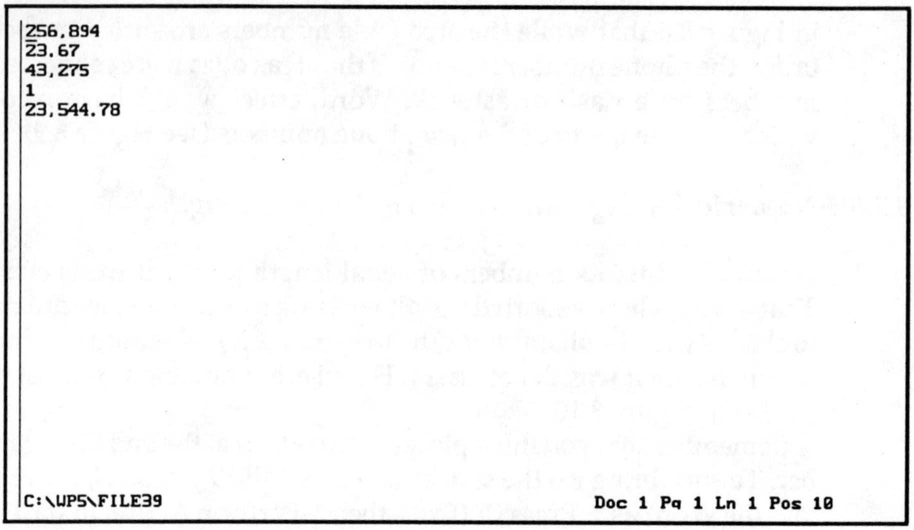

```
256,894
23.67
43,275
1
23,544.78




C:\WP5\FILE39                                    Doc 1 Pg 1 Ln 1 Pos 10
```

Figure 8.10 *Numbers of Unequal Length to be Sorted*

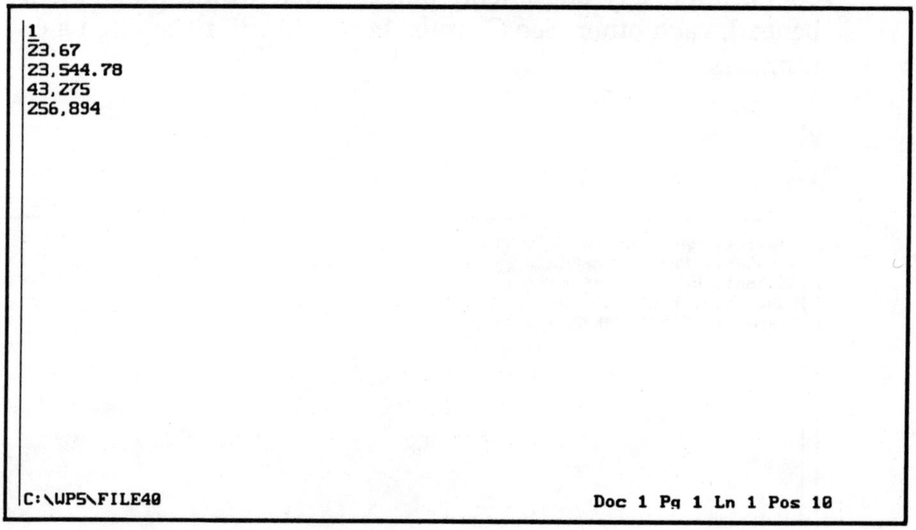

```
1
23.67
23,544.78
43,275
256,894




C:\WP5\FILE40                                    Doc 1 Pg 1 Ln 1 Pos 10
```

Figure 8.11 *Sorted Numbers*

8.1.5.2 Sorting into Descending Order

The process and all the rules for sorting numbers in ascending order apply to descending order. Follow the same steps, and select **6-Order**, then **2-Descending**. WordPerfect will then sort the largest numbers first (see Figure 8.12).

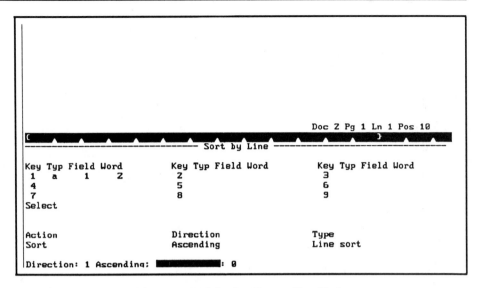

Figure 8.12 *Selecting Descending Order*
(Ctrl-F9, 2-Sort, Enter, Enter, 6-Order, 2-Descending)

8.1.6 Key Word Selection from the End of a Line

A phone book is a good example of a need to specify the key word by its position from the end of the line rather than the beginning. In the example above, everyone had only two names and no one had initials or three names. In a list where the number of words in each field varies, you might be better able to select the key word measuring right to left along the line (see Figure 8.13).

While the last names do not consistently fall in one position measuring left to right, they do fall into the consistent position of second from last. The phone numbers comprise one "word" because there are no spaces between the numbers. Therefore, when specifying the **key word**, we can enter it as **-2**, which tells WordPerfect to count backward. -2 is the second word from the end; -4 is the fourth word from the end (see Figure 8.14).

One of the problems with sorting people's names is that some will use title suffixes, such as Esq., Jr., M.D., Chairman (see Figure 8.15). This makes it impossible to designate a key word from right to left. The only way to handle this obstacle is to set up a separate field in a merge file (see Chapter 7) and sort using Merge sort rather than Line sort.

```
Margaret Hopkins McCarthy 202×385-8311
Phyllis Schwitzer 713×258-3684
Henry A. Gallant 613×436-9385
Perry Blontsky 202×463-9364
Sarah Anne Niemeyer 746×248-3896
```

Doc 1 Pa 1 Ln 1 Pos 10

Figure 8.13 *Records with Varying Numbers of Words*

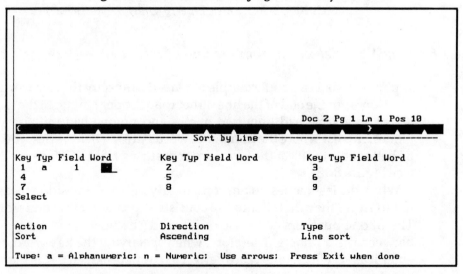

Figure 8.14 *Designating Keys Words from Right to Left*

8.1.7 *Sorting with Two Keys*

In any extensive telephone book there will be people with the same last names. In order to alphabetize them correctly, you will tell WordPerfect that the first sort key is the last name and the second sort key is their first name. In Figure 8.16 the last names are listed first. Key1 will sort by Word

```
Margaret Hopkins McCarthy.      202×385-8311
Phyllis Schwitzer 713×258-3684
Henry A. Gallant.        613×436-9385
Perry Blontsky.      202×463-9364
Sarah Anne Niemeyer 746×248-3896




                                          Doc 1 Pa 1 Ln 1 Pos 10
```

Figure 8.15 *Names with Titles*

```
Hopkins. Margaret 202×385-8311
Blontsky. Perry 202×463-9364
Gallant, Henry 613×436-9385
Schwitzer, Phyllis 713×258-3684
Niemeyer, Sarah 746×248-3896
Hopkins, Mary Beth 904×894-8654
Simpson, David Reed 714×569-3843
Zarin, Robert 843×567-9836
Simpson, Elizabeth 726×683-5825




C:\WP5\FILE42                             Doc 1 Pa 1 Ln 1 Pos 10
```

Figure 8.16 *Names to be Sorted*

1. We'll assign Key2 to handle the familiar names. The settings sheet looks like the one shown in Figure 8.17.

WordPerfect looks only at the Key1 until it finds a duplicate. Then it looks to the Key2 to decide which name takes precedence. Using this method, WordPerfect falls to a secondary criterion when the primary criterion is inadequate (see Figure 8.18).

```
Hopkins, Margaret 202×385-8311
Blontsky, Perry 202×463-9364
Gallant, Henry 613×436-9385
Schwitzer, Phyllis 713×258-3684
Niemeyer, Sarah 746×248-3896
Hopkins, Mary Beth 904×894-8654
Simpson, David Reed 714×569-3843
Zarin, Robert 843×567-9836




                                         Doc 2 Pg 1 Ln 1 Pos 10
{                                                      }
 ^    ^    ^    ^    ^         ^  Sort by Line  ^   ^   ^   ^
-------------------------------- Sort by Line --------------------------------
Key Typ Field Word       Key Typ Field Word        Key Typ Field Word
 1   a    1    1          2   a    1    Z_          3
 4                        5                         6
 7                        8                         9
Select


Action                   Direction                 Type
Sort                     Ascending                 Line sort

Type: a = Alphanumeric; n = Numeric;  Use arrows:  Press Exit when done
```

Figure 8.17 *Settings Sheet Assigning Two Keys*

```
Blontsky, Perry 202×463-9364
Gallant, Henry 613×436-9385
Hopkins, Margaret 202×385-8311
Hopkins, Mary Beth 904×894-8654
Niemeyer, Sarah 746×248-3896
Schwitzer, Phyllis 713×258-3684
Simpson, David Reed 714×569-3843
Simpson, Elizabeth 726×683-5825
Zarin, Robert 843×567-9836












C:\WP5\FILE42                            Doc 1 Pg 1 Ln 1 Pos 10
```

Figure 8.18 *Sorted Names Using Two Keys*

8.2   Advanced Sorting: Selecting Records with Combined Keys

Before you begin this section, review structuring your database records (see Section 7.1).

The phone book examples so far have dealt with putting records in alphabetical or numerical order, but WordPerfect's real power is its ability to pick out records from a database. Using **3-Keys**, you can tell Word-Perfect to look for any combination of assigned keys. Here's how it works. We've boilerplated our database (see Section 7.2.2) so that each record contains the following fields:

```
Ms. Mr. Mrs. Dr. Rev.^R (1)
name
address
city, state, zip^R (2)
salutation^R (3)
occupation^R (4)
income^R (5)
marital status^R (6)
make of car ^R (7)
age^R (8)
years of education^R (9)
^E
```

For the first example, we'll select from the database everyone who is single. Marital status is in Field 6. We've coded marital status to be:

```
M = married
S = single
D = divorced
W = widowed
```

We want to tell WordPerfect to look for all records of single people. Calling up the Merge/Sort settings sheet, we want to set the first key to look at Field 6 (^R6). This is a two-step procedure. First, we press **Ctrl-F9** and select **2-Sort** as we did above. Then press **7-Type**. The type of sort we want to select is **1-Merge**. The terminology is a little confusing, but it means that you are picking specified fields from a multifield database rather than simply alphabetizing a database comprised of one-line records (see Figure 8.19).

When you select **1-Merge** and press **Enter**, the settings sheet is expanded to include an extra column, which is **Line** (see Figure 8.20). This setting instructs WordPerfect to look in the sixth field (R6), in the first line of the sixth field (in this field there is only one line), and to look at the first word in the field.

The second step is to tell WordPerfect what criterion we want to apply to selecting the first word in the first line of the sixth field in the database.

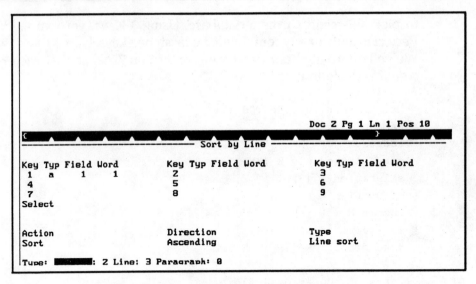

Figure 8.19 *Changing from Line Sort to Merge Sort*
(Ctrl-F9, 2-Sort, Enter, Enter, 7-Type)

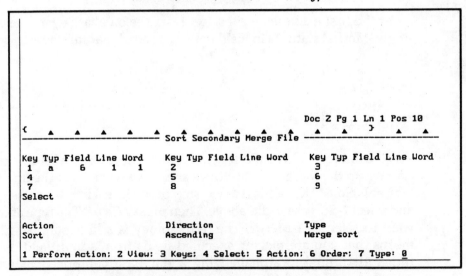

Figure 8.20 *Settings Sheet to Sort a Complex Database*
(Ctrl-F9, 2-Sort, Enter, Enter, 7-Type, 1-Merge)

To do this choose **4-Select** from the menu. This causes the cursor to jump to the center of the settings sheet. Now we can tell WordPerfect what to look for in ^R6.

This leads us to a winding road. Pay attention. We have designated the first key to look at field 6. That is, the first item that WordPerfect examines is in the sixth field. In that field we have coded four choices of marital status. We want WordPerfect to select one of those—all the single people. Therefore, we tell WordPerfect:

```
Key1=s
```

See Figure 8.21, which says, Go to the sixth field, first line, first word and select all the records where the marital code is "s" (single). Press **F7** (**Exit**), then **5-Action**. WordPerfect picks out all the single people and groups their entire records on the screen or in the file you requested (see Figure 8.22).

Notice that we used **5-Action** instead of 1-Perform Action. You use 5-Action in conjunction with **Select**.

8.3 Fields with More than One Line

The second field in our database contains three lines:

```
Ms.^R (1)
Rebecca Edwards
3415 The Boulevard
Richmond, VA 23220^R (2)
```

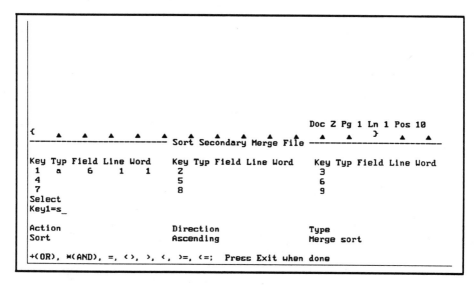

Figure 8.21 *Selecting the Code to Key On*
(Ctrl-F9, 2-Sort, Enter, Enter, 4-Select, Type Key1=s)

With a **Merge sort** we can pick out any word in any line in a multiline field. If we want to sort everyone who lives in Richmond, we tell Word-Perfect to look in the second field (R2), in the third line, and at the first word (see Figure 8.23).

```
Mr.^R
Howard Hancock
12 River Road
South Bend, IN 46779^R
Mr. Hancock^R
professor^R
$35,000^R
█
Pinto^R
41^R
20+^R
^E
Ms.^R
Rebecca Edwards
3415 The Boulevard
Richmond, VA 23220^R
Ms. Edwards^R
banker^R
$60,000+^R
█
BMW^R
31^R
18^R
^E
C:\WP5\FILES1                                    Doc 1 Pg 1 Ln 1 Pos 10
```

Figure 8.22 *Records Sorted on Field ^R6*
(Ctrl-F9, 2-Sort, Enter, Enter, 4-Select, Type Key1=s, 5-Action)

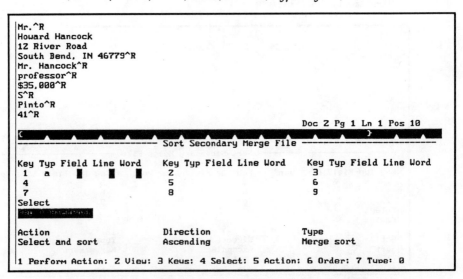

Figure 8.23 *Key Specifications for a Multiline Field*
(Ctrl-F9, 2-Sort, Enter, Enter, 7-Type, 1-Merge, 3-Keys, Type Specifications, F7, 4-Select, Type Key Specifications, F7)

We also entered the Key1 specification, which was to look for the word "Richmond." If we start the sort with these instructions, WordPerfect will find all the states with a Richmond, not just Virginia. If we wanted only Richmond, VA, we would have entered two keys (see Section 8.4).

Selecting records by a key criterion is such an important concept that you shouldn't continue to the next sections without fully understanding it. Take a few minutes to review the preceding sections of this chapter.

8.4 Using Key Combinations with Operators

Having told WordPerfect to pick out all the single people, you can combine that criterion with all the single people who drive a BMW. The make of car is filed in field 7 (R7). We've already defined Key1 as the marital status field. Now we'll define Key2 as the auto make. Moving the cursor to Key2 in the settings sheet (Ctrl-F9, 2-Sort, Enter, Enter, 7-Type, 1-Merge, 3-Key), we'll define keys as shown in Figure 8.24.

This tells WordPerfect that, if requested, it should look into two fields for data. Now you want to tell WordPerfect how to treat the data it finds in the two fields. We want WordPerfect to select only those people who are single *and* drive a BMW. Pressing **4-Select**, we'll add the second criterion (see Figure 8.25).

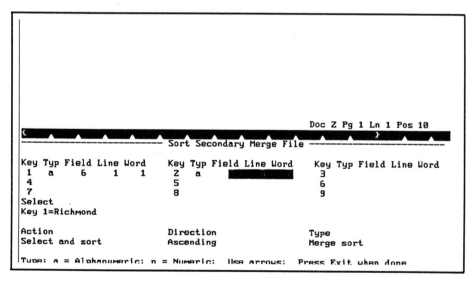

Figure 8.24 *Defining the Second Sort Key*
(Ctrl-F9, 2-Sort, Enter, Enter, 7-Type, 1-Merge, Right Arrow, Type Specifications, F7)

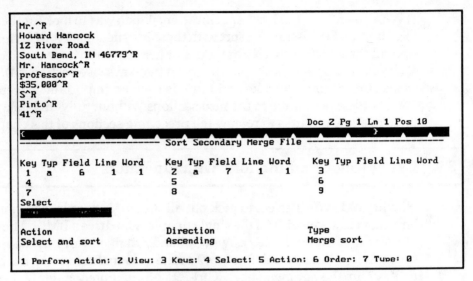

Figure 8.25 *Selecting Specifications for the Sort Keys*
(Ctrl-F9, 2-Sort, Enter, Enter, 7-Type, 1-Merge, Right Arrow, Type Specifications,
F7, 4-Select, Type Specifications, F7)

The asterisk is WordPerfect's symbol for **And**. Unless a record meets both key criteria, it will not be selected.

8.4.1 Deleting Key Settings

WordPerfect remembers key settings, and if you want to delete one, you move the cursor to the **Type** column and press **Del**. The numbers in the **Field**, **Line**, and **Word** columns disappear. When you move the cursor with the **Arrow** key, the entire key becomes vacant.

8.5 Logical Operators

With nine sort keys available and using logical operators, you can query the database for very specific records. The logical operators are:

* (And) Records meet *both* criteria: Key1 = S * Key2 = BMW
Selects only single people who drive a BMW

+ (Or) Records meet *either* criteria: Key1 = S + Key2 = BMW
Selects anyone who is single or anyone who drives a BMW

= (Equals)	Records are the same as the key data: Key3 = 27 Selects only 27-year-old people
> (Greater than)	Records are larger than the key data: Key3 > 27 Selects anyone 28 or older
< (Less than)	Records are smaller than the key data: Key3 < 27 Selects anyone 26 or younger
>= (Greater than or equal to)	Records are the same or larger than the key data: Key3 >= 27 Selects anyone 27 or older
<= (Less than or equal to)	Records are the same or smaller than the key data: Key3 <= 27 Selects anyone 27 or younger
< > (Not equal to)	Records do not match the key data: Key3< >27 Selects everyone except 27-year-olds. Key4 < > Edwards Selects everyone except people named Edwards

The operators >, <, >=, and <= can be used only with numbers; = and < > can be used with numbers or characters. The operators **Or +** and **And** ***** can be used with anything. Operators can be strung together to make complex sorting criteria. Parentheses ( ) are used to indicate the relationship between keys.

8.6   Examples Using Logical Operators

1. Select everyone named McCarthy and Byrne:

```
Key4 = McCarthy + Key4 = Byrne
```

The Or (+) operator is a little confusing. Although we want to select everyone named "McCarthy" and everyone named "Byrne," Word-Perfect must apply the Or operator to find both. It is looking for "Mc-Carthy" or "Byrne." Either name qualifies, so both names will be selected.

2. Select all single people named McCarthy:

```
Key1 = S * Key4 = McCarthy
```

With And (*), a record must meet *both* criteria to be selected, whereas with the Or (+) operator a record could meet *either* criteria and be selected.

3. Select everyone named McCarthy and Byrne who are older than 27:

```
(Key 4 = McCarthy + Key4 = Byrne) * Key3 > 27
```

The parentheses tell WordPerfect to apply the age criterion to both McCarthy and Byrne. If the key instructions had been entered without the parentheses:

```
Key 4 = McCarthy + Key4 = Byrne * Key3 > 27
```

WordPerfect would have selected everone named "McCarthy" and applied the age criterion only to "Byrne." Grouping keys within parentheses makes them function as one element in the equation.

4. Select everyone who drives a BMW who is not married:

```
Key2 = BMW * Key1 <>M
```

This would include all the single, divorced, and widowed people who drive BMWs.

5. Select everyone who drives a BMW and is over the age of 31 and everyone who is single who drives a BMW. There are two ways this equation can be entered:

```
(Key2=BMW * Key3>31) + (Key1=S * Key2=BMW)
 Key2=BMW * (Key1=S + Key3>31)
```

Equations can be as long and as complicated as you wish. If your equation is longer than the width of the screen, Wordperfect continues past the right margin.

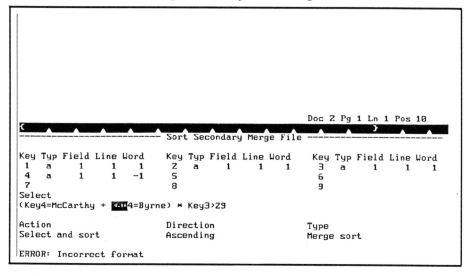

```
                                               Doc 2 Pg 1 Ln 1 Pos 10
{                                                                    }
------------------------- Sort Secondary Merge File -------------------------
Key Typ Field Line Word    Key Typ Field Line Word    Key Typ Field Line Word
 1   a    1     1    1       2   a    1     1    1       3   a    1     1    1
 4   a    1     1   -1       5                           6
 7                           8                           9
Select
(Key4=McCarthy + ████=Byrne) × Key3>Z9

Action                     Direction                  Type
Select and sort            Ascending                  Merge sort

ERROR: Key not defined
```

Figure 8.26 *Key # is Missing*

```
                                               Doc 2 Pg 1 Ln 1 Pos 10
{                                                                    }
------------------------- Sort Secondary Merge File -------------------------
Key Typ Field Line Word    Key Typ Field Line Word    Key Typ Field Line Word
 1   a    1     1    1       2   a    1     1    1       3   a    1     1    1
 4   a    1     1   -1       5                           6
 7                           8                           9
Select
(Key4=McCarthy + ███4=Byrne) × Key3>Z9

Action                     Direction                  Type
Select and sort            Ascending                  Merge sort

ERROR: Incorrect format
```

Figure 8.27 *The Word "Key" is Misspelled*

8.6.1 Correcting Mistakes in Sort Equations

When you've entered the equation, press **F7 (Exit)**, then select **5-Action** to begin the sort. If you have not abided precisely by WordPerfect's syntax for entering equations, it will give an error message and the cursor will position itself at the error, allowing you to correct the mistake. Look at some of the possible errors in Figures 8.26 through 8.29.

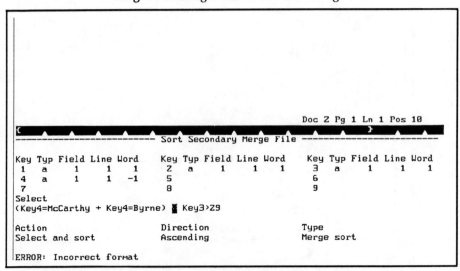

Figure 8.28 *Right Parenthesis is Missing*

```
                                              Doc 2 Pg 1 Ln 1 Pos 10
{                                                           }
------------------------- Sort Secondary Merge File -------------------------
Key Typ Field Line Word    Key Typ Field Line Word    Key Typ Field Line Word
 1   a    1    1    1       2   a    1    1    1       3   a    1    1    1
 4   a    1    1   -1       5                          6
 7                          8                          9
Select
<Key4=McCarthy + Key4=Byrne) █ Key3>Z9

Action                    Direction               Type
Select and sort           Ascending               Merge sort

ERROR: Incorrect format
```

Figure 8.29 *"&" is Not a WordPerfect Operator*

8.7 Selecting Criteria Contained in Any Field or Word Position

There might be occasions when a key word does not fall in the same position from one record to another. For example, you might want to pick out all florists from your database of companies. The words "florist" or "flowers" would appear in different positions in their company names:

Henry's Flowers
Receptions, Flowers, Inc.
The Florist Store
Florist Galore

To sort out every company whose names contain these words, enter:

```
Keyg=flowers + Keyg=florist
```

With the **g** key number, WordPerfect searches every word in every field. The **g** stands for "Global" sort.

CHAPTER 9

Columns

WordPerfect creates columns of either equal or unequal width that automatically wrap from one column to the next and from one page to the next. There are newspaper-type columns where you read down one column and then continue to the top of the next column, and there are parallel columns where text in one column corresponds to text in the next column.

You can begin and end a column format anywhere in your document. WordPerfect places code markers at the beginning and end of the column range. Within this range text is positioned in the column format you selected. As with any Block of text, you can give columns attributes different from the rest of the text, which includes such features as Bold, line justification, and type fonts. Being able to insert a column format within a document gives you the flexibility of page layouts that can include graphics with text wrapped around them. Part of the ease in using columns is WordPerfect's ability to automatically set column widths.

9.1 Laying Out Columns of Equal Widths

If you want to create columns of equal width, the only decisions you have to make are how many columns you want on a page and how much space you want between each column. WordPerfect calculates everything for you. To enter your column specifications, press **Alt-F7 (Math/Columns)** and select item **4-Column Def** (see Figure 9.1). This brings up the settings sheet for column layout (see Figure 9.2).

As you can see, you can define up to 24 columns, which you might have a need for if you're laying out math columns. WordPerfect's default is for

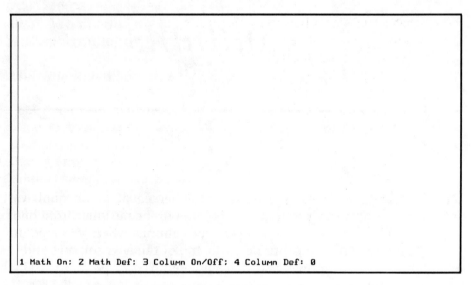

```
1 Math On: 2 Math Def: 3 Column On/Off: 4 Column Def: 0
```

Figure 9.1 *Defining and Activating Columns (Alt-F7)*

```
Text Column Definition

    1 - Type                              Newspaper

    2 - Number of Columns                 █

    3 - Distance Between Columns          ▆▆▆▆

    4 - Margins

    Column    Left     Right    Column    Left      Right
      1:      1"       4"         13:
      2:      4.5"     7.5"       14:
      3:                          15:
      4:                          16:
      5:                          17:
      6:                          18:
      7:                          19:
      8:                          20:
      9:                          21:
     10:                          22:
     11:                          23:
     12:                          24:

Selection: 4
```

Figure 9.2 *Settings Sheet for Laying Out Columns*
(Alt-F7, 4-Column Def)

two newspaper columns with a 1-inch margin at the left and right. The form (paper) size is implicit here, 8.5 inches wide. We know this because the right margin of the second column stops at 7.5 inches, leaving 1 inch for the right border. If our paper is a different size, the first step is to change the form size (see Section 2.5.2). We can also see that WordPerfect has set 0.5 inches between columns. We can, of course, change any of these settings, but first let's change the number of columns to see how Word-Perfect recalculates the settings.

In Figure 9.3 we changed the number of columns from two to three, keeping the 1-inch borders and 0.5-inch spacing between columns. Word-Perfect automatically calculated the column widths.

In Figure 9.4 we changed the distance between columns to 0.25 inches and the borders to 0.5 inches. The way we changed the borders was to make the left column begin at 0.5 inches and the right edge of the right column to end at 8 inches. WordPerfect then knew how to calculate the measurements in between (see Figure 9.4).

Whenever you Save a file and Exit, WordPerfect remembers the last column settings and Retrieves them with the document.

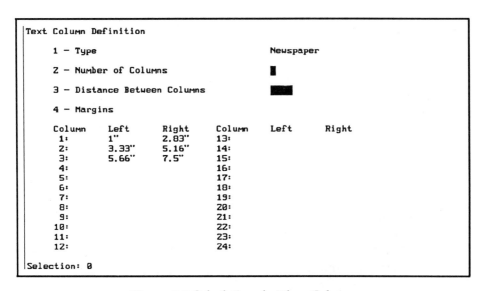

Figure 9.3 *Calculations for Three Columns*
(Alt-F7, 4-Column Def, 2-Number of Columns, Type 3, Enter)

```
Text Column Definition

    1 - Type                                Newspaper

    2 - Number of Columns                    3

    3 - Distance Between Columns             0.25"

    4 - Margins

    Column    Left      Right    Column    Left      Right
      1:      0.5"      3"         13:
      2:      3.25"     5.25"      14:
      3:      5.5"      7.5"       15:
      4:                           16:
      5:                           17:
      6:                           18:
      7:                           19:
      8:                           20:
      9:                           21:
     10:                           22:
     11:                           23:
     12:                           24:

Selection: 0
```

Figure 9.4 *Calculations for Margin and Column Spacing*
(Alt-F7, 4-Column Def, 2-Number of Columns, Change Specifications, Enter)

9.2   Turning On Columns

Once you have specified the number and size of your columns, you can begin using them at any place in your document. If you want the entire document to be columns, position the cursor at the top left margin of the first page or position it anywhere in the middle of the document. Press **Alt-F7 (Columns)** and select item **3-Column On/Off**. This places a code marker so that WordPerfect knows where to begin a column format (see Figure 9.5).

Notice that the first code **Col Def** repeats the specifications that are on the Settings sheet. We see there are two columns, the left margin is 1 inch, the first column is 3 inches wide, there is an 0.5-inch space between columns, the second column begins at 4.5 inches, is 3 inches wide, and ends at 7.5 inches, leaving a 1-inch border on the right side of an 8.5-inch piece of paper. We also see that the **[Col On]** marker has been placed.

All text entered after the marker will be formatted in columns until you place a **[Col Off]** marker. Simply press **Alt-F7** again and select **3-Column On/Off**. The marker is placed and the typing area returns to its normal format (see Figure 9.6).

Moving from column to column is accomplished by pressing **Ctrl-Home-Left/Right Arrow**.

```
You can begin and end a column        features as bolding, line
format anywhere in your               justification and type fonts.
document. WordPerfect places          Being able to insert a column
code markers at the beginning         format within a document gives
and end of the column range.          you the flexibility of page
Within this range text is             layouts which can include
positioned within the column          graphics with text wrapped
format you selected. As with          around them. Part of the ease
any Block of text you can give        in using columns is
columns attributes different          WordPerfect's ability to
C:\WP5\FILES3                                   Doc 1 Pg 1 Ln 2 Pos 10
{    ▲     ▲     ▲     ▲     ▲     ▲    ▲    ▲    ▲    ▲    ▲    ▲    }
[HRt]
[Col Def:2,1",4",4.5",7.5"][Col On]You can begin and end a column[SRt]
format anywhere in your[SRt]
document. WordPerfect places[SRt]
code markers at the beginning[SRt]
and end of the column range.[SRt]
Within this range text is[SRt]
positioned within the column[SRt]
format you selected. As with[SRt]
any Block of text you can give [SRt]

Press Reveal Codes to restore screen
```

Figure 9.5 *Looking at Column Codes Through Reveal Codes*
(Alt-F3)

```
format anywhere in your               justification and type fonts.
document. WordPerfect places          Being able to insert a column
code markers at the beginning         format within a document gives
and end of the column range.          you the flexibility of page
Within this range text is             layouts which can include
positioned within the column          graphics with text wrapped
format you selected. As with any      around them. Part of the ease
Block of text you can give            in using columns is
columns attributes different          WordPerfect's ability to
from the rest of the text, which      automatically set column widths.
includes such                         ─
                                         Col 2 Doc 1 Pg 1 Ln 13 Pos 45
{    ▲     ▲     ▲     ▲     }  {    ▲    ▲    ▲    ▲    }
WordPerfect's ability to[SRt]
automatically set column widths.[SRt]
[Col Off]




Press Reveal Codes to restore screen
```

Figure 9.6 *Turning Columns Off*
(Alt-F7, 3-Column On/Off)

9.3   Working with Columns Less than a Page Long

WordPerfect doesn't wrap text to the next column until it encounters a Page Break, and if the text is less than a page long, WordPerfect fills only one of the columns, or it fills one column completely and only partially fills the second. You have to force the columns to be filled evenly.

If you are entering new text, position the cursor, Define and turn on the column feature, and begin entering your text. When you finish entering new text, turn **Columns Off**. If you're formatting existing text, turn on Columns at the first character, move the cursor to the last character you want to appear in columns, and turn **Columns Off**. With either new or existing text, WordPerfect honors the column specifications. Now, count the lines of text in the column or use the status line to show you how many lines you've entered. In Figure 9.7 we entered 22 lines.

In order to divide the text evenly between two columns, move the cursor to the beginning of line 11, which is half the text, and press **Ctrl-Home** to enter a Page Break. Using the **Right Arrow**, move the cursor to the second column and the last half of the column of text will shift over (see Figure 9.8).

The last step is to remove the Page Break double line so that when you print, you will not skip to a new page. To do this, move the cursor to the end of the second (last) column and turn on **Reveal Codes (Alt-F3)**. Notice

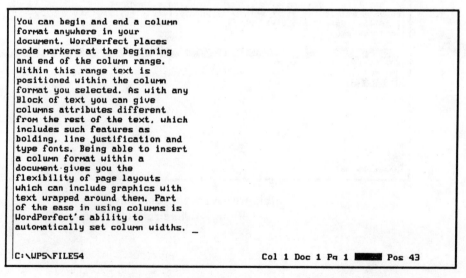

Figure 9.7 *Entering New Text into a Column*

```
You can begin and end a column          features as bolding, line
format anywhere in your                  justification and type fonts.
document. WordPerfect places            Being able to insert a column
code markers at the beginning           format within a document gives
and end of the column range.            you the flexibility of page
Within this range text is               layouts which can include
positioned within the column            graphics with text wrapped
format you selected. As with any        around them. Part of the ease
Block of text you can give              in using columns is
columns attributes different            WordPerfect's ability to
from the rest of the text, which        automatically set column widths.
includes such_
===============================================================================



C:\WPS\FILE55                           Col 1 Doc 1 Pg 1 Ln 15 Pos 23
```

Figure 9.8 *Dividing Text Evenly Between Two Columns*

```
You can begin and end a column          features as bolding, line
format anywhere in your                  justification and type fonts.
document. WordPerfect places            Being able to insert a column
code markers at the beginning           format within a document gives
and end of the column range.            you the flexibility of page
Within this range text is               layouts which can include
positioned within the column            graphics with text wrapped
format you selected. As with any        around them. Part of the ease
Block of text you can give              in using columns is
columns attributes different            WordPerfect's ability to
from the rest of the text, which        automatically set column widths.
C:\WPS\FILE55                           Col 2 Doc 1 Pg 1 Ln 11 Pos 77
{                              }  {                                }
in using columns is[SRt]
WordPerfect's ability to[SRt]
automatically set column widths.[SRt]

[Col Off][HRt]
Text which is begun after the double line Page Brake will not be[SRt]
formatted into columns.



Press Reveal Codes to restore screen
```

Figure 9.9 *Deleting the Hard Page (Page Break)*
Code Marker

in Figure 9.9 that the cursor is on the Page Break (Hard Page [HPg])
marker. Also notice that the text that follows the **[Col Off]** marker is not
formatted into columns. So we can Delete the [HPg] code, which removes
the double line Page Break but does not remove the [Col Off] marker. The
[HPg] is gone and the [Col Off] marker has moved into its place (see
Figure 9.10).

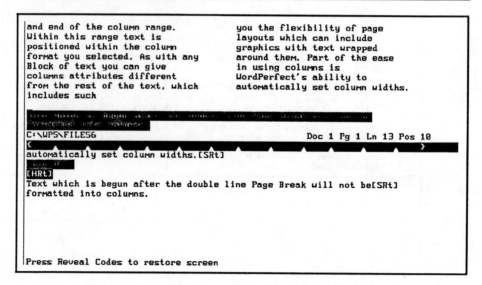

Figure 9.10 *Finished Columns with Page Break Removed*

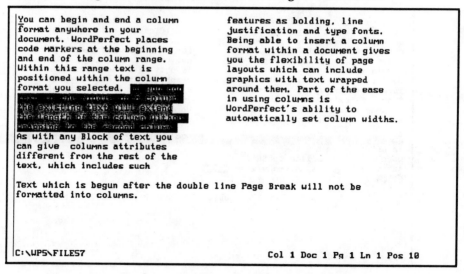

Figure 9.11 *Text Added (or Deleted) to Existing Columns*

9.4 Adding or Deleting Text from a Column

If you add or cut text from a column, the columns do not realign themselves into even lengths, and there's no handy way to use Page Breaks to align them properly (see Figure 9.11). The best way to handle this is to

Delete the current column marker codes so that the text is rearranged into standard text format. Then enter (or delete) your new text and go through the column formation process described above in Section 9.3.

9.5 Removing Columns

To eliminate a column format we simply delete the column marker codes. Move the cursor to the top of the column and turn on **Reveal Codes (Alt-F3)**. The cursor should be positioned on either [Col Def] or [Col On] (see Figure 9.12). Using the **Del or Backspace** keys, remove both code markers.

9.6 Justification Within Columns

If you are using right justification, you need to think about the appearance of your columns before you create them. As you narrow the width a line fits on, you make it more difficult for WordPerfect to evenly space words. WordPerfect's default is not to hyphenate words, which means that the entire word must fit into the spaces left at the end of the line or the entire word will be wrapped to the next line. Compare Figure 9.13, which does not use hyphenation, with Figure 9.14, which does. You can see that the

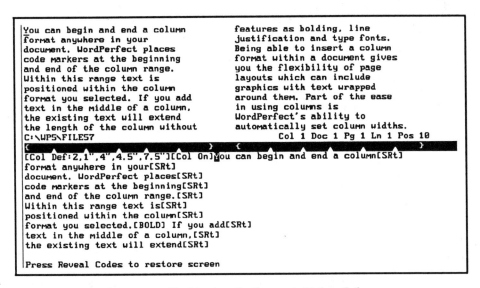

Figure 9.12 *Positioning the Cursor to Delete Column Code Markers*

```
to the next. There are newspaper type columns where you rad down
one column then continue to the top of the next column, and there
are parallel columns where text in one column corresponds to text
in the next column.

You can begin and end a column          features as bolding, line
format anywhere in your                 justification and type fonts.
document. WordPerfect places            Being able to insert a column
code markers at the beginning           format within a document gives
and end of the column range.            you the flexibility of page
Within this range text is               layouts which can include
positioned within the column            graphics with text wrapped
format you selected. As with any        around them. Part of the ease
Block of text you can give              in using columns is
columns attributes different            WordPerfect's ability to
from the rest of the text, which        automatically set column widths.
includes such

9.1.1. Laying Out Columns of Equal Widths


C:\WP5\FILE60                           Doc 1 Pg 1 Ln 5 Pos 10
```

Figure 9.13 *Columns Without Hyphenation*

```
WordPerfect creates columns of either equal or unequal width which
automatically wrap from one column to the next, and from one page
to the next. There are newspaper type columns where you rad down
one column then continue to the top of the next column, and there
are parallel columns where text in one column corresponds to text
in the next column.

You can begin and end a column          which includes such features as
format anywhere in your docu-           bolding, line justification and
ment. WordPerfect places code           type fonts. Being able to in-
markers at the beginning and            sert a column format within a
end of the column range. Within         document gives you the flex-
this range text is positioned           ibility of page layouts which
within the column format you            can include graphics with text
selected. As with any Block of          wrapped around them. Part of
text you can give  columns              the ease in using columns is
attributes different from the           WordPerfect's ability to auto-
rest of the text,                       matically set column widths.


C:\WP5\FILE59                       Col 2 Doc 1 Pg 1 Ln 11 Pos 46
```

Figure 9.14 *Columns with Hyphenation*

spacing between words is more even with Hyphenation. Also, there are 12 lines per column in Figure 9.13 and only 11 per column in Figure 9.14.

If you decide to use Hyphenation or to change the type font or size, you should make those decisions before you turn on Columns. (See Section

11.8.1 and 11.8.2 for a discussion of Hyphenation and the Hyphenation Zone, which defines the specifications for hyphenating words.)

To turn on Hyphenation, position the cursor at the beginning of the column and press **Shift-F8**. Select **1-Line**, then **1-Hyphenation**. Change the No to **Y**. You can also change the Hyphenation Zone from this menu. Move the cursor to the end of the last column and turn off Hyphenation by the same process.

9.7   Working with Columns of Uneven Widths

You can set your columns at virtually any width you want as long as the sum total of column widths is not wider than the width of the page. The setup procedure is the same as laying out columns of even widths except that you select item **4-Margins** from the Text Column Definition menu and enter the specific margins you desire. WordPerfect will not override your settings with the automatic settings.

Obviously, you need to calculate the mathematics of your column to make certain that the entire page width is accounted for, either by column widths, gutters (the space between columns), or the left and right borders. In Figure 9.15 we have changed the right margin of the first column to 5 inches. If we add up all the width specifications, we get:

```
Text Column Definition

     1 - Type                          Newspaper

     2 - Number of Columns             2

     3 - Distance Between Columns      0.5"

     4 - Margins

     Column    Left     Right    Column    Left      Right
       1:      1"       5"         13:
       2:      4.5"     7.5"       14:
       3:                          15:
       4:                          16:
       5:                          17:
       6:                          18:
       7:                          19:
       8:                          20:
       9:                          21:
      10:                          22:
      11:                          23:
      12:                          24:

Selection: 4
```

Figure 9.15 *Manually Specifying Column Widths*
(Alt-F7, 4-Column Def, 4-Margins, Type Specifications)

Width (inches)	Item
1	Left border
4	First column
0.5	Gutter
3	Second column
1	Right border
9.5	Total

This will not, of course, fit on paper 8.5 inches wide, and when you press Enter to fix the columns, WordPerfect will give an error message and will not allow you to Exit the settings sheet (see Figure 9.16).

Working with newspaper columns of unequal width that do not entirely fill a page is more difficult than working with those of equal length because it is harder to gauge where to use the Page Break (see Section 9.3). Normally documents that have columns of unequal widths are incorporating graphics (see Chapter 12) or they are parallel columns, which are not difficult to manipulate.

9.8   Parallel Columns

Whereas newspaper columns read down the column to the end, and then wrap to the top of the next column, parallel columns are designed to show

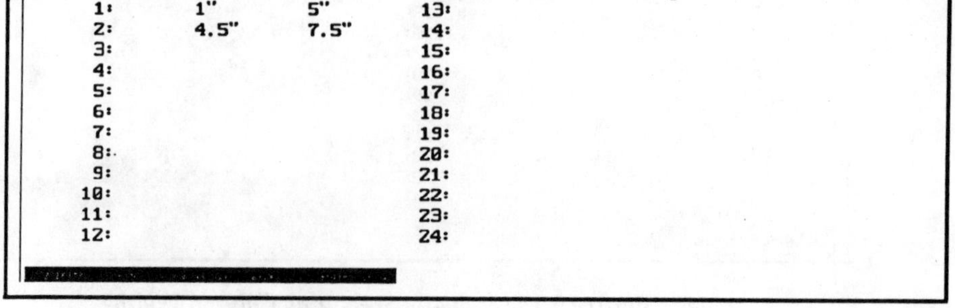

Figure 9.16 *Column Widths Incorrectly Specified*

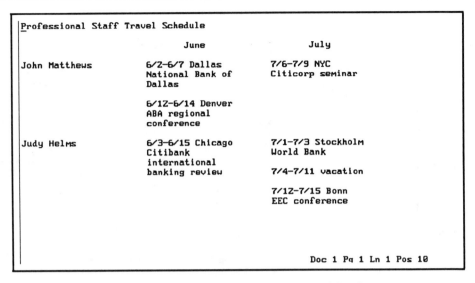

Figure 9.17 *Example Document Using Parallel Columns*

the correspondence between data in one column and across to the adjacent columns. The length of the data in one column does not have to be the same as the length in any other column (see Figure 9.17).

You can set up parallel columns with equal or unequal widths using the same settings sheet as you did with newspaper columns. Press **Alt-F7** and select **4-Column Def**. Then select **1-Type** to produce these menu choices (see Figure 9.18).

The only difference between 2-Parallel and 3-Parallel with Block Protect is that if a column extends to the following page and you do not want your records to be divided between one page and the next, you select **Block Protect**.

Choose item **2** or **3**, press **Enter**, then set **2-Number of Columns**. In our example we specified three columns of equal width and WordPerfect calculated their dimensions (see Figure 9.19)

9.8.1 *Using Parallel Columns*

Press **F7 (Exit)** or **Enter** twice to return to the typing area. Now that you've defined the columns, you can use this setting anywhere in a document. In our example we wanted a heading, so we did not activate the columns until line 3, where we positioned the cursor and turned on Columns (see Figure 9.20).

```
Text Column Definition

    1 - Type                                    Newspaper

    2 - Number of Columns                       2

    3 - Distance Between Columns

    4 - Margins

    Column    Left      Right     Column    Left      Right
      1:      1"        4"          13:
      2:      4.5"      7.5"        14:
      3:                            15:
      4:                            16:
      5:                            17:
      6:                            18:
      7:                            19:
      8:                            20:
      9:                            21:
     10:                            22:
     11:                            23:
     12:                            24:

Column Type: 1 Newspaper: ███████████████████████████████████████: 0
```

Figure 9.18 *Setting Up Parallel Columns*
(Alt-F7, 4-Column Def, 1-Type)

```
Text Column Definition

    1 - Type                              ██████████

    2 - Number of Columns                 █

    3 - Distance Between Columns

    4 - Margins

    Column    Left      Right     Column    Left      Right
      1:      1"        2.83"       13:
      2:      3.33"     5.16"       14:
      3:      5.66"     7.5"        15:
      4:                            16:
      5:                            17:
      6:                            18:
      7:                            19:
      8:                            20:
      9:                            21:
     10:                            22:
     11:                            23:
     12:                            24:

Selection: 0
```

Figure 9.19 *Specifying Three Columns of Equal Width*
(Alt-F7, 4-Column Def, 1-Type, 2-Parallel, 2-Number of Columns, Type 3, Enter)

Whatever text we type after the [Col On] marker will be placed in the first column until we enter a Hard Page [HPg] using Ctrl-Enter. Only then will the cursor move to the next column (see Figure 9.21). Notice that the [HPg] marker has been placed after "Matthews."

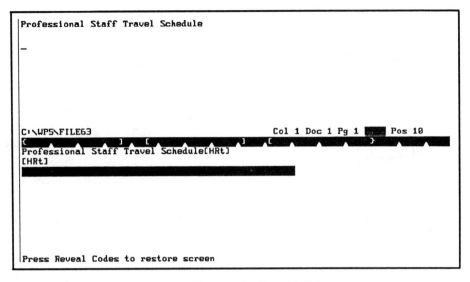

Figure 9.20 *Turning On Parallel Columns*
(Alt-F7, 3-Columns On/Off)

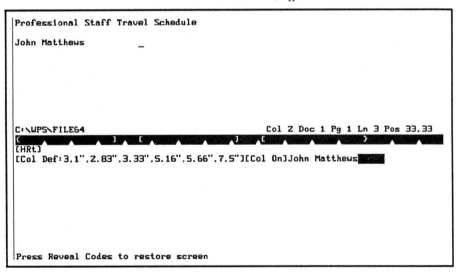

Figure 9.21 *Moving to the Second Parallel Column*
(Ctrl-Home)

Now we'll center "June" in the second column using **Shift-F6 (Center)** and enter Matthews' travel schedule for the month. Then we'll enter a **[HPg]** using **Ctrl-Enter**, which moves the cursor to the third column, where we'll center "July" and enter text. Notice that the status line tells you which column you're working in (see Figure 9.22).

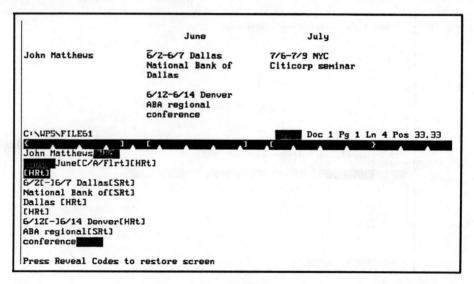

Figure 9.22 *Moving to the Third Parallel Column*
(Ctrl-Home)

Because there are only three columns defined, the next time we press
Ctrl-Enter the cursor moves back to the first column in a position to start
the second record. We'll enter Judy Helms' record the same ways as John
Matthews', but since this is our last record, we'll turn **Columns Off (Alt-
F7, 3-Columns On/Off)** when we've typed the last word in column 3. **Do
not press Enter (hard return) before turning off Columns** (see Figure
9.23).

9.8.2 Editing Parallel Columns

Unlike newspaper columns, parallel columns can be edited without wor-
rying about what will happen to the length of each column. With parallel columns, the longest column determines the length of the record. We
could move to the third column of Judy Helms' record and add as much
text as we wanted to describe her travels. As long as the new text falls
before the [Col Off] marker, all that will happen is that the column length
will be extended.

You can **Move** from one column to the next by pressing **Ctrl-Home-
Left/Right Arrow.**

Most of the features that you can use with ordinary text layouts can be
used in columns. Just remember that every record functions as a separate
page and that every column is autonomous from the other columns. That

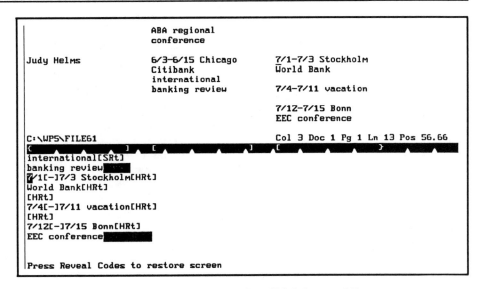

```
                      ABA regional
                      conference

Judy Helms            6/3-6/15 Chicago      7/1-7/3 Stockholm
                      Citibank              World Bank
                      international
                      banking review        7/4-7/11 vacation

                                            7/12-7/15 Bonn
                                            EEC conference

C:\WP5\FILE61                               Col 3 Doc 1 Pg 1 Ln 13 Pos 56.66
[           ]   [                    ]   [                    }
international[SRt]
banking review
7/1[-]7/3 Stockholm[HRt]
World Bank[HRt]
[HRt]
7/4[-]7/11 vacation[HRt]
[HRt]
7/12[-]7/15 Bonn[HRt]
EEC conference

Press Reveal Codes to restore screen
```

Figure 9.23 *Turning Parallel Columns Off*
(Alt-F3, 3-Columns Off)

```
Professional Staff Travel Schedule

                      June                  July

John Matthews         6/2-6/7 Dallas        7/6-7/9 NYC
                      National Bank of      Citicorp seminar
                      Dallas

                      6/12-6/14 Denver
                      ABA regional
                      conference

Judy Helms            6/3-6/15 Chicago      7/1-7/3 Stockholm
                      Citibank              World Bank
                      international
                      banking review        7/4-7/11 vacation

                                            7/12-7/15 Bonn
                                            EEC conference
```

Figure 9.24 *Deleting Text in a Column (Ctrl-PgDn)*

is, if you specify **Center** for one column, you have to specify it again for the next column.

To delete all the data in a column, use the **Delete to End of Page** command. Position the cursor at the top of the column and record you want

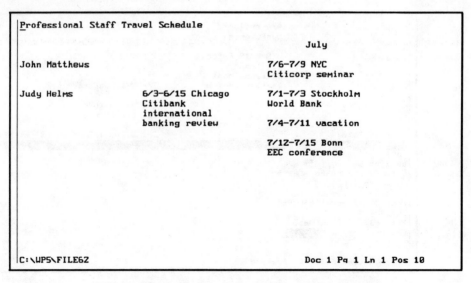

Figure 9.25 *Realigned Columns After Deleting Text*

to delete and press **(Ctrl-PgDn)** (see Figure 9.24). When you respond to the prompt with a **Y**, the text is deleted and the columns are realigned (see Figure 9.25).

CHAPTER 10

Outlines,
Contents, Indexes,
Footnotes, Tables,
Automatic Reference

WordPerfect provides a full range of features for composing a complete document including outlines, tables of contents, foot- and endnotes, indexes, cross references, and various types of lists and tables.

10.1 Outlines

The Outline feature does not create outlines from chapter or subchapter headings within the document (see Sections 10.2.4 and 10.6 for those instructions). The Outline function enables you to set up an outline, then change it any way you wish and have WordPerfect automatically renumber it.

To start an outline, position the cursor where you want the outline to begin. This can be in a new document or anywhere within existing text. Press **Shift-F5 (Date/Outline)**. This produces six menu choices:

```
1 = Date Text
2 = Date Code
3 = Date Format
4 = Outline
5 = Par Num
6 = Define
```

Select **4-Outline**. The message center indicates that you are now in the Outline mode. Press **Enter** to place the first paragraph number. If you look at this through Reveal Codes you can see that a code marker has been entered (see Figure 10.1).

To enter any text you must either press **F4 (Indent)** or use the **Space Bar** and/or **Tab**. In the example in Figure 10.2 we used indent, as you can see by the code marker. To move to the second level and insert a new outline number, press **Enter** to place a [HRt] marker. This inserts a new outline number at the *same* level as the first. To move it in one level, press **Tab** once. As you can see from Figure 10.3, each time you press **Tab** the level moves one step to the right.

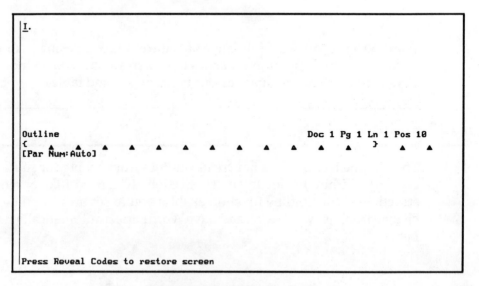

Figure 10.1 *Beginning an Outline*
(Shift-F5, 4-Outline, Enter)

```
I.   Setting Up Outline
II._




Outline                                        Doc 1 Pg 1 Ln 3 Pos 13
{          ▲   ▲    ▲    ▲    ▲    ▲    ▲    ▲    ▲    ▲    ▲    }    ▲    ▲
[HRt]▲
[Par Num:Auto][→Indent]Setting Up Outline[HRt]
[Par Num:Auto]




Press Reveal Codes to restore screen
```

Figure 10.2 *Entering Text into the Outline*
(Shift-F5, 4-Outline, Enter, F4, Type Text, Enter)

```
I.   Setting Up Outlines
     A.   Enter the Code Marker
     ■         Call Up the Menu
     Z.   Select 4-Outlines




Outline                                        Doc 1 Pg 1 Ln 1 Pos 10
{   ▲   ▲  ▲   ▲   ▲   ▲   ▲   ▲    ▲    ▲    ▲    }    ▲    ▲
[Par Num:Auto][→Indent]Setting Up Outlines[HRt]
[Tab][Par Num:Auto][→Indent]Enter the Code Marker[HRt]
                                    Call Up the Menu[HRt]
[Tab][Tab][Par Num:Auto][→Indent]Select 4[-]Outlines




Press Reveal Codes to restore screen
```

Figure 10.3 *Each Tab Moves Level One Step to the Right*

You can repeat these steps as many times as you wish. WordPerfect limits you to eight distinct levels of outlining, but there is no limit as to how long the outline can be.

If you want to turn the outlining feature off, press **Shift-F5** again. Notice that the word "Outline" disappears from the message center. Outlining will automatically turn off if you Save and Exit the file.

10.1.1 *Adding Sections to Outlines*

In order to add sections to your outline, you must turn the feature on again when you bring up the outline file. Move the cursor to the same position at which you started the outline and turn it on. Outline will appear in the message center. Move the cursor beyond the last character of the line *above* the new level you want to insert (see Figure 10.4).

When you press **Enter,** a level will be inserted. To change the level from a first level II., press **Tab** twice. This moves the level into the desired place (see Figure 10.5).

Notice that the old level 2. has not been change to 3., but it will as soon as you press the **Down Arrow.** When you type text for the new level 2., do not press Enter but use the Arrow keys to move around the outline.

10.1.2 *Changing Levels of an Existing Outline*

Once you leave a level, you cannot return to it and change the level notation. If, for example, in Figure 10.5 we wanted to make level 1. into a higher level B., which corresponds to level A., we could not use the Tab

```
I.    Setting Up Outlines
      A.    Enter the Code Marker
            1.    Call Up the Menu
II._
            1.    Select 4-Outlines




|
|
|
|
|
|
|
|
|
|
|
|Outline                                    Doc 1 Pg 1 Ln 4 Pos 13
```

Figure 10.4 *Inserting New Levels in Existing Outlines*

```
I.    Setting Up Outlines
      A.    Enter the Code Marker
            1.    Call Up the Menu
            2. _  █
            1.    Select 4-Outlines




Outline                                    Doc 1 Pg 1 Ln 4 Pos 22
{   ▲    ▲   ▲   ▲    ▲    ▲    ▲    ▲    ▲   ▲    }   ▲    ▲
[Tab][Par Num:Auto][→Indent]Enter the Code Marker[HRt]
[Tab][Tab][Par Num:Auto][→Indent]Call Up the Menu[HRt]
█████████████████████████████████████[HRt]
[Tab][Tab][Par Num:Auto][→Indent]Select 4[-]Outlines




Press Reveal Codes to restore screen
```

Figure 10.5 *Selecting the Desired Level (Tab, Tab)*

keys to move it as we did when we created the level. All you can do is insert a level B., using the method described above, and delete the existing level.

10.1.3 *Deleting Sections from Outlines*

To delete any section, turn on **Reveal Codes (Alt-F3)** and position the cursor at the right margin of the line you want to eliminate. Press **Backspace** as many times as it takes to delete all the text and codes. Or, position the cursor at the left margin and press **Ctrl-End**.

10.1.4 *Changing Numbers Styles*

WordPerfect's default system for numbering the levels of an outline is: I. A. 1. a. (1) (a) i) a), but you can easily change it to any system you wish. Press **Shift-F5** and select item **6-Define** to produce the settings sheet (shown in Figure 10.6).

You can select items 2, 3, 4, or 5 by pressing the number, or you can customize any combination by selecting **6-User-defined** and typing your selection for each level. Press **Enter** to Enter to move the cursor from one level to the next. The common number styles are listed on the bottom left of the settings sheet, but you can use any characters or numbers that you wish (see Figure 10.6).

```
Paragraph Number Definition

    1 - Starting Paragraph Number          1
          (in legal style)

                                          Levels
                             1     2     3     4     5     6     7     8
    2 - Paragraph            1.    a.    i.    (1)   (a)   (i)   1)    a)
    3 - Outline              I.    A.    1.    a.    (1)   (a)   i)    a)
    4 - Legal (1.1.1)        1     .1    .1    .1    .1    .1    .1    .1
    5 - Bullets              •     o     -     ■     ×     +     •     ×
    6 - User-defined

    Current Definition       I.    A.    1.    a.    (1)   (a)   i)    a)

        Number Style                 Punctuation
        1 - Digits                   #    - No punctuation
        A - Upper case letters       #.   - Trailing period
        a - Lower case letters       #)   - Trailing parenthesis
        I - Upper case roman         (#)  - Enclosing parentheses
        i - Lower case roman         .#   - All levels separated by period
        Other character - Bullet          (e.g.  2.1.3.4)


Selection: 0
```

Figure 10.6 *Defining Numbering for Outlines*
(Shift-F5, 6-Define)

10.1.5 *Assigning Punctuation*

From this same menu (Figure 10.6), you can customize punctuation using the number plus the punctuation marks you desire. The standard ones are listed in the bottom right of the settings sheet, but you can create your own, such as -1-. To record them, keep pressing **Enter** until you return to the typing area.

10.1.6 *Assigning the Starting Number*

WordPerfect starts an outline with 1. or I. If you're working on the same document in two files or if two people are working on different chapters, you might have an occasion to begin numbering other than with 1. To change the beginning number, select item **1- Starting Paragraph Number** and enter your starting number. You'll enter the starting number in Arabic numbers, but whatever style you've chosen will be used. For example, if you've chosen Roman numerals for the first level, you'll enter an Arabic number, such as 9, but the first level will be numbered IX.

10.2 Paragraph Numbering

You can assign code markers to paragraphs, which will automatically number them and, if you add, delete, or move paragraphs, the numbers will automatically change to reflect the new order. This is especially useful in legal documents, such as commercial leases, specifications, such as military material specs, and long lists of items that may be updated or changed. And, as with outlines, you can create up to eight levels of paragraph numbering. Paragraph numbering is the same as outlining except that WordPerfect recognizes the paragraph as an autonomous unit rather than one line in an outline.

To start paragraph numbering, position the cursor at the left margin of the first character of the paragraph. This can be done before you enter text or with existing text. However, before you enter the first paragraph number marker, be sure to define the type of numbers and punctuation you desire (see Sections 10.1.4 and 10.1.5). In Figure 10.7, we've changed the current definition.

To place the code marker, press **Shift-F5** then **5-Par Num** and **Enter**. The first-level number in the style you've chosen should appear. Whatever you type past this marker will comprise the first paragraph,

```
Paragraph Number Definition

    1 - Starting Paragraph Number          1
        (in legal style)

                                        Levels
                            1    2    3    4    5    6    7    8
    2 - Paragraph          1.   a.   i.   (1)  (a)  (i)  1)   a)
    3 - Outline            I.   A.   1.   a.   (1)  (a)  i)   a)
    4 - Legal (1.1.1)      1    .1   .1   .1   .1   .1   .1   .1
    5 - Bullets            •    o    —    ■    x    +    •    x
    6 - User-defined

    Current Definition     ██   ██   ██   ██   .1   .1   .1   .1_

        Number Style                Punctuation
        1 - Digits                  #    - No punctuation
        A - Upper case letters      #.   - Trailing period
        a - Lower case letters      #)   - Trailing parenthesis
        I - Upper case roman        (#)  - Enclosing parentheses
        i - Lower case roman        .#   - All levels separated by period
        Other character - Bullet         (e.g.  2.1.3.4)

Selection: 6
```

Figure 10.7 *Specifying the Number Style for Paragraphs*
(Shift-F5, 6-Define, 6-User-Defined, Type Specifications, Press Enter Until the Typing Area Reappears)

which is defined by WordPerfect as all text until it reaches the next paragraph number marker. In Figure 10.8 we've started a contract with five paragraphs.

If we delete a paragraph or change its level, all the other paragraphs will be renumbered accordingly. To change paragraph 3 to a new level, move the cursor to the left margin and press **Tab**. The paragraph moves to the right (see Figure 10.9.).

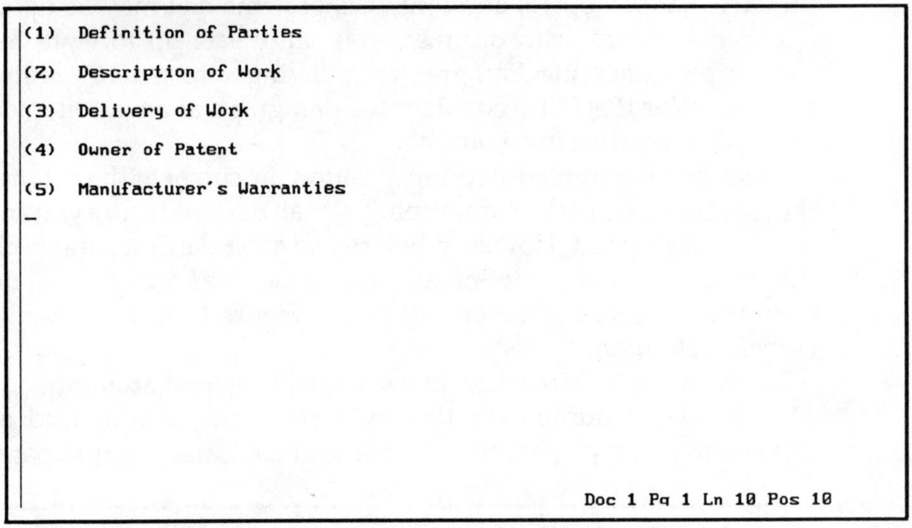

```
(1)   Definition of Parties

(2)   Description of Work

(3)   Delivery of Work

(4)   Owner of Patent

(5)   Manufacturer's Warranties
_



                                                      Doc 1 Pg 1 Ln 10 Pos 10
```

Figure 10.8 *Paragraph Headings with Number Markers*

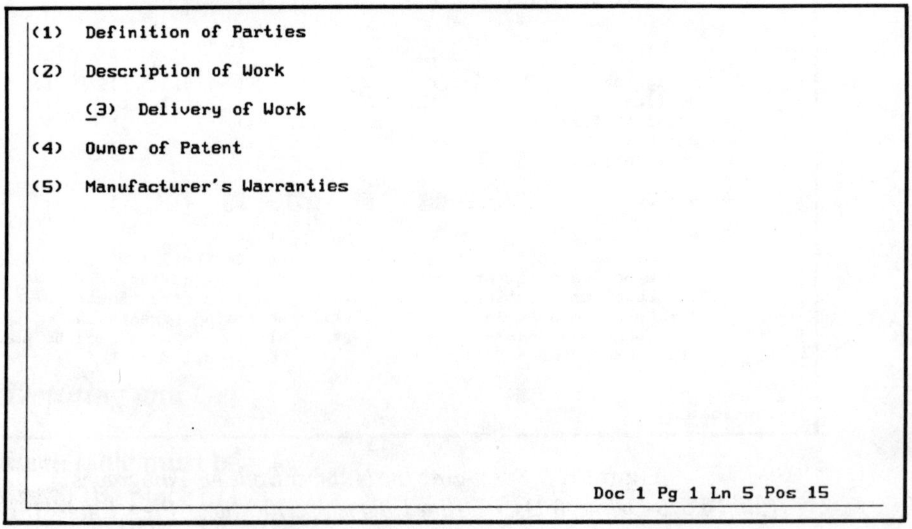

```
(1)   Definition of Parties

(2)   Description of Work

      (3)   Delivery of Work

(4)   Owner of Patent

(5)   Manufacturer's Warranties




                                                      Doc 1 Pg 1 Ln 5 Pos 15
```

Figure 10.9 *Changing a Paragraph Level (Tab)*

The paragraph numbers will change throughout the document when we press the **Home-Home-Down Arrow** (see Figure 10.10).

10.2.1 *Moving Paragraphs*

Using either **Block (Alt-F4)** or **Move (Ctrl-F5)** you can move any paragraph(s) to another position and the numbers will automatically change. Positioning the cursor as far left of the paragraph number as it will go (press Home-Home-Left Arrow to be certain you pick up the marker), **Move** the paragraph to the new position. Press **Enter** and all the paragraphs will be renumbered.

One exception is moving a paragraph to the very bottom of the document. There must a paragraph number marker beyond the paragraph you're moving. The end of the document will not have a marker, so you'll have to manually renumber it. Or, better still, place a dummy marker at the document's end, and after the final editing delete it.

10.2.2 *Deleting Paragraphs and Markers*

Using **Reveal Codes (Alt-F3)**, position the cursor on the number marker **[Par Num:Auto]** (see Figure 10.11). If you want simply to delete the automatic number, press **Del**. If you want to delete the entire paragraph, use **Block** or **Move**.

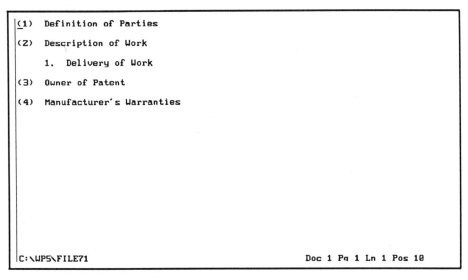

Figure 10.10 *Realigning Paragraph Numbers*

```
(1)   Definition of Parties

(2)   Delivery of Work

(3)   Owner of Patent

(4)   Description of Work

(5)   Manufacturer's Warranties


C:\WP5\FILE72                                    Doc 1 Pg 1 Ln 7 Pos 10
{                                                                      }
[Par Num:Auto]  Owner of Patent[HRt]
[HRt]
[Par Num:Auto]  Description of Work[HRt]
[HRt]
[Par Num:Auto]  Manufacturer's Warranties[HRt]
[Par Num Def][HRt]




Press Reveal Codes to restore screen
```

Figure 10.11 *Positioning the Cursor to Delete Paragraphs*

10.2.3 *Using Paragraph Numbering to Structure a Document*

Because you can add as much text to an automatically numbered paragraph as you wish, starting with a numbered structure is a good way to organize your thoughts and the document. A "working contents!" gives you the flexibility to work on sections nonsequentially and to reorganize as you go along. Automatic numbering helps you see how the document is shaping up. If you wish, you can **Mark** these headings and generate an outline (see Section 10.6).

10.3 Automatic Reference

In longer documents you might frequently refer a discussion on one page to a section on another page. When you edit the document or combine it with other documents, the page references would change drastically. However, if you tag them with WordPerfect's **Automatic Reference**, no matter where the material is moved the reference number changes to reflect its new location. You can reference text to five tie-ins:

1 = Page numbers
2 = Paragraph and Outline numbers
3 = Footnote numbers

4 = Endnote numbers
5 = Graphics Box numbers

These references are designated with **markers** of one kind or another. (WordPerfect cannot reference paragraph numbers that you've typed in manually. You must enter the "official" marker.)

The concept works like this. You're entering text and come to a reference that says "see page _." At the blank you'll place an Automatic Reference marker (see Figure 10.12). The second step is to go to the page that you are referring to and place another marker, which WordPerfect refers to as the **target**. In this example, the reference is Section 10 (see Figure 10.13).

Look at Figures 10.12 and 10.13 closely. Figure 10.12 shows that this is the Ref (reference) marker and that it is tied into a Pg ? number. Figure 10.13 shows that this is the Target marker. The text in parentheses "SOLE SOURCE" is a tag name that we gave to the reference. If the text marked by the target is moved, WordPerfect always knows to connect the reference tag "SOLE SOURCE" with the target tag "SOLE SOURCE."

In Figure 10.14 WordPerfect has referenced the target from page 1. If Section 10 is moved to page 95, WordPerfect will change the reference to "see page 95."

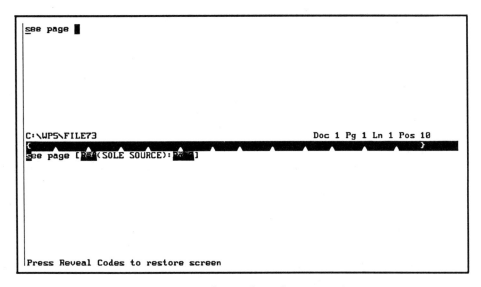

Figure 10.12 *Placing the Reference Marker*

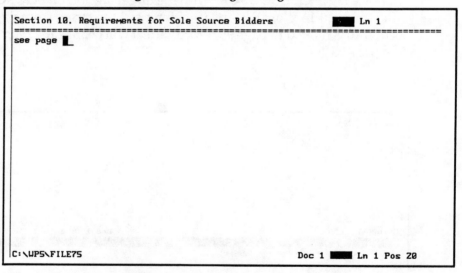

Figure 10.13 *Placing the Target Marker*

```
Section 10. Requirements for Sole Source Bidders        ▮ Ln 1
================================================================================
see page ▮
```
```
C:\WP5\FILE75                                    Doc 1 ▮▮▮▮ Ln 1 Pos 20
```

Figure 10.14 *Connecting the Reference to the Target*

10.3.1 *Procedure to Place Automatic Reference Markers*

Position the cursor at the place at which the **reference** number should appear. In our example it was at the blank in **see page _**. Then press **Alt-F5 (Mark Text)** to produce these menu items (see Figure 10.15). Select item **1-Auto Ref** to produce three choices (see Figure 10.16).

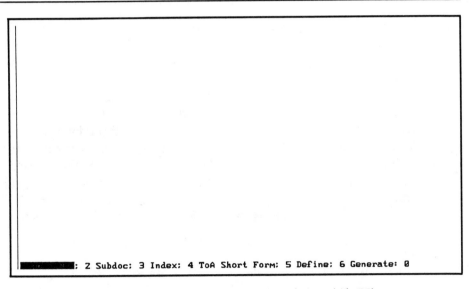

: 2 Subdoc: 3 Index: 4 ToA Short Form: 5 Define: 6 Generate: 0

Figure 10.15 *Starting Automatic Reference (Alt-F5)*

```
Mark Text: Automatic Reference

    1 - Mark Reference

    2 - Mark Target

    3 - Mark Both Reference and Target

















Selection: 0
```

Figure 10.16 *Mark Text Options (Alt-F5, 1-Auto Ref)*

The only difference between these three choices is whether you want to mark both the **reference** and the **target** at the same time. If your reference refers back to text that has already been written, it's easier to mark both at the same time, but if you haven't written the text yet, obviously you can mark only the reference. You can mark the target at any future time. Whether we mark one or both, the steps are essentially the same.

For this example we'll select item **3-Mark Both,** which produces the five choices for target numbers (see Figure 10.17). We selected **1-Page Number.** WordPerfect then asks for a target name. This is a tag for Word-Perfect to match the reference with the target but it is also your way of identifying the reference in event you want to find it later on (see Figure 10.18). It is a good idea to keep a list of the target names you've assigned.

When you type in the target name and press **Enter,** WordPerfect places both the reference and target markers at the same time, gives them the same tag name, and fills in the page reference number (see Figure 10.19). If you select a target name that already exists, WordPerfect won't accept it.

10.3.2 *Entering Target and Reference Markers Separately*

You might know ahead of time that you want to refer to particular text and so you would place a **target marker** there without having the **reference** in mind. WordPerfect will ask you to give the target a name. Type it in and press **Enter.** Nothing else is required at this time. When you finally come to the reference point, go through the steps to enter the

```
Tie Reference to:

     1 - Page Number

     2 - Paragraph/Outline Number

     3 - Footnote Number

     4 - Endnote Number

     5 - Graphics Box Number

After selecting a reference type, go to the location of the item you want to
reference in your document and press Enter to mark it as the "target".




Selection: 0
```

Figure 10.17 *Choices for Numbering References*
(Alt-F5, 1-Auto Ref, 3-Mark Both)

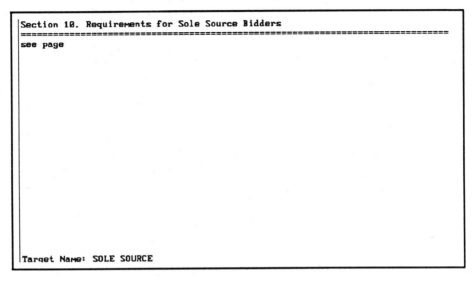

```
Section 10. Requirements for Sole Source Bidders
================================================================================
see page
```

```
Target Name: SOLE SOURCE
```

Figure 10.18 *Entering the Target Name*
(Alt-F5, 1-Auto Ref, 3-Mark Both, 1-Page, Type the Target Name)

```
Section 10. Requirements for Sole Source Bidders
================================================================================
see page 1_




C:\WP5\FILE75                                    Doc 1 Pg 2 Ln 1 Pos 20
[                                                                         ]
[ TARGET: SOLE SOURCE ]Section 10. Requirements for Sole Source Bidders[HPg]
see page [REF(TAR NAME):Pg 1]




Press Reveal Codes to restore screen
```

Figure 10.19 *Automatic Reference Markers*
(Alt-F5, 1-Auto Ref, 3-Mark Both, 1-Page, Type Target Name, Enter)

marker. WordPerfect will ask you for the target name. Be sure to give the exact name that you entered when you placed the target marker.

Similarly, you can enter a reference marker first. Without a target to refer to, WordPerfect places a ? mark in the place of a page number.

If you enter reference and target markers separately, you must **Generate** the final merge. Or, if you move text containing target markers to another page, you must **Generate** new reference numbers. It's easy. Press **Alt-F5**, select **6-Generate**, then **5-Generate** Tables. WordPerfect asks if you want to replace the old reference numbers. You do (see Figure 10.20). WordPerfect renumbers the corresponding references, tables and indexes according to their target locations.

10.3.3 *Multiple References to the Same Target*

Long documents will undoubtedly contain several references to the same sources. A good example are endnotes that contain a bibliography. You might refer to a particular book six times. With Automatic Reference you simply enter the reference marker and specify the target name. In our simple example in Figure 10.21, we entered another reference to SOLE SOURCE. Notice that WordPerfect placed a ? mark for the page number until we generated (Section 10.3.2) the final results (see Figure 10.22).

10.3.4 *Using Footnotes and Endnotes as the Target*

This is a slightly different procedure because footnotes and endnotes are not a part of the document you can readily access (see Section 10.4). In Figure 10.23 we added a reference and named it SOLE SOURCE LAWS.

```
Mark Text: Generate

    1 — Remove Redline Markings and Strikeout Text from Document

    2 — Compare Screen and Disk Documents and Add Redline and Strikeout

    3 — Expand Master Document

    4 — Condense Master Document

    5 — Generate Tables, Indexes, Automatic References, etc.




Existing tables, lists, and indexes will be replaced.   Continue? (Y/N) Yes
```

Figure 10.20 *Generating New Reference Numbers*
(Alt-F5, 6-Generate, 5-Generate Tables, Y)

```
Section 10. Requirements for Sole Source Bidders
================================================================================
see page 1

================================================================================
see page ?




C:\WP5\FILE76                                        Doc 1 Pg 2 Ln 1 Pos 10
{                                                                             }
[Target:SOLE SOURCE]Section 10. Requirements for Sole Source Bidders[HPg]
See page [Ref:SOLE SOURCE:Pg 1][HRt]
[HPg]
[HRt]
see page [Ref:SOLE SOURCE:Pg ?]




Press Reveal Codes to restore screen
```

Figure 10.21 *Multiple References to the Same Target*

```
Section 10. Requirements for Sole Source Bidders
================================================================================
see page 1

================================================================================
see page 1









C:\WP5\FILE77                                        Doc 1 Pg 3 Ln 2 Pos 10
```

Figure 10.22 *Multiple References After Generation*

To name the **target** we must call the endnote to the screen, then proceed
through the steps to name it. Press **Ctrl-F7** and select either **1-Create** or **2-
Edit a foot/endnote**. When the note is on the screen, press **Alt-F5** to Mark
the text. Select **2-Mark Target** and follow the prompts. WordPerfect will
ask you to name the target, which must have the exact name as the
reference (SOLE SOURCE LAWS) (see Figure 10.24).

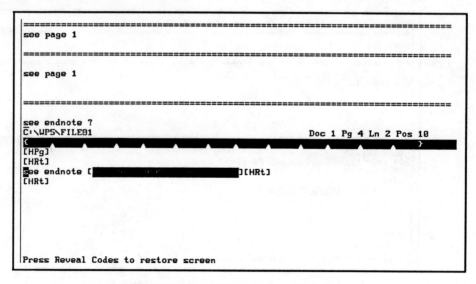

Figure 10.23 *Endnote Reference Marker*
(Alt-F5, 1-Auto Ref, 3-Mark Both, 1-Page, Type Target Name, Enter)

```
Mark Text: Automatic Reference

      1 - Mark Reference

      2 - Mark Target

      3 - Mark Both Reference and Target




















Target Name: ▒▒▒▒▒▒▒▒▒▒▒
```

Figure 10.24 *Naming an Endnote as the Target*
(Ctrl-F7, 2-Endnote, 2-Edit, Endnote 1, Alt-F5, 1, 2-Mark Target, Enter,
Type Target Name)

When we press **Enter** and look at Reveal Codes, we see how the marker has been placed (see Figure 10.25). Press **F7 (Exit)** to record the marker and return to the typing area. To connect the reference to the target, **Generate** a merge (see Section 10.3.2).

```
1.Meese. Edwin. "Attorney General's Report to Congress."
Congressional Quarterly, May 1986.




Press Exit when done                                    Ln 1 Pos 10
{                                                               }
[Target(SOLE SOURCE LAWS)][Note Num]Meese, Edwin, "Attorney General's Report to
Congress,"[SRt]
[UND]Congressional Quarterly,[und] May 1986.




Press Reveal Codes to restore screen
```

Figure 10.25 *Looking at the Target Marker Through Reveal Codes*

10.3.4.1 *Marking Both the Target Endnote and the Reference Text*

When you select **3-Mark Both Reference and Target** and the target is a foot- or endnote, you mark the **reference** first. When WordPerfect asks you to move the cursor to the **target**, press **Ctrl-F7** to call up the note. With the note on the screen press **Enter** twice, then **F7**. Reveal Codes show how the markers look (see Figure 10.26).

10.4 Creating Footnotes and Endnotes

Footnotes and endnotes are created and edited the same way. The main difference is in the text appearance when the document is printed: footnotes are at the bottom of the page on which they appear; endnotes are all grouped together at the end of the document.

Entering a note is simply a matter of placing a code marker at the desired place in the document and creating the text for the note. Notes can be entered while you're typing text or with existing text.

Position the cursor and press **Ctrl-F7**. WordPerfect will ask if you want to work with **1-Footnote** or **2-Endnote**. Select **1** (see Figure 10.28).

When you select **1-Create**, WordPerfect places a footnote number in the text and immediately switches to the typing area where you will enter the

```
================================================================
see page 1


================================================================
see endnote 1
================================================================

see endnote 1
C:\WP5\FILE79                                    Doc 1 Pg 3 Ln 2 Pos 10
<                                                                      >
[HPg]
[HRt]
See page [Ref(SOLE SOURCE):Pg 1][HRt]
[HRt]
[HPg]
see endnote [                               )][Note Num]Meese, Edwin, "Attorn
ey ... ][HPg]
[HRt]
[HRt]
see endnote [                      ]
Press Reveal Codes to restore screen
```

Figure 10.26 *Marking Both the Reference and Target Endnote*

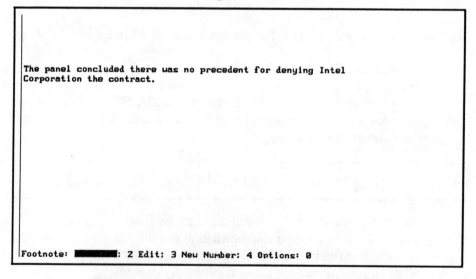

```
The panel concluded there was no precedent for denying Intel
Corporation the contract.
```

```
Footnote:          : 2 Edit: 3 New Number: 4 Options: 0
```

Figure 10.27 *Creating a Footnote (Ctrl-F7, 1-Footnote)*

footnote text. Only the footnote number appears on this screen (see Figure 10.28).

Enter the text and press F7 (Exit). Do not press any other key or the footnote will not be recorded. If you do not want to enter text at this time, leave the screen blank or make a note to yourself as to what the footnote

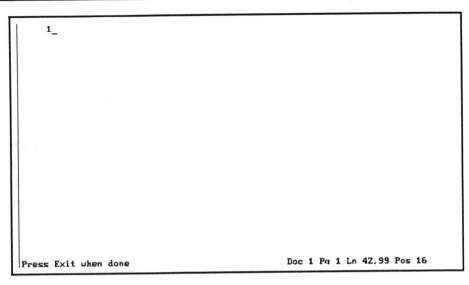

Figure 10.28 *Footnote Typing Area*
(Ctrl-F7, 1-Footnote, 1-Create)

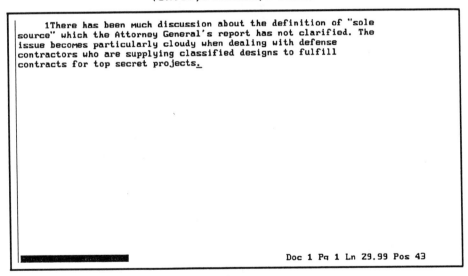

Figure 10.29 *Entering Footnote Text*

will contain. You can add the text later (see Figure 10.29). Footnote text can be as long as you wish. If the footnote text is too long to fit on a page when printed, WordPerfect will divide it between pages.

When you press F7 and return to the document typing area, you'll see that the footnote number has been placed in the text. Through Reveal

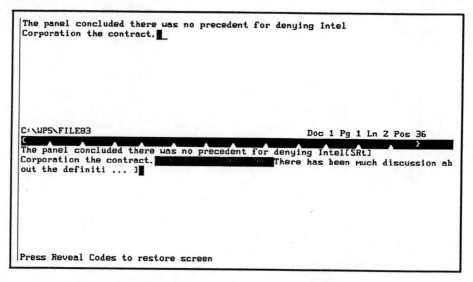

Figure 10.30 *Code Marker for Footnotes*

Codes you can see the code marker (see Figure 10.30). Notice that the footnote itself does not appear on the document screen, and it never will. WordPerfect has allocated room for the footnote on the page.

10.4.1 Printing and Viewing Notes

You cannot see notes on the document screen, but there are three ways to produce them. The first, of course, is to print the page that contains the note. During printing, WordPerfect merges the note text into the document and creates a separator line that divides the footnote from the document (see Figure 10.31).

If you want to see the footnote before you print it, you can use WordPerfect's **View** feature. This actually recreates on the screen the page as it will appear when printed. Press **Shift-F7 (Print)**, then **6-View** (see Figure 10.32). You can view only the page on the screen and you cannot do anything to it other than look. F7 returns to the typing area.

The third way to look at a footnote is through the note editing function, as well as through Reveal Codes. You can see the first line of the footnote through Reveal Codes (see Figure 10.33).

10.4.2 Editing Foot- and Endnotes

You can call up a footnote by positioning the cursor on the footnote number or by remembering and entering the footnote number. Press **Ctrl-F7,**

The panel concluded there was no precedent for denying Intel Corporation the contract.[1]

---

[1]There has been much discussion about the definition of "sole source" which the Attorney General's report has not clarified. The issue becomes particularly cloudy when dealing with defense contractors who are supplying classified designs to fulfill contracts for top secret projects.

Figure 10.31 *Example of a Printed Footnote*

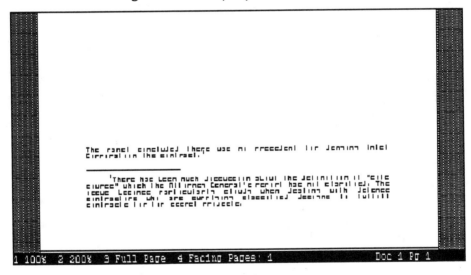

Figure 10.32 *Looking at Footnotes Through View*
(Shift-F7, 6-View)

select **1-Footnote,** then **2-Edit.** WordPerfect will suggest a footnote number. If it's the footnote you want to see, press **Enter**; otherwise, type the footnote number.

You are now in the footnote typing area where you created the text. You can change it any way you want. Press **F7 (Exit)** to record the changes and return to the document typing area.

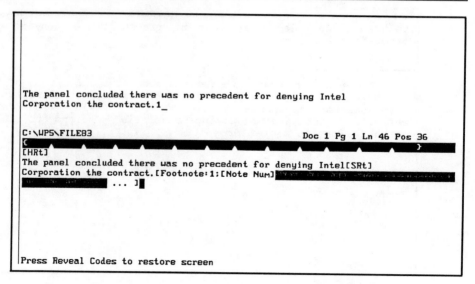

Figure 10.33 *Looking at a Footnote Through Reveal Codes*

10.4.3 Deleting Notes

Deleting a Note marker not only deletes the reference but also all of the text in the note itself. Position the cursor on the **note number,** turn on **Reveal Codes (Alt-F3)** to double check the cursor position, and press **Del.** If you accidentally delete a note number (and thus the note text), you can Restore it with the Undelete feature. Press **F1** and select **1-Restore.** Both the reference number and the Note text will be restored.

10.4.4 Options for Formatting Foot- and Endnotes

Press **Ctrl-F7,** select **1-Footnote** (or 2-Endnote) and choose **4-Options** to bring up this settings sheet (see Figure 10.34).

The format for footnoting that WordPerfect has preset is standard and acceptable, but you can change every element of style. As with all Word-Perfect codes, the style is changed at the code marker where you want the new style to begin. Therefore, if you want the style of *all* notes to change, position the cursor at the top of the document before bringing up this settings sheet. If you want to change only one note, position the cursor on that note, change it, and change the next note back to the default.

Most of the items on the settings sheet are self-explanatory. You can change **1-Spacing** to any decimal number. A 2 double spaces the lines in the note, while .25" leaves a quarter inch between notes.

```
Footnote Options

    1 - Spacing Within Footnotes              1
               Between Footnotes               0.16"

    2 - Amount of Note to Keep Together        0.5"

    3 - Style for Number in Text               [SUPRSCPT][Note Num]

    4 - Style for Number in Note                     [SUPRSCPT][Note

    5 - Footnote Numbering Method              Numbers

    6 - Start Footnote Numbers each Page       No

    7 - Line Separating Text and Footnotes     2-inch Line

    8 - Print Continued Message                No

    9 - Footnotes at Bottom of Page            Yes




Selection: 0
```

Figure 10.34 *Options Setting Sheet for Notes*
(Ctrl-F7, 1-Footnote, 4-Options)

2- tells WordPerfect that if it must divide a note, this amount (0.5 inches) must be held together.

3-/4- determines whether the note number will appear as a superscript or on the same level as the text.

5- gives the option of changing note numbers to letters, to characters, or not to have any number notation at all. This doesn't mean that the footnote will not have an assigned number, only that the number won't print.

6- the default, is to continue numbering consecutively throughout the document. Changing this item to Y causes each page to start footnote numbering with 1.

7- is the separator line between the document text and footnote text; it can be set to any length you wish.

8- If a footnote is divided between pages, WordPerfect will add the message "Continued" if you change this item to Y.

9- If the document text doesn't fill an entire page, you can elect to print the footnote immediately beneath the text. The default is to print it at the bottom of the page.

10.4.4.1 Beginning with Numbers Other than "1"

Footnotes can be set to begin on any number you wish. This is useful if you're working on sections of the same document in different files, such as chapters of a book being filed under different names. To start a new numbering order, press **Ctrl-F7, 1-Footnote** (or 2-Endnote), **3-New Number**. Type the new number and press **F7**.

10.4.5 Placing Endnotes in the Document Text

You must tell WordPerfect where you want Endnotes to be printed if it's anywhere other than right after the last sentence of your document. You can, in fact, print Endnotes anywhere, not just at the end, and you can print some of them in one place and the rest somewhere else. For example, you might want to collect the notes at the end of each chapter.

Position the cursor at the place where the endnotes should start. Press **Ctrl-F7** and select **3-Endnote placement**. Now Generate the notes by pressing **Alt-F5** and selecting **6-Generate**.

WordPerfect will highlight the number of lines necessary to contain all the Endnotes that have been entered *to this point in the document*. When printed, they will fit the space. The next time you enter the Endnote placement code in the document, it will include all the notes *after* the first marker through this position in the document.

To print Endnotes on a separate page at the end of the document, move the cursor to a blank page (press Ctrl-Enter) and enter the Endnote placement marker.

10.4.6 Summary of Footnote Rules

1. Markers for notes can be placed anywhere in a document, either at the time text is entered or with existing text.

2. Notes are automatically numbered. If new notes are inserted or some are deleted, the remaining notes are renumbered.

3. To merge the note markers with the notes themselves, you must run a procedure that WordPerfect calls "Generate."

4. No matter where text is moved, if the note marker goes with it, the note will be correctly numbered.

5. Footnotes cannot be seen in the document typing area. They can be viewed only through Note Edit, View, Reveal Codes, and by printing the page on which the note resides.

6. Notes can be any length. If a note is too long to fit on a page, Word-Perfect divides it between two pages. WordPerfect will not separate a footnote reference from the note text. That is, if there are several footnotes on a page and not enough room to print them all, Word-Perfect will not leave the marked text on one page and print the footnote on the following page.

7. To delete notes, simply delete the note marker from the document.

10.5 Tables of Contents

The principle for creating automatic tables of contents is the same as for automatic reference. You mark the text in the document that should appear in the table of contents and when you generate the results, Word-Perfect automatically connects that marker with the page number and produces the table. No matter how often or dramatically text is shifted or edited, WordPerfect keeps track of where it is by the code marker and can generate an updated table anytime you wish. Using this same procedure you can produce any other kinds of tables, such as a table of figures. Tables can also be generated in levels to correspond to the levels of the document.

10.5.1 *Marking Text for Tables*

You can mark text at the time you enter it or once the document is finished. You can include as much or little of the document headings in the table as you wish, or you can pick out phrases from within the text. You're simply placing a mark on each side of the text that will appear in the table.

Position the cursor and **Block** the text that you want to appear in the table. Then press **Alt-F5** to bring up the Mark Text menu (see Figure 10.35). If you have not Blocked any text, this menu will not come up. Select **1-ToC**. WordPerfect will ask what **level** the heading should appear on.

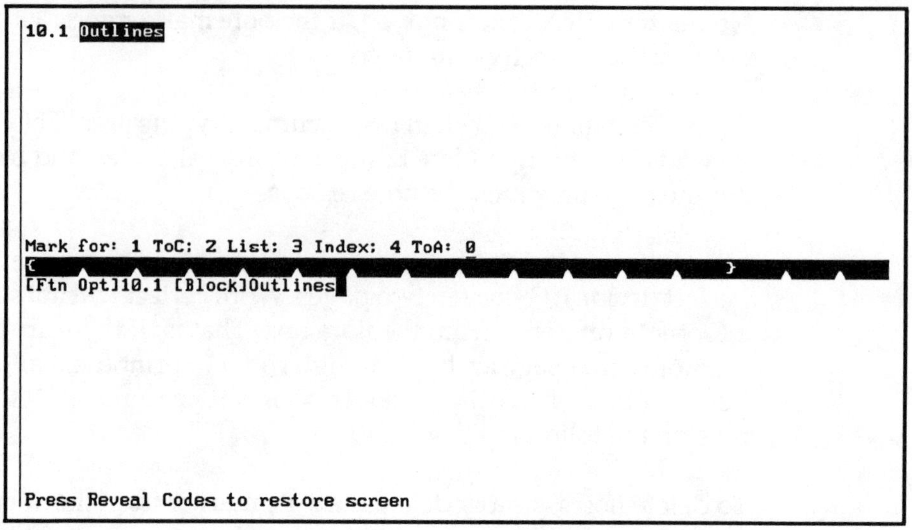

```
10.1 Outlines




Mark for: 1 ToC: 2 List: 3 Index: 4 ToA: 0
{                                                                    }
[Ftn Opt]10.1 [Block]Outlines




Press Reveal Codes to restore screen
```

Figure 10.35 *Mark Text Menu (Block Text, Alt-F5)*

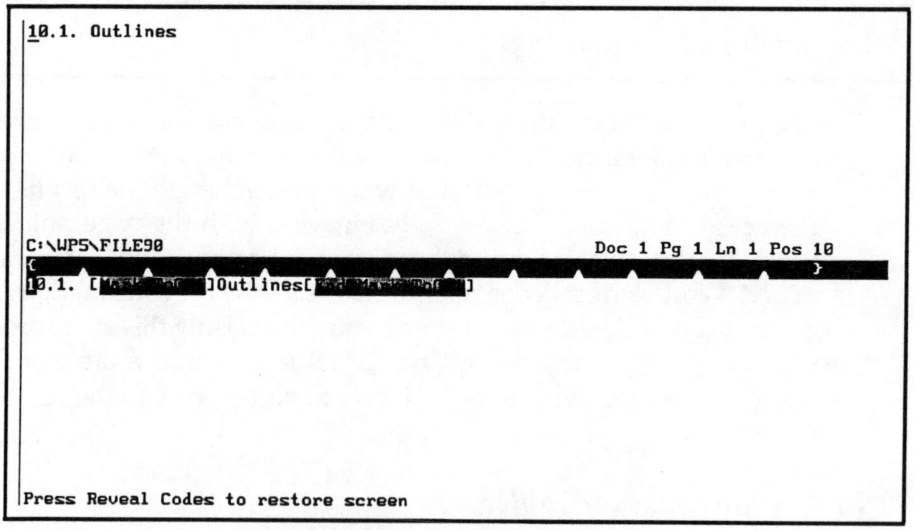

```
10.1. Outlines




C:\WP5\FILE90                                    Doc 1 Pg 1 Ln 1 Pos 10
{                                                                    }
10.1. [        ]Outlines[            ]




Press Reveal Codes to restore screen
```

Figure 10.36 *Text Marked for a Table*
(Block Text, Alt-F5, 1-ToC, Level 1)

For this heading we'll select **1**. WordPerfect then marks the text (see Figure 10.36).

Now we'll go through the entire document and repeat the marking process for every heading. For our example we'll assign some headings to level 2. In Figure 10.37 you can see the markers with Reveal Codes. [Mark:ToC,2] indicates level 2.

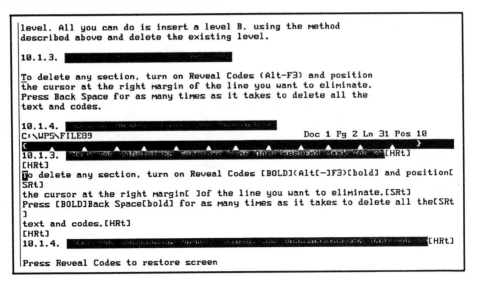

Figure 10.37 *Text Marked for Level 2 in the Table*
(Block Text, Alt-F5, 1-ToC, Level 2)

10.5.2 *Defining the Table*

Before you Generate the table, WordPerfect requires that you **Define** it. Move the cursor to the top of the document and press **Ctrl-Enter** to establish a Page Break. Move the cursor into the empty page and type a heading, such as Table of Contents. You can center it if you wish. Press **Enter** twice to position the cursor. Bring up the Mark Text menu (**Alt-F5**) and select **5-Define** (see Figure 10.38). Select **1-Define Table of Contents**. (Notice that we'll use this same menu to define other sorts of tables.) This brings up another menu to specify the table format (see Figure 10.39).

In our example there are two levels, so we'll change item 1 in this menu. The default page numbering layout for a table is to run periods from the last character to the right margin, where the page number is inserted flush right. However, there are four other choices that appear at the bottom of the screen if you press **3-Page Number Position**. You can elect to have no page numbers, numbers that follow the last character, numbers in parentheses that follow the last character, numbers without a leader that are flush right, as well as the default numbers with leaders flush right.

When you've filled out this settings sheet, press **Enter** or F7 to return to the typing area.

```
Mark Text: Define

     1 - Define Table of Contents

     2 - Define List

     3 - Define Index

     4 - Define Table of Authorities

     5 - Edit Table of Authorities Full Form














Selection: 0
```

Figure 10.38 *Menu to Define a Table of Contents*
(Alt-F5, 5-Define)

```
Table of Contents Definition

     1 - Number of Levels              1

     2 - Display Last Level in         No
         Wrapped Format

     3 - Page Number Position - Level 1   Flush right with leader
                                Level 2
                                Level 3
                                Level 4
                                Level 5









1 None; 2 Pg # Follows; 3 (Pg #) Follows; 4 Flush Rt; 5 Flush Rt with Leader
```

Figure 10.39 *Specifications for a Table*

10.5.3 *Generating the Table*

You may Generate or regenerate tables any time you wish. This is WordPerfect's process of connecting code markers to page numbers. Press **Alt-F5** and select **6-Generate**. WordPerfect will ask if you want to replace the current generated tables. Answer **Y**. While it is generating,

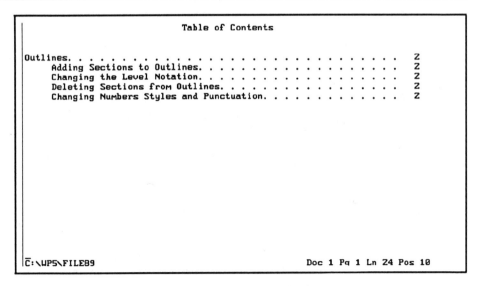

```
                        Table of Contents


Outlines. . . . . . . . . . . . . . . . . . . . . . . . . . . . . .    2
        Adding Sections to Outlines. . . . . . . . . . . . . . . .    2
        Changing the Level Notation. . . . . . . . . . . . . . .     2
        Deleting Sections from Outlines. . . . . . . . . . . . .     2
        Changing Numbers Styles and Punctuation. . . . . . . . .     2














C:\WP5\FILE89                                Doc 1 Pg 1 Ln 24 Pos 10
```

Figure 10.40 *A Generated Table of Contents*
(Alt-F5, 6-Generate)

WordPerfect gives an account of its progress in the message center. Our example generated the table shown in Figure 10.40.

10.5.4 Correcting the Page Numbers

Notice in Figure 10.40 that our section headings are generated as being on page 2 when in fact they are on page 1 in the document. This happened because of the empty page we created in order to Define the table. This became page 1 and the real first page became page 2. This problem can be easily corrected by assigning the table page a different number. Position the cursor at the top left margin of the table page. Press **Shift-F8 (Format)** and select **2-Page** (see Figure 10.41).

Through this menu you can elect not to number the table page at all, or you can assign it a Roman numeral. Select item **7-Page numbering,** then **9-No numbers** to turn off numbering, or select item **6-New page number** to set up Roman numerals.

The next step is to position the cursor at the top left margin of the first page of the document and turn on page numbering through the same process. When you Generate the table again, the page numbers will reflect the true position of the headings.

```
Format: Page

    1 - Center Page (top to bottom)        No

    2 - Force Odd/Even Page

    3 - Headers

    4 - Footers

    5 - Margins - Top                       1"
                  Bottom                    1"

    6 - New Page Number                     1
          (example: 3 or iii)

    7 - Page Numbering                      No page numbering

    8 - Paper Size                          8.5" x 11"
            Type                            Standard

    9 - Suppress (this page only)

Selection: 0
```

Figure 10.41 *Page Format Settings Sheet*
(Shift-F8, 2-Page)

10.6 Producing Tables for Figures, Maps, Illustrations, Etc.

This process is exactly the same as making a table of contents, with two modifications. (Review all of Section 10.5.) **Block** the text and press **Alt-F5**, but this time select **2-List** instead of **1-Table of Contents**. WordPerfect will ask you to number the list (1 to 5). Enter a number. WordPerfect places code markers which identify the list number (see Figure 10.42).

When you Define the list (see Figure 10.38), select **2-Define List**. Word-Perfect asks what list number you want to Define. In our example it is **3**. When you **Generate** the list, you'll also enter the list number. You can produce five different lists in addition to the table of contents and index.

10.7 Indexes

Creating an index is essentially the same process as creating a table. You **Mark** the word or phrases you want to include in the index, **Define** the index, and eventually **Generate** it. Review Section 10.5 for the details of creating a table.

```
Figure 10.41. Page Format Settings Sheet (Shift-F8, 2-Page)




C:\WP5\FILE92                                        Doc 1 Pg 1 Ln 1 Pos 10
[                                                                         ]
                    Figure 10.41. Page Format Settings Sheet         (Shift[-]
F8, 2[-]Page)




Press Reveal Codes to restore screen
```

Figure 10.42 *Marking Text for List #3*

10.7.1 *Marking Words to be Indexed*

There are two levels of indexing, one for primary terms and one for all the other terms related to it. For example, "how to index" might be a principal term while the steps to complete the index are grouped beneath it as secondary terms. WordPerfect calls these "Index heading" and "Subheading." Here's how they work.

Position the cursor anywhere within the word you want to index, or Block a group of words. Press **Alt-F5** and select **3-Index**. In the example in Figure 10.43 we positioned the cursor on the word "Index." When you press **3-Index**, the message center displays the word.

Now we have some choices. If we want the word "Index" to be listed in the index as a primary term, we can press **Enter** twice. If, however, we want to index the word "Index" but call it something else, such as "Learning to Index," we can type in the phrase we want to use. When we elect this option, WordPerfect keys on the word in the document, in this case "Index," but lists it by the name we entered, "Learning to Index." If you index the same word scattered throughout the document as a primary term, WordPerfect will recognize it and list the various pages on which it appears, such as:

```
Learning to Index 2,9,34
```

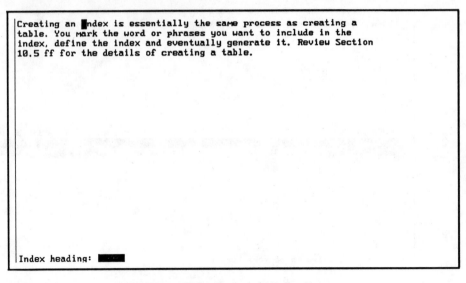

Figure 10.43 *Beginning the Index Process*
(Position Cursor, Alt-F5, 3-Index)

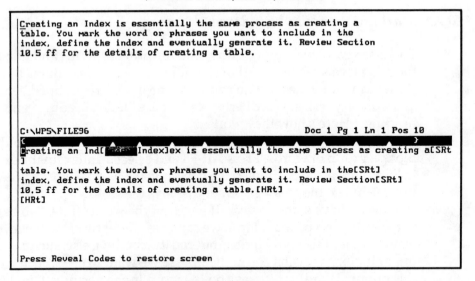

Figure 10.44 *Index Codes*

Looking at Figure 10.44 through Reveal Codes, we can see the marker that WordPerfect has placed. Because the cursor was positioned in the middle of the word, the indexed word is split on either side of the code marker:

```
Ind[Index:Index]ex
```

Inside the marker we see that the Index word (i.e., the word that will appear when printed) is the word "Index." We'll say more about this in a minute.

When you press **Enter,** WordPerfect gives you the opportunity to enter a **Subheading.** If the term you are indexing is a primary listing, you will not enter any subheading. Just press **Enter** to return to the typing area.

If the term you're indexing is to be grouped under a primary term, the first step is to tell WordPerfect what that primary term is. In our example above the index word is "Index." It's the key word under which subterms will be grouped. Continuing the example, we want to index the term "mark" under the key word "index." When WordPerfect asks us for the **Index heading,** we fill in:

```
Index heading: Index
```

and press **Enter.** Then, WordPerfect asks for the **Subheading,** which we'll fill in:

```
Subheading: mark
```

Actually, the word "mark" isn't very descriptive, so we'll add a better term:

```
Subheading: marking text
```

Look at Reveal Codes again to see what happened (see Figure 10.45). Notice how the main heading and subheading codes correspond:

```
[Index:Index]
[Index:Index:marking text]
```

The first one is a main heading; the second one is a subheading called "marking text" that falls under the word "Index."

We'll mark two other words, "defining" and "generating," for our example index (see Figure 10.46).

10.7.1.1 *Marking a Word as Both a Heading and Subheading*

This is a two-step process. First mark the word as a heading, then go through the entire process again and mark it as a subheading. In our example, we told WordPerfect to include "generating" as a subheading

```
Creating an Index is essentially the same process as creating a
table. You mark the word or phrases you want to include in the
index, define the index and eventually generate it. Review Section
10.5 ff for the details of creating a table.




C:\WP5\FILE96                                    Doc 1 Pg 1 Ln 2 Pos 22
[                                                                    ]
Creating an Ind[Index:Index]ex is essentially the same process as creating a[SRt
]
table. You m[                    ]ark the word or phrases you want to includ
e in the[SRt]
index, define the index and eventually generate it. Review Section[SRt]
10.5 ff for the details of creating a table.[HRt]
[HRt]


Press Reveal Codes to restore screen
```

Figure 10.45 *Code Markers for Subheadings in an Index*

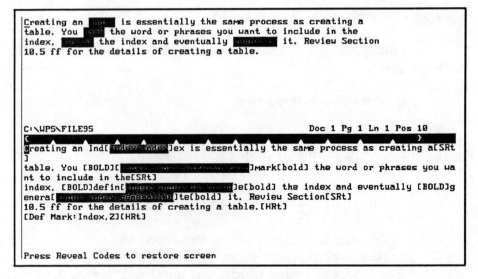

```
Creating an [   ] is essentially the same process as creating a
table. You [   ] the word or phrases you want to include in the
index, [   ] the index and eventually [   ] it. Review Section
10.5 ff for the details of creating a table.




C:\WP5\FILE95                                    Doc 1 Pg 1 Ln 1 Pos 10
[                                                                    ]
Creating an Ind[           ]ex is essentially the same process as creating a[SRt
]
table. You [BOLD][                        ]mark[bold] the word or phrases you wa
nt to include in the[SRt]
index, [BOLD]defin[                    ]e[bold] the index and eventually [BOLD]g
eneral[                        ]te[bold] it. Review Section[SRt]
10.5 ff for the details of creating a table.[HRt]
[Def Mark:Index,2][HRt]


Press Reveal Codes to restore screen
```

Figure 10.46 *Marking Other Words for the Index*

under "Index." Now we'll tell it to create a primary heading but we'll call it "Generating an Index." When we regenerate and print our index, it will look like Figure 10.47.

```
┌─────────────────────────────────────────────────────────────────────┐
│Creating an Index is essentially the same process as creating a       │
│table. You mark the word or phrases you want to include in the        │
│index, define the index and eventually generate it. Review Section    │
│10.5 ff for the details of creating a table.                          │
│                                                                       │
│=======================================================================│
│                                  Index                                │
│                                                                       │
│Index  1                                                               │
│     defining  1                                                       │
│     generating  1                                                     │
│     marking text  1                                                   │
│                                                                       │
│                                                                       │
│                                                                       │
│                                                                       │
│                                                                       │
│                                                                       │
│                                                                       │
│                                                                       │
│                                                                       │
│                                                                       │
│C:\WP5\FILE94                                   Doc 1 Pg 1 Ln 1 Pos 10 │
└─────────────────────────────────────────────────────────────────────┘
```

Figure 10.47 *The Same Term Indexed as Both a Heading
and a Subheading*

10.7.2 *Defining and Generating Indexes*

Move the cursor to the end of the document and press **Ctrl-Enter** to create
a Page Break. Type a heading for the index, press **Enter** twice to position
the cursor, then **Alt-F5**. Select **5-Define**. When you're ready to produce
the index, Generate it by selecting **6-Generate**. The results in our example
are shown in Figure 10.48.

10.8 Concordances

One of the most useful indexing features in WordPerfect is its ability to
automatically mark words through a concordance. You simply make a
list of the terms you want indexed, Save them in a regular text file, and
when the index is generated, all the words in the list will be marked and
indexed. Using the concordance also assures that no references to a term
will be missed.

The only rule for making the concordance is that each term must be
separated by a hard return. Usually, there will be only one word or phrase
on a line. When you Define the index, WordPerfect asks for the name of
the concordance. You can add or edit words in the concordance as often
as you wish. It isn't until the index is generated that the words in the document are marked (see Figures 10.49 and 10.50).

```
Creating an Index is essentially the same process as creating a
table. You mark the word or phrases you want to include in the
index, define the index and eventually generate it. Review Section
10.5 ff for the details of creating a table.

==============================================================================
                                Index


Generating an Index  1
Index  1
      defining  1
      generating  1
      marking text  1






C:\WP5\FILE98                                    Doc 1 Pg 1 Ln 1 Pos 10
```

Figure 10.48 *Generating a Final Index*

```
zoning ordnance 43Z
Philadelphia Housing Authority
1976 Restoration Act
Designer's Handbook













C:\WP5\FILE100                                   Doc 1 Pg 1 Ln 1 Pos 10
```

Figure 10.49 *A Sample Concordance*

10.9 Tables of Authority

Tables of authority, which are really specialized indexes, list citations in legal documents. You can mark and create up to 16 tables of authority.

```
                                 Index
_
1976 Restoration Act   4, 9
Designer's Handbook   5, 6
Philadelphia Housing Authority   3, 8
zoning ordnance 432   1, 7
```

```
C:\WP5\FILE101                              Doc 1 Pg 1 Ln 1 Pos 10
```

Figure 10.50 *Index Generated with a Concordance*

Because citations can be quite long, WordPerfect provides a shortcut for marking the second occurrence of the same citation. The first time requires several steps:

Block the citation
Press **Alt-F5**
Select **4-ToA** (meaning To Authorities)

WordPerfect now asks what section number you want the citation to appear in. This is one of the 16 possible lists you can create:

```
ToA Section Number:
```

The citation that you've Blocked appears on a special editing screen. If you want to modify the citation for the table of authorities, you can change it here without altering its full title in the document. Press F7 to leave the editing screen.

Now WordPerfect wants you to give this citation an abbreviated name so that the next time you mark it you can reduce the number of steps. Select any unique word from the citation as the **short form**. Press **Enter** to return to the typing area. See Figure 10.51 to look at the code marker through Reveal Codes.

```
Civil Rights Act of 1965
=================================================================================
Brown vs. The Board of Education
=================================================================================
Housing Rights Act of 1972
=================================================================================




C:\WP5\FILE103                                    Doc 1 Pg 1 Ln 1 Pos 10
{                                                                         }
[         ]]Civil Rights Act of 1965[HPg]
Brown vs. The Board of Education[HPg]
Housing Rights Act of 1972[HPg]




Press Reveal Codes to restore screen
```

Figure 10.51 *Table of Authorities Code Markers*

The code tells us that this citation has been designated for table of authorities #1 [ToA:1] and that its abbreviated name is "1965." Its full form name is "Civil Rights Act of 1965." If we had changed the name in the editing screen, the new name would appear in this code.

The second time we mark this citation is much easier. Position the cursor anywhere in the citation and press **Alt-F5**. Select **4-ToA Short Form**. Enter the abbreviated name, which in our example is **1965**, and press **Enter**. The citation will be fully marked with the same code as the first time you marked it. If you want to assign a citation to two different tables, simply mark it twice using different table numbers (see Figure 10.52).

You can use WordPerfect's **Extended Search** feature to locate all your citations. Press **Home-F2** to begin the search. Extended Searches look for citations in footnotes, endnote, and graphics, as well as throughout the text. If you create tables of authority often, you'll want to make a macro to help you mark text (see Chapter 15).

Marking the rest of our example citations, we'll assign "Brown vs. The Board of Education" to Table 2 (see Figure 10.53).

10.9.1 *Defining and Generating Tables of Authority*

Each table must be Defined before it can be Generated. Position the cursor at the place in the document where you want the table to be printed. Type a title. Then press **Alt-F5**, select **5-Define**, and **4-Table of Authorities**. WordPerfect will ask which section number you want to

```
Civil Rights Act of 1965
===================================================================
Brown vs. The Board of Education
===================================================================
Housing Rights Act of 1972
===================================================================
Civil Rights Act of 1965
===================================================================



C:\WP5\FILE104                                Doc 1 Pg 1 Ln 1 Pos 10
{                                                                  }
[                                           ][HPg]
Brown vs. The Board of Education[HPg]
Housing Rights Act of 1972[HPg]
[ToA:;1965;][                                            ][HPg]



Press Reveal Codes to restore screen
```

Figure 10.52 *Marking the Second Occurrence of a Citation*

```
Civil Rights Act of 1965
===================================================================
Brown vs. The Board of Education
===================================================================
Housing Rights Act of 1972
===================================================================
Civil Rights Act of 1965
===================================================================



C:\WP5\FILE105                                Doc 1 Pg 1 Ln 1 Pos 10
{                                                                  }
[ToA:1;1965;[Full Form]]Civil Rights Act of 1965[HPg]
[ToA:2;Brown;[Full Form]]Brown vs. The Board of Education[HPg]
[ToA:1;1972;[Full Form]]Housing Rights Act of 1972[HPg]
[Def Mark:ToA,1][ToA:;1965;]Civil Rights Act of 1965[HPg]



Press Reveal Codes to restore screen
```

Figure 10.53 *Document Fully Marked for Table
of Authorities*

define for this table. In our example we'll select 1. Press **Enter** and a settings sheet comes up that permits you to select 1-Dot Leaders, 2-Underlining, 3-Blank Lines Between Authorities. Make your selections or press **Enter** to keep the default selections.

This completes the table definition. Whenever you're ready, **Generate** the table. Press **Alt-F5**, select **6-Generate** and **5-Tables**. Answer **Y** to

```
Civil Rights Act of 1965
==========================================================================
Brown vs. The Board of Education
==========================================================================
Housing Rights Act of 1972
==========================================================================
Civil Rights Act of 1965
==========================================================================
                         Table 1: Case Precedents

Civil Rights Act of 1965. . . . . . . . . . . . . . . . . . . . .1, 4

Housing Rights Act of 1972. . . . . . . . . . . . . . . . . . . 3




C:\WP5\FILE106                              Doc 1 Pg 1 Ln 1 Pos 10
```

Figure 10.54 *Generated Table of Authorities*

replacing existing tables. WordPerfect now generates the table as shown in Figure 10.54.

You'll remember that we assigned "Brown vs. The Board of Education" to Table 2, so it does not show up in Table 1. If the Table of Authorities is on a separate page, you might want to turn off the page numbering (see Section 10.5.4). If you don't, WordPerfect reminds you of that when you Generate the table.

10.9.2 Editing Citations

If you want to edit the citation that appears in the table of authorities, position the cursor on the first occurrence, press **Alt-F5**, select **5-Define**, then **5-Edit Table of Authorities Full Form**. The citation appears on the editing screen. Change it and press **F7** to continue.

CHAPTER 11

Bells and Whistles of Editing Features

11.1 Dual Screens and Windows

WordPerfect offers two methods for working on different files at the same time. You can **Split** the screen, which divides one screen into upper and lower halves, or you can **Switch** screens. **Switch** hides the first screen and produces a second, full screen. Because a Split screen can be expanded into a full screen, the only difference between Split and Switch screens is the ability to see two Split screens at the same time. You cannot use both Split and Switch screens together. Therefore, you can work on only two files, not three or four.

Dual screens are especially useful for moving text from one document to another, creating an outline for the document you're working on, cutting text out of a document and Saving it in an auxiliary file, creating charts and tables that you'll later merge into the document, and laying out page designs.

Each screen functions entirely separately from the other. You can Create, Edit, Format, Delete, or Save a document on one screen without affecting the other screen. The only functions they have in common are the ones involving the computer's internal memory, such as moving text from one document to another. If you perform an internal memory task in one screen, then switch to the second screen, whatever is in memory functions in the second screen. In other words, if you Delete text from a document, it remains in the computer's memory until you Delete more text or Exit the program. When you Switch to the second screen, that text still remains in memory, so you can Restore it in the other screen.

11.1.1 *Switching Screens*

To **Switch** screens, press **Shift-F3** from anywhere within the document. An empty screen appears whose status line indicates that this is Doc 2 (see Figure 11.1).

To return to the first screen, just press **Shift-F3** again. You can Switch between documents as often as you wish. If two screens are open and you Exit the program, you are Exiting only the file on the screen. Once you have Exited it, WordPerfect switches to the other screen, where you can continue working or Exit.

11.1.2 *Splitting Screens*

To **Split** a screen, press **Ctrl-F3** to bring up a three-item menu:

```
0-Rewrite, 1-Window, 2-Line Draw
```

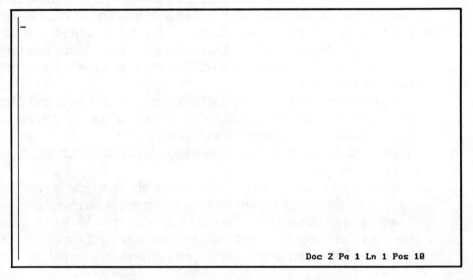

```
                                                    Doc 2 Pg 1 Ln 1 Pos 10
```

Figure 11.1 *Switching Screens (Shift-F3)*

Select **1-Window**.

A prompt asks how many lines long you want the screen to be. Since most PC monitors display 24 lines, you must enter 22 or less to Split the screen. Entering 12 divides the screen evenly (see Figure 11.2). You can also use the Arrow keys to enlarge or narrow the screen.

To move between screens, press **Shift-F3**. As with **Switch** screens, whatever work you perform in one screen is treated autonomously from the other screen. You must **Save** the second screen under a **different file name** if you want to keep your work.

To **close** a screen, position the cursor in the **screen you want to keep open**, press **Ctrl-F3**, select **1-Window**, and type the number of lines to equal any number larger than the total line capacity of your monitor, such as 25. This "pushes" the text of the second screen out of view, but the text still resides in the computer's memory until you Exit the program. You can bring it back by opening a window again. Even if you Exit the other document, the text in the second screen remains in memory until you Exit the program. But remember, if you've "hidden" the second screen, you must Save it separately or it will be lost when you leave WordPerfect.

11.2 Rewriting the Screen

WordPerfect automatically formats the screen. That is, no matter how much text you add or delete, WordPerfect adjusts the revised text to fit

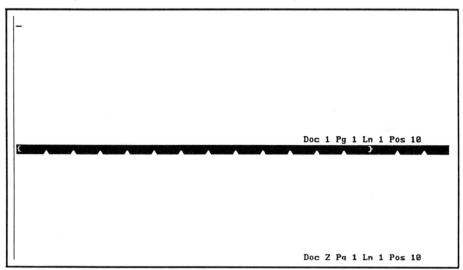

Figure 11.2 *A Screen Split Evenly*

whatever format you've specified, including right justification and hyphenation. You can turn off Automatic Rewrite through the Setup menu:

Press **Shift-F1 (Setup)**
Select **3-Display**
Select **1-Automatic Rewrite**
Type **N**

If you want WordPerfect to Rewrite a screen, press **Ctrl-F3** and select **0-Rewrite**.

11.3 Headers and Footers

These are principally labeling devices that can appear on the top or bottom of every page, on odd pages only, or on even pages only. As with footnotes, headers and footers are created in a separate typing area and merged with the document when printed. You can elect to place one or two headers and one or two footers on a page. Creating headers and footers is straightforward.

Position the cursor at the top of the first page of the document where you want the headers or footers to begin, then:

Press **Shift-F8 (Format)**
Select **2-Page**
Select **3-Headers** or **4-Footers**
Select **1-Header A** or **2-Header B**

WordPerfect allows two headers on the same page. However, you must position them on the page. Select **1-Every Page, 2-Odd Pages,** or **3-Even Pages**. WordPerfect switches to the Header/Footer typing area. This is a full screen that allows you to create a header or footer that can be as long as you wish and can be formatted with attributes such as center, bold, or special type fonts.

Press **F7 (Exit)** to Save the header or footer. If you want to create a second header or footer, you can do it now or later. If you create header A to appear at the top left margin and header B to appear at the top left margin, they will overlap. Therefore, you might place one of them flush right. Remember not to place a header or footer in a position where you have specified a page number.

```
SOLE SOURCE LAWS                              VENDOR RESTRICTIONS

10.1 New Regulations Requiring 60-Day Approval




C:\WP5\FILE107                                Doc 1 Pg 1 Ln 3 Pos 10

[Header A:1:SOLE SOURCE LAWS][Header B:1:[     ]VENDOR RESTRICTIONS]SOLE SOURC
E LAWS[       ]VENDOR RESTRICTIONS[C/A/Flrt][HRt]
[HRt]
10.1 New Regulations Requiring 60[-]Day Approval




Press Reveal Codes to restore screen
```

Figure 11.3 *Header A Placed Flush Left;*
Header B Flush Right

You can look at a header or footer through Reveal Codes (Alt-F3) (see Figure 11.3) and you can edit them by selecting **5-Edit** from the menu.

11.4 Document Comments

These are notes inserted anywhere in a document; they do not print and do not affect the format of the page layout. They are useful for making notes to yourself, such as ideas for revisions or private thoughts and information that you wouldn't want to appear in the printed document. If several people are working on a revision, Document Comments are good ways to call attention to sections that need work. Document comments are placed in boxes:

```
This is an example of a comment box.
```

Notice that when we continue entering text after the Comment box, it appears just past the text entered before the Comment. If you move through the text using the Arrow key, the cursor jumps over the Comment box as though it didn't exist.

To create a Comment Box, press **Ctrl-F5**, select **1-Create Comment**, and type your comment. Press **F7** to return to the typing area. You can edit an existing comment through the same menu by selecting **2-Edit Comment**.

Looking at Reveal Codes, you can see that WordPerfect places a [Comment] marker in the text, but it does not display the comment itself. You can delete a comment by deleting the marker. You can also copy the comment by **Blocking** the marker and using the **copy** procedure. If you decide that you want a comment to print with the document, position the cursor anywhere past the comment you want printed, press **Ctrl-F5**, and select **3-Convert to Text**.

11.5 Document Compare

Although this feature has practical limitations, it allows you to see how one document differs from a similar version. This is useful if one editor has made changes that you want to show a second editor or if you want to evaluate the accuracy of the edited document. Document Compare is not very useful for documents that have undergone serious revisions. While it will find the changes, the results can be very confusing.

WordPerfect compares a document on the screen with one that's on disk. WordPerfect doesn't care if the older version is on screen or disk, but you should be certain which is which. That is, if you want the edited sections in the older version to be Redlined, that is the document on disk, while the more recent version is on the screen.

With one version on screen, press **Alt-F5**, select **6-Generate** and **2-Compare Screen and Disk Document**. WordPerfect will ask you to enter the name of the document on disk that you want to compare. Type the file name and press **Enter**. It is a good idea to Save the document on screen before you Compare it (see Figures 11.4 through 11.6).

WordPerfect examines the changes and prints segments of the text that have been changed alongside the edited text. A "segment" is defined as text that falls between punctuation marks. For example, if the only change we made was:

We hold these truths to be universal:
We hold these truths to be self-evident:

WordPerfect would print both these phrases and Redline the outdated one, but it would not reprint the entire sentence because the colon (:) designates the phrase since the last period (see Figure 11.7).

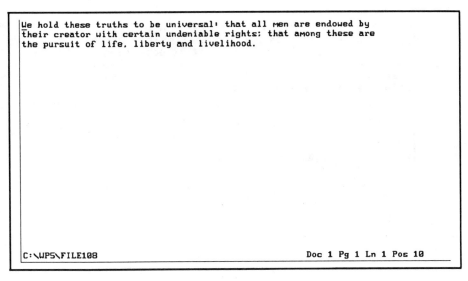

```
We hold these truths to be universal: that all men are endowed by
their creator with certain undeniable rights: that among these are
the pursuit of life. liberty and livelihood.




C:\WP5\FILE108                                    Doc 1 Pg 1 Ln 1 Pos 10
```

Figure 11.4 *Document On Disk to be Compared*

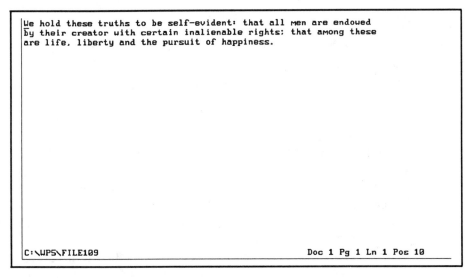

```
We hold these truths to be self-evident: that all men are endowed
by their creator with certain inalienable rights: that among these
are life. liberty and the pursuit of happiness.




C:\WP5\FILE109                                    Doc 1 Pg 1 Ln 1 Pos 10
```

Figure 11.5 *Document On Screen*

To remove Redlining from the compared document, which will return you to the original on-screen document, press **Alt-F5**, select **6-Generate**, select **1-Remove Redline Markings**, and press **Y**.

If you have Saved the document on screen, you can Retrieve it instead of removing the Redline markings.

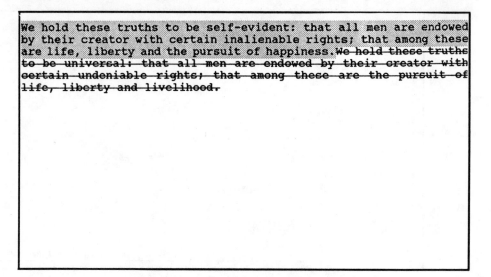

Figure 11.6 *Document After Comparison*

11.6 Redlining Text

You might have a document that you would like to Redline without actually Deleting the text. One editor might want to show another editor what might be cut out. It could be Redlined and later WordPerfect can be told to automatically delete it. You can also Redline text that you might want to transfer or add to another document.

You cannot see Redlined text on the screen although you can see the markers through Reveal Codes. When you do mark text for Redlining, you'll tell WordPerfect how you want it to appear on the printed copy. You can mark it with a bar in the margins, with any character of your choice, in color if you have a color printer, or with Strikeout, which draws a line through the marked text.

You can Redline or Strikeout existing text or text that you're ready to enter. If it already exists, Block it. Press **Ctrl-F8 (Font)**, select **2-Appearance** and either **8-Redline** (for color printers) or **9-Strikeout**. If you're entering new text, press **Right Arrow** to move past the [Font Attribute Off] code marker. Press **F7** to return to the typing area.

When you print the Redlined or Strikeout document, WordPerfect defaults to your printer's method of Redlining, whatever that is. If you

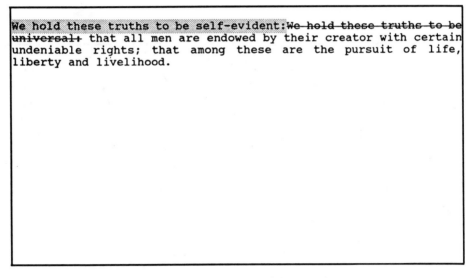

Figure 11.7 *Redlining Segments of Compared Documents*

don't like it, press **Shift-F8**, select **3-Document**, and then **4-Redline Method**. You can then change the settings to suit your needs. The choices are to place a bar at the left margin of every page or alternating left and right margins of odd or even pages. For color printers you can elect to Redline in red ink.

11.7 Overstriking Text

Although this feature has limited uses, you can create some specialized symbols by printing two or more characters in the same position. Press **Shift-F7**, select **4-Other**, **5-Overstrike**, and **1-Create**. The message line will indicate [Overstrike]:. Type your first layer of characters; then, using the **Arrow** keys, move along the line, and superimpose the second and third layers. Press **Enter** to return to the typing area. If you want to return to this screen to edit the overstrike, go through the same steps and press **2-Edit**. WordPerfect searches backward to locate an Overstrike. If this isn't the one you want to edit, press **2-Edit** again.

The overstrike does not appear in the typing area, only the last character in the string does. You can get a more complete idea of the Overstrike through Reveal Codes.

11.8 Formatting Lines

In addition to changing margins and tabs (see Section 2.5 and 2.6), you can change WordPerfect's default settings to create more precise justification for unusual documents; you can change the line spacing and line height, and number lines. These functions, plus Widow/Orphan protection, are accessed through the **Shift-F8 (Format)** menu (see Figure 11.8):

> Press **Shift-F8**
> Select **1-Line**

All of the features described in the 11.8 sections below are set through this menu.

11.8.1 Hyphenation

WordPerfect's default is to right justify lines (see Section 11.8.3 for instructions to turn it off). With Justification **On**, WordPerfect examines the words contained in a line and attempts to space them evenly apart. Obviously, this spacing will vary from one line to the next depending on the number and length of words in the line.

```
Format: Line

    1 - Hyphenation                        Off

    2 - Hyphenation Zone - Left            0.7"
                           Right           0.25"

    3 - Justification                      Yes

    4 - Line Height                        Auto

    5 - Line Numbering                     No

    6 - Line Spacing                       1

    7 - Margins - Left                     1"
                  Right                    1"

    8 - Tab Set                            0", every 0.5"

    9 - Widow/Orphan Protection            No


Selection: 0
```

Figure 11.8 *Line Format Settings Sheet*
(Shift-F8, 1-Line)

To reduce the variations of spacing between words, which is particularly important in text columns, you can elect to hyphenate the last word on the line, giving WordPerfect a few optional characters to work with. WordPerfect continually calculates how much space remains on a line and decides if the next word of text is too long to fit the space. When Hyphenation is turned on, WordPerfect divides and hyphenates the last word. When you turn on Hyphenation, you're given the choice of **2-Manual** or **3-Automatic** hyphenation. **2** will prompt you at every word before it hyphenates. You press **Esc** to accept the hyphenation. **3** automatically hyphenates every word without asking you unless it encounters a word where WordPerfect is not sure of the correct division.

If WordPerfect is unsure of the correct hyphenation, it presents its choice in the message center and asks you to decide. Move the **Left Arrow** key to the correct hyphenation position and press **Esc**. WordPerfect does not decide on its hyphenation by checking the word in its dictionary but uses internal logic to decide. Occasionally you'll find a word incorrectly hyphenated.

11.8.2 *Hyphenation Zone*

This is a second tier of refinement for spacing words more evenly between lines. WordPerfect has preset its Hyphenation Zone to hyphenating words more or less in the center. A word like "agitation" might be hyphenated "agita-tion." If the word can't be hyphenated near the center, WordPerfect wraps it to the next line. This is to prevent dividing words into "a-gain" or "occasional-ly."

WordPerfect's Hyphenation Zone is a scale to measure where and if words should be hyphenated. Here's how it works.

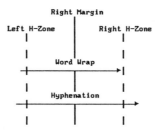

A word that starts left of the Left H-Zone and runs through the Right H-Zone will be hyphenated. The distance between the Left H-Zone and the Right Margin has been preset to be 10% of the length of the line. From the Right Margin to the Right H-Zone is 4%. By changing these percentages, you control where and how often words are hyphenated.

The narrower the H-Zone settings, the more often words will be hyphenated. That is, many words would cross the Left and Right H-Zones if the settings were 4%, 2% while few words are long enough to cross 15%, 10%. You can experiment with the settings to find a happy medium for your document. Too much hyphenation is distracting; too little creates unwanted spaces between words.

Note: If you change the Hyphenation Zone and wish to change it again, you should delete the first setting by turning on Reveal Codes, positioning the cursor, and pressing the Del key. WordPerfect does not automatically delete the first code when you set the second one and so it might not recognize the setting you want.

11.8.3 *Justification*

The Hyphenation feature works only in documents that are **right justified**. If you turn off Justification, you turn off Hyphenation as well. In more formal documents, reports and text columns, you'll probably elect Justification On. For a less formal and formidable look you'll turn it off. Change **3-Justification** from Yes to **N**.

11.8.4 *Line Numbering*

WordPerfect offers several options for placing numbers by lines. These numbers appear only when printed, although you can see the [Ln Num:On] marker through Reveal Codes. Line Numbering can be turned on or off at any place in the document, allowing you to number a few lines in the middle of a page. Select **5-Line Numbering** and type Y (see Figure 11.9).

WordPerfect's default is to place consecutive numbers beginning with 1 by all lines that contain any text. In other words, it does not number blank lines. If you want to count blank lines, change N to Y. Or, you can request that it number every so many lines, either counting or not counting blank lines. If you wanted to number every fourth line that contained text, item **1-Count Blank Lines** would be set to N and item **2-Number Every n Lines** is set to 4. You can enter a left margin where the number will be placed. The default is .6 inches. You need to coordinate this setting with the left margin setting for the document. The default margin of 1 inch allows enough space for the line numbers to be inserted.

WordPerfect is preset to start line numbering on every page with 1, but you can change that to continuously number throughout the document. You can also begin numbering with any number you wish, not just 1.

```
Format: Line Numbering

     1 - Count Blank Lines                    No

     2 - Number Every n Lines, where n is     1

     3 - Position of Number from Left Edge    0.6"

     4 - Starting Number                      1

     5 - Restart Numbering on Each Page       Yes




Selection: 0
```

Figure 11.9 *Line Numbering Settings Sheet*
(Shift-F8, 1-Line, 5-Line Numbering, Y)

Press **F7** to return to the typing area. Turn Numbering Off at the position in the document where you want it to stop.

11.9 Page Breaks

Ctrl-Enter places a hard Page Break at the position of the cursor. This is especially useful for isolating tables and charts, starting new sections or chapters, and creating columns. A new page number is indicated in the status line after the Page Break. Page Break code markers can be deleted by moving the cursor to the last position above the Page Break line and pressing Del.

If you do not want the new page to be numbered, turn off Page Numbering (see Section 10.5.4) for this page.

11.10 Repeat Key

When you press Esc, the message center prompts:

```
Repeat value = 8
```

You can change the default of 8 to any number you wish. Then, with Repeat turned on, many operations that you can perform in WordPerfect will be repeated that number of times. For example, if you want to delete six lines, set **Repeat = 6** and press **Ctrl-End**, which is the command to delete one line. Repeat then deletes one line six times. To type a row of dashes across the page set **Repeat = 73**, then type one dash.

11.11 Compose

Compose is used to create special characters such as digraphs and diacritical marks. To activate Compose press **Ctrl-2** (not F2), type the first character, then the second, such as **a'** to produce á.

WordPerfect has also created a list of special characters that you can generate by entering their number. These character sets are listed in Section 16.3. To generate one, press **Ctrl-2** and enter the character set, such as **1** and the character reference, such as **23**.

For example, to create the German ss, press **Ctrl-2**, then type **1,23** to produce β.

11.12 Automatic Date and Time

To use this feature you must enter the correct date and time when you boot DOS, or your computer must be equipped with a clock that enters it for you.

There are three methods for using the Date and Time feature. First, you may bring into your document the current Date and Time and place it at the position of the cursor. This date will not be changed in later printings. Second, you may enter a code that updates the Date and Time every time you print the document. Third, you may place a **^D** in the **primary file** of a merge document, which prints the current date during a merge.

To place today's date in the text that will remain that date in all future printing:

Position the cursor where you want the date to appear
Press **Shift-F5**
Select **1-Date Text**

To place a data code that will correct the date each time you print:

Position the cursor
Press **Shift-F5**
Select **2-Date Code**

11.12.1 Formatting Date and Time

WordPerfect's default is to bring in the date only in its full format, such as June 23, 1988. You can change that date format and also include the time. Press **Shift-F5** and select **3-Date Format** to produce this settings sheet (see Figure 11.10).

Using any appropriate combination of date and time options presented on the settings sheet, enter up to 29 characters of formula and text. For example, the following setting shows:

```
3 1, 4              8:90


Month  Day  Year  Hour  Minutes  am/pm
```

This setting comes into the text as the current date and time in the format of:

```
June 23, 1988      2:43pm
```

```
Date Format

       Character   Meaning
          1        Day of the Month
          2        Month (number)
          3        Month (word)
          4        Year (all four digits)
          5        Year (last two digits)
          6        Day of the Week (word)
          7        Hour (24-hour clock)
          8        Hour (12-hour clock)
          9        Minute
          0        am / pm
          %        Used before a number, will:
                       Pad numbers less than 10 with a leading zero
                       Output only 3 letters for the month or day of the week


       Examples:  3 1, 4     = December 25, 1984
                  %6 %3 1, 4 = Tue Dec 25, 1984
                  %2/%1/5 (6) = 01/01/85 (Tuesday)
                  8:90       = 10:55am

Date format: 3 1. 4
```

Figure 11.10 *Date and Time Settings Sheet*
(Shift-F5, 3-Date Format)

The comma after 23 and the colon in 2:43 are entered into the formula as text and not automatically assigned by WordPerfect. You may also enter other text, such as:

```
3 1, 4      Time: 8:90
```

This is translated into:

```
June 23, 1988    Time: 2:43pm
```

You cannot place Date and Time codes on separate lines.

CHAPTER 12

Graphics

Version 5.0, for the first time, allows you to combine graphics images from numerous sources with text in a document. WordPerfect has been tested with some 50 graphics packages on the market today, 12 of which it directly supports. This means you don't have to convert the image or picture into another format before WordPerfect can read it. Another 40 of the tested graphics packages have file-exporting capability that WordPerfect understands. An extremely handy feature is WordPerfect's ability to capture an image from the screen of another graphics package and bring that image directly into your document. Some 30 graphics packages have been tested for this powerful feature in WordPerfect. See Section 16.4 for a complete listing of supported graphics products.

The graphics feature in WordPerfect makes it easy for you to create newsletters that contain company logos, financial reports with multiple graphs, or charts surrounded by text. There are many applications for using graphics with text in a business environment. You'll find that reports containing tables of numerical data supported by charts are much easier to read. The ability to display a table with a border surrounding it gives the document a neater appearance, especially when combined with laser printer technology for high-quality output.

12.1 Uses for Graphics Boxes

In order to use the graphics feature, you first create a box on the screen. The text will wrap around the box as it is drawn. The location of the box can be adjusted and sized according to your needs. You can retrieve a graphics image from another program inside the box or place another document inside of it. You may also create an empty box and later enter text inside it. Horizontal or vertical lines can also be drawn in your document with the graphics feature.

Graphics boxes can be placed almost anywhere in a document with the exception of:

1. Tables of authority

2. Inside other graphics boxes. (However, you can place two or more graphics boxes on top of each other.)

3. Comments

Graphics boxes are most useful when placed in the main body of the document, but they can be effective when used in headers, footers, footnotes, endnotes, and styles. The examples we use will incorporate graphics boxes in each of these areas.

12.2 Graphics Box Types

There are four categories of boxes you can create (see Figure 12.1), although the only practical difference is the numbering system for captions:

1. Figure. Figure boxes are useful for graphic pictures or for images, charts, and diagrams. WordPerfect automatically numbers the graphics boxes and displays the number on the screen while you are editing the document. The default numbering system for figures is Arabic (i.e., Figure 1, Figure 2). The number only prints if you define a caption for the graphics box.

2. Table. You may want to use table boxes for numerical information, statistical data, or maps. The default numbering system for tables is Roman numerals (i.e., Table I, Table II).

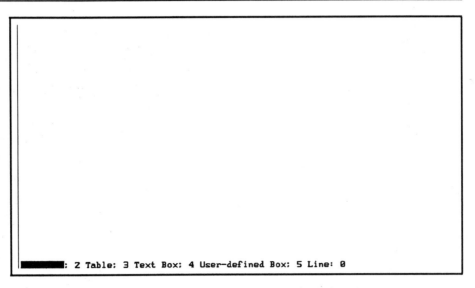

: 2 Table: 3 Text Box: 4 User-defined Box: 5 Line: 0

Figure 12.1 *Menu to Select Box Type (Alt-F9)*

3. Text. Text boxes may be used for text you may want emphasized, such as quotes of endorsement for a product in a newsletter or marketing brochure.

4. User defined. This option is for your discretion for images that do not fall into one of the other three categories.

The reason for these different box types is so that you can generate a separate list for each one by using the List feature. If you are writing a report with several tables, charts, or maps, it would be useful to print a listing of these at the end of your report for general reference.

There is a fifth option you will notice in the Graphics menu, Lines, which is not a box at all but is a feature allowing you to place vertical or horizontal lines, as well as shaded rectangles in the document. A full explanation of the lines option is given in Section 12.4.

12.3 Choosing a Box Type

To create a box, position the cursor where you want the box to begin, then press **Alt-F9 (Graphics)**, and choose a box type. Select **1-Figure** (see Figure 12.2), and then **1-Create**. WordPerfect displays a menu of options (see Figure 12.3).

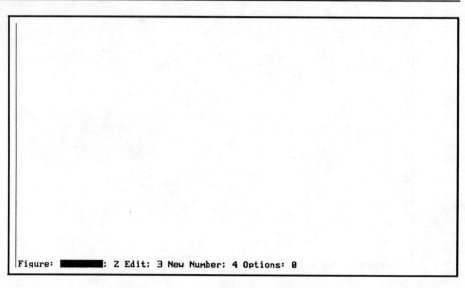

Figure: ▇▇▇▇▇▇▇: 2 Edit: 3 New Number: 4 Options: 0

Figure 12.2 *Creating a Figure Type Box*
(Alt-F9, 1-Figure)

```
Format: Paper Type

    1 - Standard

    2 - Bond

    3 - Letterhead

    4 - Labels

    5 - Envelope

    6 - Transparency

    7 - Cardstock

    8 - Other








Selection: 2
```

Figure 12.3 *Settings Sheet for Figure Type Boxes*
(Alt-F9, 1-Figure, 1-Create)

WordPerfect sets certain defaults for the vertical and horizontal position of the graphics box based on the distance the cursor is located from the top of the current paragraph. Also, the options for the vertical and horizontal positioning are dependent on the choice you make for the Type option. A more detailed discussion of these menu selections is given in Sections 12.3.5 and 12.3.6.

12.3.1 *Filename*

With the Filename option (see Figure 12.3), you may either retrieve a WordPerfect document into the box by simply typing the name of the file, or you may retrieve a graphics image into the box by typing the name of the graphics file. Section 16.4 lists the types of graphics files supported directly and indirectly by WordPerfect. If the file you specify was not created in a WordPerfect-supported graphics package, an error message is displayed.

There may be an occasion when you want the box to remain empty. In that case, do not enter a file name. You can enter your own text inside the box by selecting Edit and simply typing the text and/or codes you desire. Following is an example of a box with a graphics .PIC file from Lotus Symphony.

By selecting the following keystrokes, we have instructed WordPerfect to create a box using the default settings for size and positioning in the current paragraph. If the box is too large to fit between the cursor position and the end of the page, WordPerfect moves the box to the following page. Here are the keystrokes for opening a Figure box:

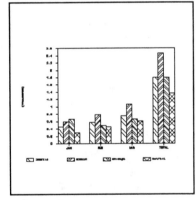

Fig. 1

Press **Alt-F9**
Select **1-Figure**
Select **1-Create**
Select **1-Filename**

When prompted by WordPerfect, type the name of the graphics file you want to retrieve inside the box. In this case, the file name is QTR1.PIC. WordPerfect then gives you a Please Wait message while it searches the disk for the file (see Figure 12.4). After the flashing Please Wait stops, select **F7** to quit and return to your document.

```
Definition: Figure

    1 - Filename                    QTR1.PIC (Graphic)

    2 - Caption                     Fig. 1

    3 - Type                        Paragraph

    4 - Vertical Position           0"

    5 - Horizontal Position         Right

    6 - Size                        2" wide x 1.49" (high)

    7 - Wrap Text Around Box        Yes

    8 - Edit




Selection: 0
```

Figure 12.4 *Naming a Graphics File to Merge*
(Alt-F9, 1-Figure, 1-Create, 1-Filename, Type File name)

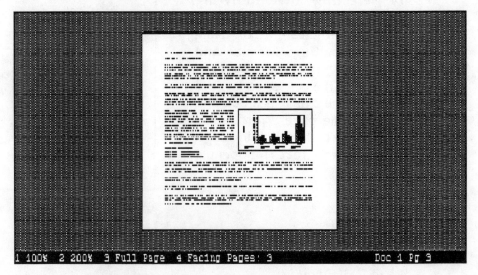

Figure 12.5 *Looking at a Graph Through View Document*
(Shift-F7, 6-View Document)

You'll notice that you do not see the graphics image inside the box. This is because we are in a text mode while editing; however, you can see the graphics image if you now select **Shift-F7 (Print)**, followed by **6-View Document** (see Figure 12.5). This feature allows you to view the document as either (1) 100%, (2) 200%, (3) Full Page, or (4) Facing Page. The

Page Up and Page Down keys will allow you to scroll through the document page by page.

This is the moment of truth when you learn whether or not WordPerfect followed all of your keystrokes as you meant them. Happily, in Figure 12.5 our bar chart is inside the box and everything looks like we imagined it would.

12.3.2 *Entering Text Inside a Box*

Let's take the same box but this time just enter text of our own rather than a graphics image. Follow the same steps as you did to create the first box, but do not enter a file name:

Press **Alt-F9**
Select **1-Figure**
Select **1-Create**
Select **F7** to exit to the typing area

In order to add text to this new box we need to edit the contents. Follow these keystrokes to get to this point:

Press **Alt-F9**
Select **1-Figure**
Select **2-Edit**

```
THIS  IS  AN  EXAMPLE
OF  ENTERING  TEXT  IN
A BOX.

WP PLACED THE CURSOR
INSIDE     A     BLANK
SCREEN   WHERE   TEXT
ARE ENTERED.

PRESS  F7  TO  RETURN
TO THE TYPING AREA.

USE VIEW DOCUMENT TO
SEE THE TEXT INSIDE
```

When prompted, type the figure number you're working with, in this case, Figure 2, followed by the Enter key. **Select 8-Edit.** You are now looking at a blank screen with the cursor positioned inside the box on the first line.

Enter your text here. When finished, press F7 to exit to the typing area. Once again, we do not see our text on the screen, but you may go to the Print menu in order to view the box with text inside. It may be annoying at first not to be able to see those graphics images and text inside the boxes, but it saves a great deal of time while in the edit mode for WordPerfect not to merge all the images and bring them into view at once. You'll get used to this method very quickly.

12.3.3 Creating a Caption

You may want to create a caption to identify the graph. You are allowed to do this with all of your graph boxes with the exception of any boxes that are located inside of headers, footers, footnotes, and endnotes. When you select **2-Caption**, WordPerfect displays an editing screen with the current figure number (see Figure 12.6).

Now you have three options: (1) If you want to print "Figure 1" without any caption, press **F7**. (2) If you want to print a caption, but without "Figure 1," delete "Figure 1 " with the **Backspace** key, then type the caption and press **F7**. (3) If you want to print both "Figure 1" and the caption, type the caption one space beyond "Figure 1" and press **F7**. Figure 1" is printed in Bold type, and the caption in normal type, unless you change the font specifications. The numbering system will automatically update the other Captions as you create other boxes of the same type.

The default display position of the caption is immediately beneath the graphics box. You can change this position to above the location of the box from the **4-Options** submenu selection. The following example shows the inclusion of a caption for our first box chart with the Lotus .PIC file. The keystrokes are:

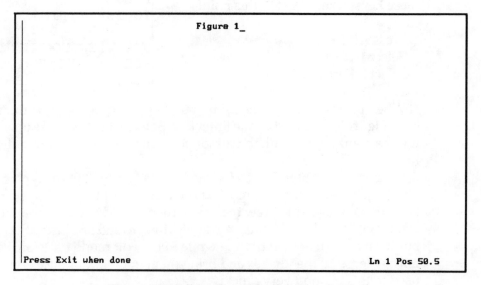

Figure 12.6 *Editing Screen for Entering Captions*
(Alt-F9, 1-Create, 2-Caption)

Press **Alt-F9**
Select **1-Figure**
Select **1-Create**
Select **1-Filename (QTR1.pic)**
Select **2-Caption** and begin entering the text for the caption of the figure. The text wraps according to the width of the graphics box you've created.

Remember, the position of the caption text defaults below the outline of the box. If you want to see the caption at the top of the graphics box, you must change this under the Options submenu.

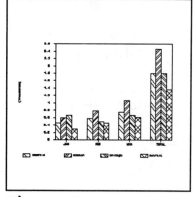

Figure 3
Qtr 1, FY 88 Sales
Times   Journal
Telemarketing

12.3.4 *Graphics Box Type*

There are three selections under the Type submenu that determine how or if the box moves in your document. Item **3-Type** will access the menu (see Figure 12.7).

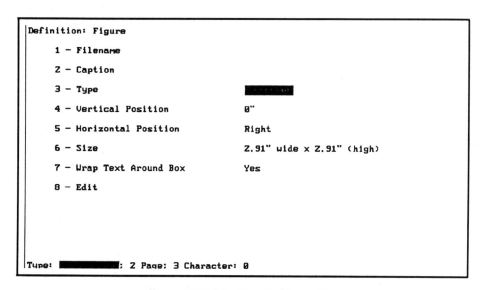

Figure 12.7 *Selecting the Type of Box*
(Alt-F9, 1-Figure, 1-Create, 3-Type)

12.3.4.1 Paragraph Box Types

If you want the graphics box to remain with its surrounding text, select **1-Paragraph.** Select this option at the beginning of the paragraph. The text and box stay together when the document is edited. The box will move to the top of the following page if the paragraph is too close to the bottom of the page for the entire box to fit.

12.3.4.2 Page Box Types

Select the **2-Page** option when you want the graphics box to stay at a fixed location on the page (see Figure 12.8).

The selection for Page is made at the cursor location. Do not begin typing any text you want to wrap around the box before selecting Page. If you do, the box will move to the next page. In other words, if you want to place a page-type box at the top of the page, you must position the cursor at the top of the page before creating the box and entering text to go along with it.

The graphics box on page 265 is a Page box and is contained in a fixed position on the page. It will not move as the text is written around the box. This is useful when you want to devote an entire page to the image for emphasis.

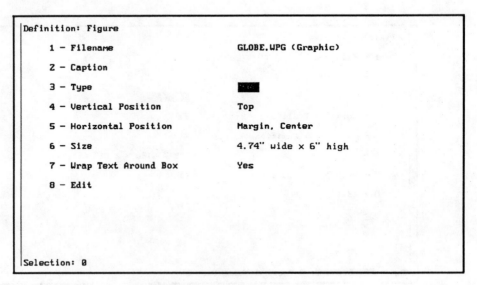

```
Definition: Figure

      1 - Filename              GLOBE.WPG (Graphic)

      2 - Caption

      3 - Type

      4 - Vertical Position     Top

      5 - Horizontal Position   Margin, Center

      6 - Size                  4.74" wide x 6" high

      7 - Wrap Text Around Box  Yes

      8 - Edit




Selection: 0
```

Figure 12.8 *Page Type Settings Sheet*
(Alt-F9, 1-Figure, 1-Create, 3-Type, 2-Page)

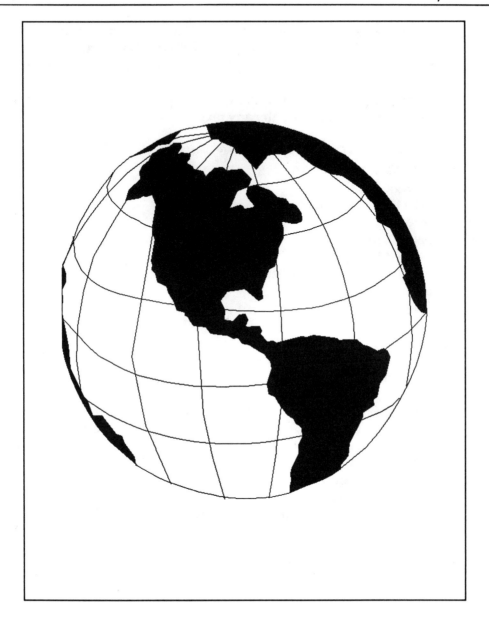

The globe in this figure is one of thirty "clip-art" images that come with WordPerfect. These files are easily identified with a .WPG file extension and can be retrieved into graphics boxes. Section 16.5 lists the clip-art images.

To create the **Page** graph with the clip-art globe, we move to the beginning of a page before we enter any text. The keystrokes are:

Press **Alt-F9 (Graphics)**
Select **1-Figure**
Select **1-Create**
Select **3-Type (Page)**
Select **5-Horizontal**
Select **1-Margins**
Select **3-Center**
Select **1-Filename (Globe.wpg)**
Select **6-Size**
Select **2-Height**
Type **8.0**
Press **F7** to return to the typing area

12.3.4.3 Character Box Types

Character-type boxes are the only type allowed inside footnotes and endnotes. This is because the character-type box is treated as a single character, regardless of the size of the box (see Figure 12-9). WordPerfect wraps text around the specified Block, as illustrated in the footnote below.

First let's write a footnote that will contain the graphics box we'll create. Bring up the Footnote menu (Ctrl-F7) (see Figure 12.10).

The ability to easily incorporate footnotes into a report is an invaluable feature of a word processing package. We'll begin the third footnote now.[3] The keystrokes for incorporating a footnote into your document, along with a character-type graphics box are:

Press **Ctrl-F7**
Select **1-Footnote**
Select **1-Create**

---

[3] This is an example of a character-type graphics box which, you will recall, is the only type allowed inside footnotes or endnotes. ☐ It is necessary for you to identify the size of the box while you are creating the footnote.

```
Definition: Figure
     1 - Filename
     2 - Caption
     3 - Type                    Character
     4 - Vertical Position       Top
     5 - Horizontal Position
     6 - Size                    1.7" wide x 1.7" (high)
     7 - Wrap Text Around Box     Yes
     8 - Edit



Selection: 0
```

Figure 12.9 *Settings Sheet for Character Type Boxes*
(Alt-F9, 1-Figure, 1-Create, 3-Type, 3-Character)

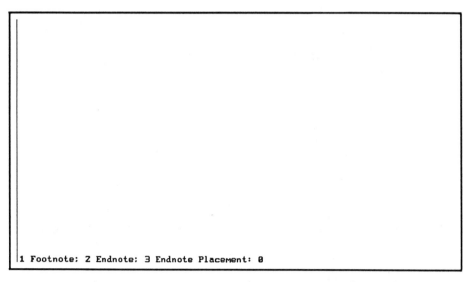

```
1 Footnote: 2 Endnote: 3 Endnote Placement: 0
```

Figure 12.10 *Footnote Menu (Ctrl-F7)*

```
Definition: Figure

    1 - Filename

    2 - Caption

    3 - Type                    Character

    4 - Vertical Position       Top

    5 - Horizontal Position

    6 - Size                    1" wide x 0.25" high

    7 - Wrap Text Around Box     Yes

    8 - Edit




Selection: 0
```

Figure 12.11 *Settings Sheet for Character Type Box*
(Alt-F9, 1-Figure, 1-Create, 3-Type, 3-Character)

This moves you inside an editing area with the footnote number appearing to the left of the cursor. Begin typing the text for the footnote at this point and, when you are ready to enter the graphics box, follow these keystrokes:

Press **Alt-F9**
Select **1-Figure**
Select **1-Create**
Select **3-Type**
Select **3-Character**

This brings up the settings sheet for a character-type box (see Figure 12.11). Specify the size of the box at this point because you cannot edit the size later:

Select **6-Size**
Select **3-Both Width and Height**

We want to specify both height and width because the character-type graphics box will be used for emphasis inside the footnote and we don't want it to be too large.

12.3.5 *Options for Vertical Positioning*

WordPerfect sets defaults for both the vertical and horizontal positions of the graphics box you create. This is based on the type of box you select. After you create the box, WordPerfect displays a default for the vertical position that is the distance the cursor is located from the top of the current paragraph.

If you want to override the default, simply enter an "offset" for the vertical position, such as 1.5 inches, which would place the box 0.5 inches below the first line of the paragraph (see Figure 12.12).

If you select an offset position for the graphics box that causes the box not to fit on the page because the paragraph is very close to the bottom of that page, WordPerfect alters the setting to keep the box within the paragraph. There is an option within the Graphic Options menu that allows you to control how far the box can move in the paragraph before being moved to the next page. We will fully describe this option on page 281.

Let's create a paragraph-type graphics box that is positioned 0.5 inches below the beginning of the current paragraph of text. We will also bring into this graphics box another one of the clip-art files that comes with WordPerfect. In this example, we are using the Book.wpg file. The steps to recreate this graphics box are:

```
Definition: Figure

     1 - Filename                 BOOK.WPG (Graphic)

     2 - Caption

     3 - Type                     Paragraph

     4 - Vertical Position        0.5"

     5 - Horizontal Position      Right

     6 - Size                     1.54" wide x 1.07" (high)

     7 - Wrap Text Around Box     Yes

     8 - Edit




Selection: 0
```

Figure 12.12 *Setting the Vertical Position*
(Alt-F9, 1-Figure, 1-Create, 1-Paragraph, 4-Vertical Position)

Press **Alt-F9**
Select **1-Figure**
Select **1-Create**
Select **1-Filename**
Type **filename:Book.wpg**
Select **3-Type**
Select **1-Paragraph**
Select **4-Vertical Position** Type **0.5**
Select **F7** to exit to the typing area

If you are working with a Page graphics box, the menu choices for vertically aligning the box are: 1) full page, 2) top, 3) center, 4) bottom, or you can specify the location of the box by choosing option 5) set position and specifying the offset in inches.

Vertical alignment also applies to Character boxes. Character boxes can be aligned to correspond with lines of text in the footnote or endnote. The footnote text can be aligned with either the top, center or bottom of the box.

12.3.6 *Options for Horizontal Positioning*

Like the vertical position choices, horizontal positions are also dependent on the choice you make in the Type option. For example, if you select Paragraph as the graphics box type, the box can be aligned with the left or right margins or can be centered. Our previous Paragraph boxes have been right aligned, which is the default setting.

In this example, we are illustrating a paragraph graphics box which is positioned 0.1 inch from the beginning of the current paragraph and contains a graphic image from the clip-art files that come with WordPerfect. We have selected the left position, which means the box begins at the left margin (see Figure 12.13).

If we select Page as the graphics box type, we have three options for horizontal positioning to choose from: (1) Margins, (2) Columns, or (3) Set Position. Each of these choices is discussed below.

12.3.6.1 *Margins*

The Margins option allows you to align the graphics box with the left or right margin, center it between the margins, or expand the box to fill the page between the left and right margins. Figure 12.14 indicates that the

```
Definition: Figure

    1 - Filename

    2 - Caption

    3 - Type                    Paragraph

    4 - Vertical Position        .5"

    5 - Horizontal Position      Left

    6 - Size                     .5" wide x .25" (high)

    7 - Wrap Text Around Box     Yes

    8 - Edit



Horizontal Position: 1 Left: 2 Right: 3 Center: 4 Both Left & Right: 0
```

Figure 12.13 *Setting the Horizontal Position*
(Alt-F9, 1-Figure, 1-Create, 2-Paragraph, 5-Horizontal Position)

```
Definition: Figure

    1 - Filename                HOURGLAS.WPG (Graphic)

    2 - Caption

    3 - Type                    Page

    4 - Vertical Position        Top

    5 - Horizontal Position      Margin, Center

    6 - Size                     2" wide x 2.46" (high)

    7 - Wrap Text Around Box     Yes

    8 - Edit




Selection: 0
```

Figure 12.14 *Settings for Centering an Image*
(Alt-F9, 1-Figure, 1-Create, 1-Page, 5-Horizontal Position)

hourglas.wpg image is centered between the left and right margins on the page and is set at 2 inches wide.

12.3.6.2 *Columns*

If you have defined text columns, you will designate which column, and the position within the column, for the graphics box. WordPerfect asks you for the column number(s) and then you select how you want the graphics box aligned with those columns (see Figure 12.15). If you want to specify more than one column, use a dash to specify the range (i.e., 1–3).

12.3.6.3 *Set Position*

The Set Position feature is used to set a specific measurement in inches from the left edge of the page to position the box horizontally.

Bring up the settings sheet with the following keystrokes:

Press **Alt-F9**
Select **1-Figure**
Select **1-Create**
Select **1-Filename (hourglas.wpg)**
Select **3-Type**
Select **2-Page**
Select **5-Horizontal Position**
Select **3-Set Position (3")**

We see in Figure 12.16 that the hourglass image from the clip-art figures is contained in a Page-type graphics box and that the box is 3 inches from the left edge of the page.

```
Definition: Figure

     1 - Filename

     2 - Caption

     3 - Type                        Page

     4 - Vertical Position           0"

     5 - Horizontal Position         Column(s) 1, Right

     6 - Size                        3.25" wide x 3.25" (high)

     7 - Wrap Text Around Box        Yes

     8 - Edit




Selection: 0
```

Figure 12.15 *Settings for Placing an Image in a Column*
(Alt-F9, 1-Figure, 1-Create, 1-Page, 5-Horizontal Position)

```
Definition: Figure

     1 - Filename                    HOURGLAS.WPG (Graphic)

     2 - Caption

     3 - Type                        Page

     4 - Vertical Position           Top

     5 - Horizontal Position         3"

     6 - Size                        1.5" wide x 2" high

     7 - Wrap Text Around Box        Yes

     8 - Edit




Selection: 0
```

Figure 12.16 *Setting the Position of an Image*

12.3.7 *Size Options*

When you select **6-Size**, WordPerfect gives you three choices for sizing
the graphics boxes: (1) Set Width, (2) Set Height, and (3) Set both Width
and Height.

WordPerfect calculates the height of the box automatically when you select **Set Width** and specify a certain width. It does this so that the original shape of the graphics image is preserved and the proportions are correct.

Alternatively, if you want WordPerfect to calculate the box width, you select **Set Height** and specify the height of the box you want.

If you want to customize the height and width, select **Set Both Width and Height** and enter the measurements in inches (see Figure 12.17).

If you have told WordPerfect that you want to set the width, the height is calculated according to the number of lines of text in the box or by the size of the graphics image specified for the box.

12.3.8 *Turning Off Text Wrapping in Graphics*

The default is to wrap text around graphics boxes, but if a box occupies most of the space between margins or if you want the image to stand out, you will not want to wrap text around the box. To turn off automatic wrapping, select item **7-Wrap Text Around Box** and change Yes to N (see Figure 12.18). You will notice that when the option is set to No, you cannot see the box on the page. It is necessary to view the document through **Shift-F7, 6-View Document**.

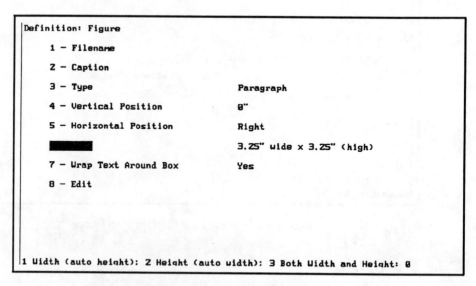

Figure 12.17 *Setting Both Width and Height for an Image*
(Alt-F9, 1-Figure, 1-Create, 1-Page, 6-Size)

```
Definition: Figure

     1 - Filename

     2 - Caption

     3 - Type                      Page

     4 - Vertical Position         Top

     5 - Horizontal Position       Margin, Right

     6 - Size                      3.25" wide x 3.25" (high)

     ████████████████████          █

     8 - Edit




Selection: 0
```

Figure 12.18 *Turning Off Automatic Wrapping*
(Alt-F9, 1-Figure, 1-Create, 1-Page, 7-Wrap Text Around Box)

12.3.9 Editing a Graphics Box

Editing the graphics boxes you create is easy with the editing choices in WordPerfect. We have already used some of these choices and will explain them fully here.

Our first example will edit a previous image from the clip-art files. We have four editing options available as well as a percent change option. The keystrokes to edit an existing graphic are:

Press **Alt-F9**
Select **1-Figure**
Select **2-Edit**
Select Box Number to Edit
Select **8-Edit**

In the example in Figure 12.19, Applause.wpg is the image we will edit. Choosing **8-Edit**, we see the screen change to the graphics mode and display the image. Each of the options for editing is now explained.

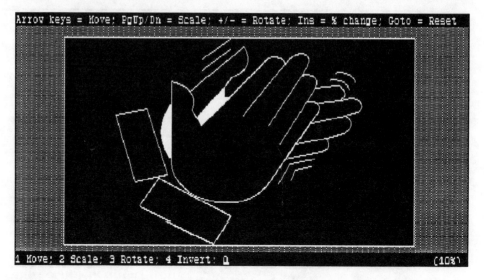

Figure 12.19 *Editing a Clip Art Image*

12.3.9.1 Move Figure

With the Move option, the figure can be moved both horizontally and vertically in the graphics box. This is accomplished in two ways. The lower right-hand corner of the screen indicates a percentage that you can select by pressing the Arrow keys on your keyboard. The percentages are either 1, 5, 10, or 25, and they indicate the image will move by that amount in the direction of the Arrow keys. The Insert key (Ins) allows you to toggle through these percentage choices.

You can also move the figure by selecting Move from the menu choices at the bottom of the screen and then entering both the horizontal and vertical measurements in positive or negative numbers.

12.3.9.2 Scale Option

With the Scale option, the image can be expanded or contracted in a horizontal or vertical direction. By pressing PgUp, you can expand the image in both directions. Pressing PgDn contracts the image in both directions. Once again, the percentage of change affected is indicated in the lower right-hand corner of the screen and can be changed with the Ins key. The percentage change you can specify is either 1, 5, 10, or 25.

12.3.9.3 Rotating an Image

To rotate a graphics image, use the Rotate option, which allows you to enter a number of degrees for the rotation (0 to 360). WordPerfect asks you if you want to mirror the image. If you select Y for yes, the dots in the image change so they display from right to left instead of left to right.

If you don't want to enter the number of degrees, WordPerfect also allows you to use the + or − keys to rotate the figure counterclockwise or clockwise, respectively.

Graphics images imported from .wpg files, HPGL files, .pic files, CGM metafiles, and .DXF files are considered to be line drawings by Word-Perfect. Images from all other WordPerfect-supported graphics programs are considered to be bit-mapped images.

If the image in the graphics box is a bit-mapped image, as opposed to a line drawing, the Rotate option has no effect. However, you can mirror the image from left to right.

12.3.9.4 Percentage (%) Change

This option has been explained in Section 12.3.9.2. The percentage of change (1, 5, 10, or 25) is entered by the Arrow keys or Page Up and Down keys. The Insert key is used to toggle between the percentage ranges. These percentage numbers appear in the lower right-hand corner of the screen. You'll recall that to turn the image, press the plus or minus key on the keyboard.

12.3.10 New Number

If you want to change the numbering of your graphics boxes, which are numbered consecutively according to box type, first move the cursor to where you want to enter the new number. Press **Alt-F9**, and select the type of box you want to renumber; then select **3-New Number** and enter that number (see Figure 12.20).

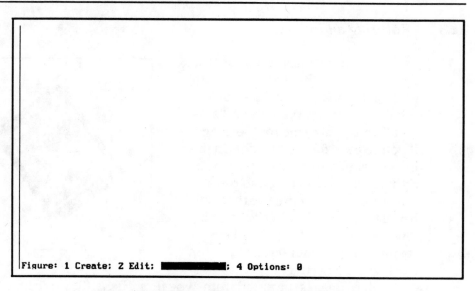

Figure: 1 Create; 2 Edit; ▮▮▮▮▮▮▮; 4 Options: 0

Figure 12.20 *Changing the Number of a Graphics Box*
(Alt-F9, 1-Figure, 3-New Number)

From this point forward, all graphics boxes of the type you selected (figure, table, etc.) are renumbered starting with this new number. If you are using two-level numbering such as 1–a, you have the capability of indicating a starting point for both levels.

12.3.11 Graphics Options

There are other settings you can change for each graphics box you've created. Select 4-Options (see Figure 12.20) to bring up the Options settings sheet (see Figure 12.21).

Select an option and make the changes. Press **F7** to return to the typing area. Options are changed from the cursor forward in the document.

Now let's take a close look at each of the settings you can change.

12.3.11.1 Border Style

The Border Style option sets the line style for the four borders of the graphics box (see Figure 12.22). There are seven options: (1) None, (2) Single, (3) Double, (4) Dashed, (5) Dotted, (6) Thick, and (7) Extra Thick. Make your choice or use the default and continue to the next setting.

```
Options:    Figure

     1 - Border Style
             Left                              Single
             Right                             Single
             Top                              Single
             Bottom                            Single
     2 - Outside Border Space
             Left                              0.16"
             Right                             0.16"
             Top                              0.16"
             Bottom                            0.16"
     3 - Inside Border Space
             Left                              0"
             Right                             0"
             Top                              0"
             Bottom                            0"
     4 - First Level Numbering Method          Numbers
     5 - Second Level Numbering Method         Off
     6 - Caption Number Style                  [BOLD]Figure 1[bold]
     7 - Position of Caption                   Below box, Outside borders
     8 - Minimum Offset from Paragraph         0"
     9 - Gray Shading (% of black)             0%

Selection: 0
```

Figure 12.21 *Settings Sheet for Graphics Options*
(Alt-F9, Box Type, 4-Options)

```
Options:    Figure

     1 - Border Style
             Left                              Single
             Right                             Single
             Top                              Single
             Bottom                            Single
     2 - Outside Border Space
             Left                              0.16"
             Right                             0.16"
             Top                              0.16"
             Bottom                            0.16"
     3 - Inside Border Space
             Left                              0"
             Right                             0"
             Top                              0"
             Bottom                            0"
     4 - First Level Numbering Method          Numbers
     5 - Second Level Numbering Method         Off
     6 - Caption Number Style                  [BOLD]Figure 1[bold]
     7 - Position of Caption                   Below box, Outside borders
     8 - Minimum Offset from Paragraph         0"
     9 - Gray Shading (% of black)             0%
```

Figure 12.22 *Selecting Borders for Graphics*

12.3.11.2 Outside Border Space

The Outside Border Space refers to the amount of space (specified in inches) you want between each border of the box and the text surrounding the outside of the box. Once again, you can enter a desired setting or use the default.

12.3.11.3 Inside Border Space

The Inside Border Space is a measurement referring to the amount of space you want between each border of the box and the text or image located inside the box.

12.3.11.4 Level Numbering Methods

WordPerfect allows you to define two levels of numbering for captions (see Figure 12.23). Select a level (menu items 4 or 5) and then define the number style for that level. The options are:

1. Off

2. Numbers

```
Options:    Figure

          1 - Border Style
                  Left                        Single
                  Right                       Single
                  Top                         Single
                  Bottom                      Single
          2 - Outside Border Space
                  Left                        0.16"
                  Right                       0.16"
                  Top                         0.16"
                  Bottom                      0.16"
          3 - Inside Border Space
                  Left                        0"
                  Right                       0"
                  Top                         0"
                  Bottom                      0"
          4 - First Level Numbering Method    Numbers
          5 - Second Level Numbering Method   Off
          6 - Caption Number Style            [BOLD]Figure 1[bold]
          7 - Position of Caption             Below box, Outside borders
          8 - Minimum Offset from Paragraph   0"
          9 - Gray Shading (% of black)       0%

1 Off: 2 Numbers: 3 Letters: 4 Roman Numerals: 0
```

Figure 12.23 *Numbers for Graphics Boxes*

3. Letters

4. Roman numerals

At the first level, letters or Roman numerals are indicated in uppercase. At the second numbering level, they are indicated with lowercase letters or numerals.

12.3.12 *Caption Number Style Definition*

WordPerfect allows you to further define caption (menu item 6) numbers by entering text and codes for font attributes. Let's go through the keystrokes to create a graphics box with a caption that is in italics and is numbered with Roman numerals for the first level and letters for the second level:

Press **Alt-F9**
Select **1-Figure**
Select **1-Create**
Select **Filename** and enter **Qtr1.pic**
Select **2-Caption** and press the **Backspace** key until the figure
   number is erased
Enter **Fig. I-a**
Press **F7** to exit to the Definition Menu
Select **5-Horizontal** and choose **Left**
Select 6-Size and enter **2"** for width
Press **F7** to exit to the typing area

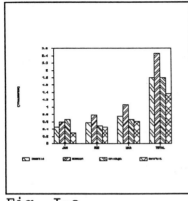

Fig. I-a

At this point, we see our graphics box take shape on a new page. The caption we have identified is a two-level caption with the first level identified as a Roman numeral and the second one as a lowercase letter. We can now go to the Options menu under **Alt-F9 (Graphics)**, and change the attributes of the caption. The keystrokes for this selection are:

Press **Alt-F9**
Select **4-Option**

Select **6-Caption Number Style**
Press the **Backspace** key to erase the default
Type the text as you want it displayed, i.e.,
"Fig. I–a"
Select **Ctrl-F8**
Select **2-Appearance**
Select **4-Italic**
Press **F7** to return to the typing area

It may seem that a significant number of steps are required to accomplish this particular style for the caption. However, WordPerfect does give the user a great deal of flexibility with these features. Once you have used the graphics features to their fullest capability, you will find it becomes much easier to create your graphs and enjoy using this feature. And with the added benefit of the macro function (see Section 15.3), you can automate many of these keystrokes to be recalled over and over again.

12.3.12.1 Position of Caption

This feature allows you to place the caption either above or below the box and outside or inside the box. Select item **7** and enter your choice. Once you decide if the caption will be placed below or above the box, WordPerfect will ask if you want it to appear inside or outside of the border (see Figure 12.24).

12.3.12.2 Minimum Offset from Beginning of Paragraph

You will recall that when you create a Paragraph box and specify an offset distance from the current paragraph, WordPerfect will honor that setting unless there is not sufficient room on a page to fit both the graphics box and the paragraph. If there is not enough room, WordPerfect automatically moves the graphics box to the top of the next page or column.

The minimum offset feature (menu item 8) allows you to have some degree of control over how far the graphics box can move up into the paragraph when WordPerfect needs to make an adjustment to the original offset measurement you defined.

As an example, if you told WordPerfect to recognize 1/2 inch (.5") as the minimum offset, the graphics box could move up to within 1/2 inch of the top of the paragraph before WordPerfect moved it to the next page.

```
Options:    Figure

    1 - Border Style
            Left                        Single
            Right                       Single
            Top                         Single
            Bottom                      Single
    2 - Outside Border Space
            Left                        0.16"
            Right                       0.16"
            Top                         0.16"
            Bottom                      0.16"
    3 - Inside Border Space
            Left                        0"
            Right                       0"
            Top                         0"
            Bottom                      0"
    4 - First Level Numbering Method    Numbers
    5 - Second Level Numbering Method   Off
    6 - Caption Number Style            [BOLD]Figure 1[bold]
                                        Below box, Outside borders
    8 - Minimum Offset from Paragraph   0"
    9 - Gray Shading (% of black)       0%
```

Figure 12.24 *Positioning the Caption*

There may be a case where you would want your original offset measurement honored regardless of how close to the bottom of the page the text appeared. In that case, you need to set the minimum offset to a large value.

12.3.12.3 *Gray Shading*

Menu selection **9 (Gray Shading)** is used when you want the graphics box to be shaded. The higher the percentage, the blacker the box is shaded. If you select 100 percent, the entire box would be black. Gray Shading has become a popular feature with the advent of laser printers. It gives your graphics image a different quality and makes it stand out on the page.

12.4 Graphics Lines

Another flexible option of the Graphics feature in WordPerfect is the Lines feature. The lines you create can be either horizontal or vertical and can be shaded or black.

12.4.1 *Horizontal Position*

The following keystrokes to create a horizontal line (see Figure 12.25) are:

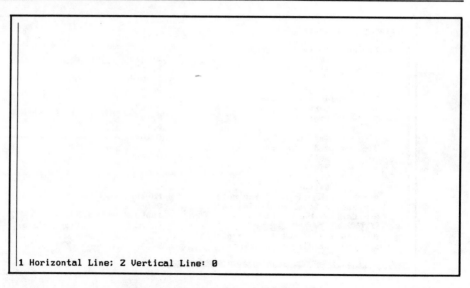

1 Horizontal Line; 2 Vertical Line: 0

Figure 12.25 *Menu to Select Line Draw*
(Alt-F9, 5-Line)

Press **Alt-F9**
Select **5-Line**

Select **1-Horizontal Line** to bring up a menu to define your line (see Figure 12.26). Enter your line specifications and press **F7** to exit to the typing area.

The tricky thing here is that you cannot see the line in the typing area, nor do you see a marker of any kind to indicate a line is there. You cannot edit a graphics line once it is defined. The only way to deal with it is to select **Reveal Codes (Alt-F3)** and delete the line, which is clearly identified there.

You may see how the line will be printed by selecting the View Document feature from the Print menu.

If you are creating a vertical line, which we will discuss in the next section, the horizontal position feature allows you to place the line slightly to the left of the left margin or slightly to the right of the right margin.

If you have defined a column layout, WordPerfect asks you to enter a column number to place the line between that column and the one to the right of it. The Set Position option allows you to identify a specific horizontal offset from the left edge of the page for the vertical line (see Figure 12.27).

```
Graphics: Horizontal Line

     1 - Horizontal Position          Left & Right

     2 - Length of Line

     3 - Width of Line                0.01"

     4 - Gray Shading (% of black)    100%









Horizontal Pos: 1 Left 2 Right 3 Center 4 Both Left & Right 5 Set Position: 0
```

Figure 12.26 *Setting the Specifications for the Line*
(Alt-F9, 5-Line, 1-Horizontal)

```
Graphics: Horizontal Line

     1 - Horizontal Position          Left & Right

     2 - Length of Line

     3 - Width of Line                0.01"

     4 - Gray Shading (% of black)    100%









Offset from left of page: 1"
```

Figure 12.27 *Setting the Position of a Vertical Line*
(Alt-F9, 5-Line, 1-Horizontal, 1-Horizontal Position)

12.4.2 *Vertical Position*

The Vertical Position option is available to you on the Graphics: Vertical Line menu when you have told WordPerfect that the line you want to draw is a vertical one. It allows you to place the line against the top of the margin, against the bottom margin, centered between the top and bottom margins, or at some absolute measurement from the top of the form (see Figure 12.28).

12.4.3 *Length of Line*

To specify the length of the line, simply type the number in inches. If you are drawing horizontal lines, WordPerfect's default line length is calculated from the current cursor position to the margin specified in the horizontal position option. If you have chosen the horizontal position as left and right, the line length is calculated automatically for you.

12.4.4 *Width of Line*

You have the ability to specify the thickness of the line by typing the width in inches. It's useful to use the Switch Screen function key to try some of these different line widths before you enter them into your document.

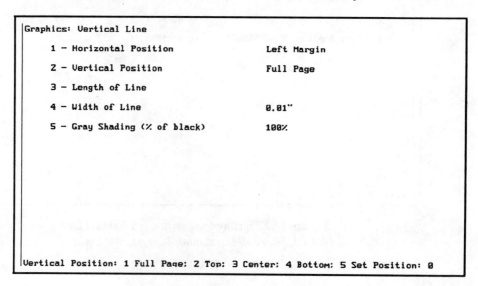

Figure **12.28** *Vertical Line Settings Sheet*
(Alt-F9, 5-Line, 2-Vertical)

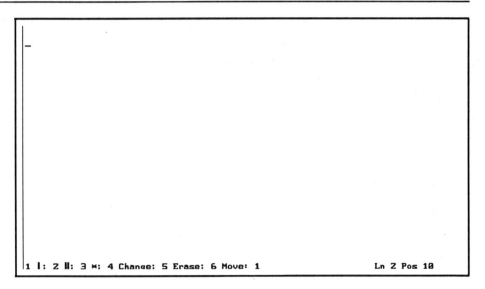

1 I: 2 II: 3 ×: 4 Change: 5 Erase: 6 Move: 1   Ln 2 Pos 10

Figure 12.29 *Menu Choices for Drawing Lines*
(Ctrl-F3, 2-Line, Draw)

12.4.5 *Gray Shading*

Once again, gray shading is an option to determine the blackness of the line. The higher the percentage, the darker the line, with 100 percent being completely black.

12.5 Free-Hand Line Drawing

If you want to create boxes such as you would use in an organizational chart, you would not use any of the features through the Alt-F9 (Graphics) key. Instead, position the cursor where you want the line to begin, then press **Ctrl-F3 (Screen)** and select **2-Line Draw** (see Figure 12.29).

Items 1, 2, 3, and 4 allow you to select the appearance of the line. As soon as you select one of these, the Arrow keys are activated, and whenever you press one of them, a line is drawn in that direction. Figure 12.30 is an example of drawing with the right and down Arrow keys.

The only way to stop drawing is to press **F7**. And the only way to correct a mistake is to erase a line and start over. To erase or move a line,

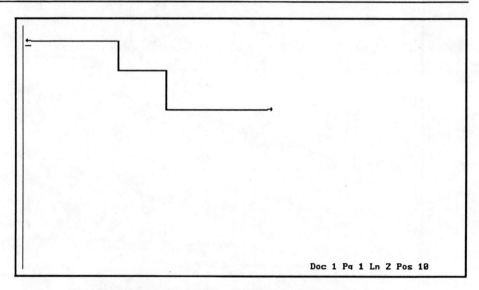

Figure 12.30 *Lines Drawn with the Free-hand Feature*

position the cursor where you want to make corrections, then press **Ctrl-F3** and select **5-Erase** or **6-Move**. Again, you use the Arrow keys to perform operations.

Advanced Page Formatting and Desktop Publishing Features

"Desktop publishing" is a loosely bantered term defined differently by almost everyone who uses it. Software manufacturers, who have achieved varying degrees of sophistication in their products' abilities to simulate genuine typesetting through PC-based software, continue to make marked improvements toward combining word processing functions with desktop publishing capabilities. While WordPerfect 5.0 doesn't attempt to be a page layout program in the sense of PageMaker or Ventura, it does provide excellent features for designing documents with good-looking print quality. It also provides excellent graphics capabilities, which is one of the most important features for desktop publishing. Refer to CHapter 12 for WordPerfect's graphics.

The ultimate quality of your document depends, of course, on the capabilities of your printer. Version 5.0 supports PostScript, and printer drivers have been written for many of the leading laser printers. Version 5.0 takes advantage of all the type fonts and sizes, kerning abilities, and proportional space features that your printer offers. The list of printers that the first release of WordPerfect 5.0 supports is in Section 16.5.

However, WordPerfect Corporation is continually adding drivers to the list; you can add them to your printer disk.

This chapter divides itself between page formatting features and typesetting and printing features. Be sure to review Chapter 12 for WordPerfect's graphics features, an important part of desktop publishing.

13.1 Additional Formatting Features for Controlling Pages

In order to control the appearance of a finished document, WordPerfect provides features that adjust the placement of text on the page.

13.1.1 *Widows and Orphans*

In printing terminology, a widow is the first line of a paragraph printed by itself on the last line of a page. An orphan is the last line of a paragraph printed on the first line of a page. Most book designers agree that widows and orphans create an unbalanced feel to a page and so they require that at least two lines of text appear at the top and bottom of pages. The consequence of removing widows and orphans is that the space that the widow or orphan would have occupied must be compensated for by the spacing between other paragraphs on the page.

If widows and orphans are undesirable in your document, press **Shift-F8**, select **1-Line**, then **9-Widows/Orphans**. Turn on Widow/Orphan protection by entering **Y**. The widowed and orphaned lines will be shifted between pages as you add or delete text.

13.1.2 *Conditional End of Page*

In order to prevent contiguous lines from being divided as you edit your document and change the format, WordPerfect allows you to "glue" any number of lines together with Conditional End of Page. This is different from widow and orphan protection in that Conditional End of Page will never allow the specified lines to be separated. To use it:

Position the cursor one line *above* the first line you want to glue
Press **Shift-F8 (Format)**
Select **4-Other**
Select **3-Conditional End of Page**

Enter the number of lines you want to glue together
Press **F7 (Exit)**

Now the number of lines you specified will always remain together on a page no matter what else happens to the document. However, Word-Perfect only glues together the exact number of lines you specify, so if you add text within the glued lines, some of your original text might now fall outside of the Conditional End of Page range. Holding Blocks of text together is a different procedure called "Block Protect."

13.1.3 Block Protect

To ensure that a block of text remains glued together no matter how much text is added or deleted from it, use **Block Protect**. Position the cursor at the beginning of the text and Block it (Alt-F4). Do not include a hard return [HRt] at the end of the paragraph. With the Block **on**, press **Shift-F8**. The prompt will ask:

```
Block protection? (Y/N):No
```

Change the No to **Y**.

13.1.4 Hard Spaces: Keeping Characters Together

Words, equations, and symbols that should not be separated, such as $a + b = c$, are glued together with a hard space. To enter a hard space, type the last character of the first word, press **Home-Space Bar** and enter the first character of the second word. WordPerfect then knows to make line adjustments based on keeping these characters or words together.

13.2 Forcing Printing at a Specified Position

If your printer is able to take advantage of this feature, you can **Advance** the print head to any specified position in the document. If, for example, you want to print a chart four lines below a paragraph, it's better to use **Advance** than hard returns because the four lines will not be reformatted by Page Breaks. In this use, **Advance** is Block Protect in reverse. It guarantees that the last line of the paragraph and the chart will always be separated by four lines.

```
Format: Other

    1 - Advance

    2 - Conditional End of Page

    3 - Decimal/Align Character     .
        Thousands' Separator        .

    4 - Language                    EN

    5 - Overstrike

    6 - Printer Functions

    7 - Underline - Spaces          Yes
                    Tabs            No




Advance: 1 Up: 2 Down: 3 Line: 4 Left: 5 Right: 6 Column: 0
```

Figure 13.1 *Advance Menu*
(Shift-F8, 4-Other, 1-Advance)

Advance distances are given in number of lines up or down or in number of characters right or left *from the position of the Advance marker* or to a specific line number. Column distances are given in inches to correspond with the column margin settings. To begin **Advance** press **Shift-F8**, select **4-Other**, then **1-Advance** to bring up the menu choices in Figure 13.1.

Look at the menu items along the bottom of the screen in the figures. Item **3-Line** and **6-Column** are absolute positions. For example, you Advance to Line 36 or to the column whose left margin is at 4 inches. Items 1 and 2 move up or down the number of specified lines from the position of the Advance marker. Items 4 and 5 move left or right the specified number of characters. Press **F7** twice to return to the typing area.

13.3 Forcing Printing On Odd or Even Pages

To ensure that a page will appear on one side of a book or the other, regardless of the charts and inserts that might cause its placement to change, position the cursor at the top of the page you want to encode, press **Shift-F8**, select **2-Page**, then **2-Force Odd/Even Pages**. WordPerfect will force the correct page number. For example, if you want an odd page and the current number is 84, WordPerfect changes it to 85 and renumbers the rest of the document.

13.4 Adjusting Margins for Bindings

This feature is used only when two-sided copies are being printed. If you plan to photocopy your document on a copying machine that has this same feature, you will find it easier to shift the bindings there rather than through WordPerfect. However, if what you need are two-side originals that leave appropriate margins for binding on odd and even pages, you'll use WordPerfect's binding feature. When you're ready to print your document, press **Shift-F7 (Print)** and select **B-Binding** as you enter your print instructions. The margin measurement is in inches. Right-hand pages are odd numbered. WordPerfect recognizes numbering systems for front and end matter so be certain that your page numbers reflect the right- and left-hand positions you want. You might have to create some "blank" pages to ensure correct binding positions.

13.5 Paper Size and Type

WordPerfect is preset to print on a standard 8.5-by-11-inch sheet of paper, but it can be set to print on virtually any size. Press **Shift-F8**, select **2-Page Format,** then **7-Paper Size** to produce these choices (see Figure 13.2).

```
Format: Paper Size

      1 - Standard                 (8.5" x 11")

      2 - Standard Landscape       (11" x 8.5")

      3 - Legal                    (8.5" x 14")

      4 - Legal Landscape          (14" x 8.5")

      5 - Envelope                 (9.5" x 4")

      6 - Half Sheet               (5.5" x 8.5")

      7 - US Government            (8" x 11")

      8 - A4                       (210mm x 297mm)

      9 - A4 Landscape             (297mm x 210mm)

      0 - Other

Selection: 0
```

Figure 13.2 *Paper Size Menu*
(Shift-F8, 2-Page, 7-Paper Size)

```
Format: Paper Type

     1 - Standard

     2 - Bond

     3 - Letterhead

     4 - Labels

     5 - Envelope

     6 - Transparency

     7 - Cardstock

     8 - Other




Selection: 0
```

Figure 13.3 *Paper Stock Menu*
(Shift-F8, 2-Page, 8-Paper Size, F7)

Select any of WordPerfect's commonly used sizes, or press **O-Other** (that's "O" not zero) and enter the width and height. Press **F7** to Save these settings. A second menu comes up asking for paper stock type. The type stock may tell your printer how hard to strike the paper (see Figure 13.3).

13.6 Working While Printing

If you print from disk rather than from memory, you can continue working in WordPerfect. The printing is being accomplished through DOS, which frees WordPerfect's program. In order to print from disk you cannot **Fast Save** the document (see Section 5.2). All of WordPerfect's features are available while printing except Exiting the program or exiting to DOS through Shell. However, you might notice that some features work more slowly or that printing is temporarily interrupted while certain screen operations, such as merge, are in progress. These interruptions are nothing to be concerned about.

13.7 Refining the Appearance of Type

The following sections discuss your options for changing type styles and sizes, as well as spacing letters and lines. These features are entirely dependent on your printer's capabilities. For many users, these are the features soon-to-be-available in the PC environment.

13.7.1 *Line Height and Leading*

Back in the days when movable type was set by hand, printers inserted a bar of lead between lines to separate them. A narrow bar placed lines close together; wide leading made lines easier to read. With the advent of electronic typesetting, "leading" continued to be used to denote the distance between the baseline of one line to the baseline of the next. Certain type styles look best with specified leading and WordPerfect is preset to automatically select those.

However, if your printer has the capability to print it, WordPerfect can change the leading to any setting you wish. And, as with most WordPerfect markers, you can change the leading for any portion or all of a document. Press **Shift-F8**, select **3-Line Height**, then **2-Fixed**. Enter the leading setting you desire. To return to the default settings, select **1-Auto** from the menu.

13.7.2 *Pitch*

Pitch is the width specified to hold one character, which in turn determines the number of characters per inch. Different type styles require different pitches. Italics, for example, require less width than Roman type. WordPerfect automatically determines the standard pitch unless you turn it off and specify your own. There might be times when spreading characters apart lends clarity or an improved appearance to your text. You can change the pitch at any position and return to automatic pitch as easily. WordPerfect enters beginning and ending code markers.

To enter your own pitch, press **Shift-F8**, select **3-Document**, then **1-Display Pitch**. Change Yes to N and type the pitch you desire. Press F7 to return to the typing area. Turn pitch **off** when you want to return to automatic pitch.

When you change automatic pitch to an exact width, every character will occupy the same space regardless of its size. This is an **absolute** pitch size and does not permit relative spacing between letters and words. It is more useful for entering formulas than for text. To refine pitch settings more precisely for text, turn on Kerning (see Section 13.7.3) or Customized Word and Letter Spacing (see Section 13.7.4).

13.7.3 *Kerning*

Pitch assumes that all letters occupy the same amount of width, which is not true, of course. An *m* occupies more width than an *i*. Kerning determines the absolute width of letter pairs and spaces them proportionately. This is one of the most difficult and impressive accomplishments of electronic typesetting. Like Pitch, you can turn Kerning on or off anywhere in the document by placing code markers (see Figure 13.4):

Press **Shift-F8**
Select **4-Other**
Select **6-Printer Functions**
Select **1-Kerning**
Change No to **Y**
Press **F7** to return to the typing area

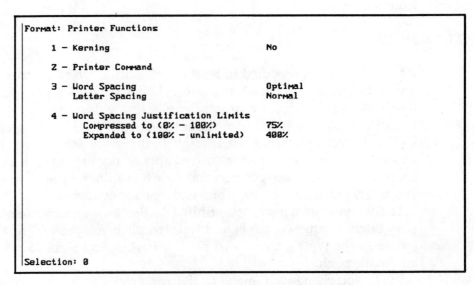

```
Format: Printer Functions

    1 - Kerning                          No

    2 - Printer Command

    3 - Word Spacing                     Optimal
        Letter Spacing                   Normal

    4 - Word Spacing Justification Limits
        Compressed to (0% - 100%)        75%
        Expanded to (100% - unlimited)   400%




Selection: 0
```

Figure 13.4 *Printer Functions Menu*
(Shift-F8, 4-Other, 6-Printer Functions)

13.7.4 *Customized Word and Letter Spacing*

From the Printer Functions menu (see Figure 13.4) you can refine your pitch settings. These settings can operate with or without kerning. When you choose a type font, what the printer manufacturer feels is most appropriate pitch has been set for it. WordPerfect calls this "normal" spacing. If you select this option, WordPerfect allows the printer to use its predetermined spacing between letters and words. WordPerfect, however, frequently disagrees with the printer manufacturer's suggestions and offers you the option of selecting its pitch recommendations, which it calls "optimal." With the optimal setting you can then influence WordPerfect's pitch by increasing or decreasing it by a percentage:

Press **Shift-F8**
Select **4-Other**
Select **6-Printer Functions**
Select **3-Word Spacing**

Look at the menu items along the bottom of the screen in Figure 13.5. To enter a percentage of optimal, select item **3** and type the percentage you wish. Percentages less than 100 decrease the pitch while percentages greater than 100 increase it.

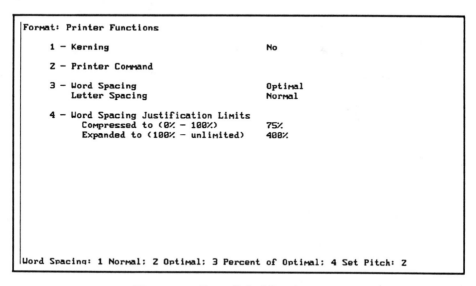

```
Format: Printer Functions

    1 - Kerning                         No

    2 - Printer Command

    3 - Word Spacing                    Optimal
        Letter Spacing                  Normal

    4 - Word Spacing Justification Limits
        Compressed to (0% - 100%)       75%
        Expanded to (100% - unlimited)  400%












Word Spacing: 1 Normal; 2 Optimal; 3 Percent of Optimal; 4 Set Pitch: 2
```

Figure 13.5 *Letter/Word Spacing Menu*
(Shift-F8, 4-Other, 6-Printer Functions, 3-Word/Letter Spacing)

If you want to specify a pitch setting in characters per inch, select item **4-Set pitch** and enter any decimal number.

13.8 Fonts: Type Styles and Sizes

WordPerfect offers options for varying the appearance of your text by changing the type font, the size of type, and the attributes, such as bold or italics. Your printer will limit the options you have, but when you selected your printer, WordPerfect recorded the fonts that your printer uses and will not allow you to specify incompatible fonts. You may turn Font on and off at any position in the document, giving you the opportunity to change the appearance of specific words, formulas, headings, or the entire text. You may select fonts, sizes, and attributes as you enter text, or you can Block existing text before pressing Ctrl-F8.

13.8.1 *Changing the Current Font Style*

To see the fonts available through your printer, press **Ctrl-F8 (Font)** and select **4-Base Font**. The font with the asterisk is the current font, or the one your printer is currently using. The selections available on the Epson FX-86e/286e are shown in Figure 13.6.

```
Base Font

* Roman (10 CPI)
  Roman (12 CPI)
  Roman (17 CPI)
  Roman (20 CPI)
  Roman (5 CPI)
  Roman (6 CPI)
  Roman (8.5 CPI)
  Roman (PS)
  Roman Dbl-High (10 CPI)
  Roman Dbl-High (12 CPI)
  Roman Dbl-High (17 CPI)
  Roman Dbl-High (20 CPI)
  Roman Dbl-High (5 CPI)
  Roman Dbl-High (6 CPI)
  Roman Dbl-High,Wide (PS)
  Roman Dbl-Wide (PS)
  Roman Italic (PS)
  Roman Subscript (10 CPI)
  Roman Subscript (12 CPI)
  San Serif (10 CPI)
  San Serif (12 CPI)

1 Select: N Name search: 1
```

Figure 13.6 *Selecting a Current Font from the Available Base Fonts (Ctrl-F8, 4-Base Font)*

Using the **Arrow** keys, highlight the font you want to make current, then press **1-Select**.

13.8.2 *Changing the Type Size*

Selecting another font style does not change the size of type, which is measured in "point" sizes. Normal text size is 10 or 12 point, while normal heading or headline sizes range from 14 to 24 points. Although you can enter exact point sizes through Printer Commands (see Section 13.11), WordPerfect also provides a more friendly selection menu (see Figure 13.7).

1-Suprscpt (Superscript) and **2-Subscpt (Subscript)** are proportional to the size of the type, but this is the means for marking it. You may mark as few or as many characters as you wish to be subscripted or superscripted.

Menu items 3 through 7 set the type size: 3 and 4 are smaller than the normal size while 5, 6, and 7 are larger. You'll want to print a test page of varying type fonts and sizes for reference.

To reset the normal type size, press **Ctrl-F8** and select **3-Normal**.

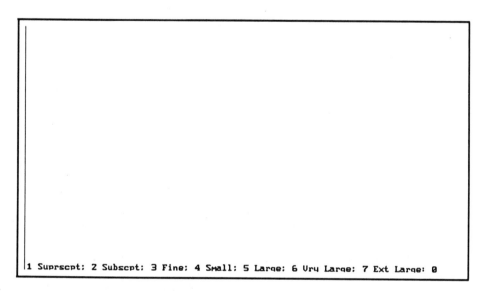

1 Suprscpt: 2 Subscpt: 3 Fine: 4 Small: 5 Large: 6 Uru Large: 7 Ext Large: 0

Figure 13.7 *Selecting Type Size*
(Ctrl-F8, 1-Size)

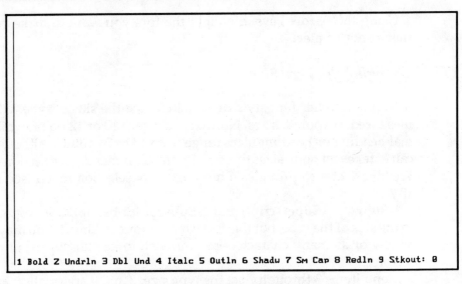

1 Bold 2 Undrln 3 Dbl Und 4 Italc 5 Outln 6 Shadw 7 Sм Cap 8 Redln 9 Stkout: 0

Figure 13.8 *Text Attributes Menu*
(Ctrl-F8, 2-Appearance)

```
Select Printer: Edit

        Filename              HPLASEII.PRS

  1 - Name                    HP LaserJet Series II

  2 - Port                    LPT1:

  3 - Sheet Feeder            None

  4 - Forms

  5 - Cartridges and Fonts

  6 - Initial Font            Courier 12pt 10 pitch (PC-8)

  7 - Path for Downloadable
        Fonts and Printer
        Command Files




Selection: 0
```

Figure 13.9 *Edit Select Printer Menu*
(Shift-F7, S-Select, 3-Edit)

13.8.3 Changing the Attributes of Type

Press **Ctrl-F8** and select **2-Appearance** to produce the menu choices in
Figure 13.8. If you have entered Bold or Underline codes with the F6 or
F8 keys, you will not enter them again through this menu. However, items

3 through 7 offer the only means of altering the appearance of text through these special attributes.

13.9 Specifying Cartridges and Fonts for Advanced Printers

Many printers offer a wide variety of optional fonts that you can purchase. In many of these printers you change fonts manually with cartridges or print wheels that are inserted into a slot. Some other printers are equipped with font files that can be downloaded. You must tell WordPerfect which fonts you plan to use with your printer. You can do this when you go through the printer selection installation or any time later, perhaps as you purchase more fonts for your library.

Press **Shift-F7** to access the Printer menu, then select **S-Select printer**. If you have already defined your printer, select **3-Edit**; otherwise go through the entire definition. At the appropriate step, select **5-Cartridges and Fonts**. In Figure 13.9, we are defining the HP LaserJet Series II.

Pressing **5-Cartridges and Fonts** produces the menu in Figure 13.10. It shows us that the LaserJet Series II comes with the potential of two cartridge slots as well as downloadable memory of 350K. You will not change these defaults unless you've added slots or memory to your printer. To continue our selection, press **1-Select Fonts** (see Figure 13.11).

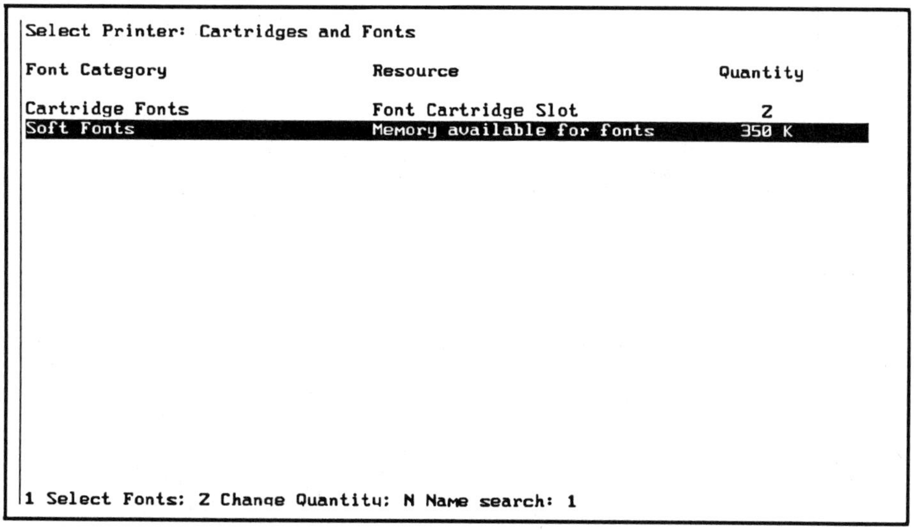

```
Select Printer: Cartridges and Fonts

Font Category                Resource                    Quantity

Cartridge Fonts              Font Cartridge Slot            2
Soft Fonts                   Memory available for fonts    350 K












1 Select Fonts; 2 Change Quantity; N Name search: 1
```

Figure 13.10 *Cartridges and Fonts Menu*
(Shift-F7, S-Select, 3-Edit, 5-Cartridges and Fonts)

```
Select Printer: Cartridges and Fonts

                                        Total Quantity:      2
                                    Available Quantity:      2

Cartridge Fonts                                        Quantity Used

   A Cartridge                                              1
   B Cartridge                                              1
   C Cartridge                                              1
   D Cartridge                                              1
   E Cartridge                                              1
   F Cartridge                                              1
   G Cartridge                                              1
   H Cartridge                                              1
   J Cartridge                                              1
   K Cartridge                                              1
   L Cartridge                                              1
   M Cartridge                                              1
   N Cartridge                                              1
   P Cartridge                                              1
   Q Cartridge                                              1

Mark Fonts:  * Present when print job begins        Press Exit to save
                                                    Press Cancel to cancel
```

Figure 13.11 *Available Fonts for the HP LaserJet Series II*
(Shift-F7, S-Select, 3-Edit, 5-Cartridges and Fonts, 1-Select Fonts)

```
Print Color

                            Primary Color Mixture
                          Red      Green      Blue

     1 - Black            0%        0%         0%
     2 - White            100%      100%       100%
     3 - Red              67%       0%         0%
     4 - Green            0%        67%        0%
     5 - Blue             0%        0%         67%
     6 - Yellow           67%       67%        0%
     7 - Magenta          67%       0%         67%
     8 - Cyan             0%        67%        67%
     9 - Orange           67%       25%        0%
     A - Gray             50%       50%        50%
     N - Brown            67%       33%        0%
     O - Other

     Current Color        0%        0%         0%




Selection: 0
```

Figure 13.12 *Color Menu*
(Ctrl-F8, 5-Color)

This is the entire list of fonts available for the HP LaserJet Series II. Two fonts can reside in the printer at the same time. Place an asterisk by each of the fonts you plan to use if you intend to use only these fonts during a print job. If you plan to switch fonts *during* printing, mark the fonts with a + (plus) sign.

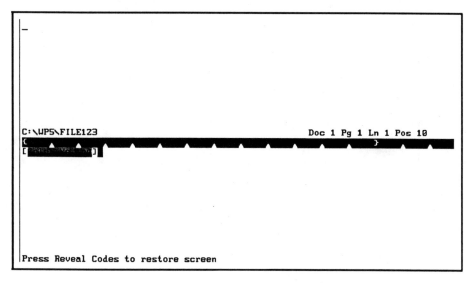

Figure 13.13 *Looking at a Color Marker Through*
Reveal Codes

The fonts that you mark become your **base font** selections through the **Font (Ctrl-F8)** menu.

13.10 Printing in Color

Depending on your printer's capabilities, WordPerfect can specify almost any mix of colors. Using color is simply a matter of placing color codes in the document just as you would place any other WordPerfect markers. Position the cursor where you want color to begin, press **Ctrl-F8** and select **5-Color** to produce the color menu (see Figure 13.12).

By typing a number corresponding to a color number, you place a marker in the text. Press **F7** to record the color request. If you look through Reveal Codes, you'll see the color marker displayed (see Figure 13.13). All text entered after this marker will be printed in yellow until you switch colors or return to black. You can also enter color codes for existing text by Blocking it before pressing Ctrl-F8.

13.10.1 Creating Your Own Color Mix

As Figure 13.13 shows, colors are determined by a percentage mix of the primary colors. By changing these percentages, you can alter the color

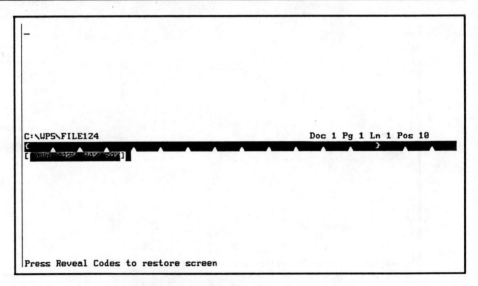

Figure 13.14 *Color Marker with Color Mix*

and intensity. Select a color, then press **O-Other** ("O" not zero) to change it. Type in the percentages you want and press **F7** to Save it. Or, you can create any color not listed by selecting **O-Other** and entering your mix. When you press **F7**, Reveal Codes will display what is shown in Figure 13.14.

13.11 Printer Commands

Any of the features of your printer can be activated whether or not Word-Perfect has included them as a menu item. Your printer manual lists the features and a corresponding code. When the printer encounters this code, it knows how to respond. An example is shown in Figure 13.15.

To enter a printer command code, press **Shift-F8**, select **4-Other, 6-Printer Functions, 2-Printer Command**, and **1-Command**. Printer commands are entered between angle brackets, such as <28>. Press **F7** to return to the typing area. If you have turned on a feature with a command code and want to turn it off, you'll enter another code specified by your printer manual.

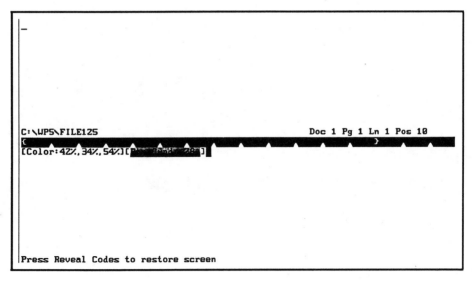

Figure 13.15 *Printer Command Code*

13.11.1 Downloadable Files

If you use a series of codes often, you might want to create a file that contains them, then load the entire file into your document. Following the steps to the Printer Command, select **2-Filename** and type the name. If you plan to use printer command files, list the path name during the printer selection process (see Figure 13.9) (Shift-F7, S-Selection, 3-Edit, 7-Path for Downloadable Files).

CHAPTER 14

Using WordPerfect's Math Features

Just as WordPerfect isn't a database manager, neither is it intended to be a spreadsheet. But WordPerfect does have the ability to easily format numbers into columns and perform some limited operations with them. It is especially useful for formatting text with numbers, such as sales reports and travel expenses. However, with WordPerfect 5.0, which can import graphics and thus spreadsheets, it is often easier to create your numbers in a software system that's specifically designed as a spreadsheet.

14.1 Establishing Columns

Although the Alt-F7 key is for both text and math columns, you cannot use text columns if you want to calculate numbers. The first step for math columns is to set tabs for the number of columns you want. Press **Shift-F8**, select **1-Line**, then **8-Tabs Set** to produce the Tab Ruler (see Figure 14.1).

Remove all the default tabs by pressing **Ctrl-End**, then move the cursor with the **Arrow** key to the position where the first column of numbers

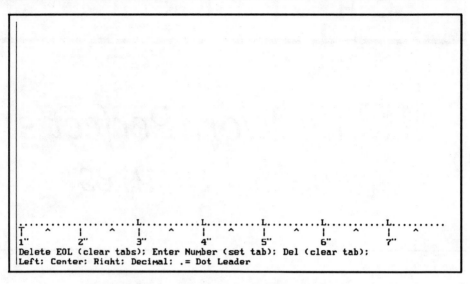

```
·······································L··········L········L··········L··········L·· ·······
T       ^     |     ^     |     ^     |     ^     |     ^     |     ^     |    ^
1"            2"          3"          4"          5"          6"          7"
Delete EOL (clear tabs); Enter Number (set tab); Del (clear tab);
Left: Center: Right: Decimal: .= Dot Leader
```

Figure 14.1 *Setting Tabs for Math Columns*
(Shift-F8, 1-Line, 8-Tab Set)

will be entered. Leave enough space at the left margin for any text you might want to enter that identifies the numbers. Press **Tab** or **L** to enter the tab. Set the rest of the tabs in the same way. Try to determine the widest number in the column so you can make the column wide enough to hold it. However, you can widen columns at any time simply by moving the tab marker.

With the cursor at the left margin, press **Alt-F7 (Math/Columns)** and select **2-Math Def** to produce the following settings sheet (see Figure 14.2). This settings sheet is the only complicated part of using math. Here's how it works. Every column that you've set with tabs can serve only one function. It can (1) add all the numbers in that column, (2) add subtotals, and then add the subtotals into totals, (3) calculate formulas, or (4) contain text as well as numbers. Text columns cannot perform math functions. The reason to designate a text column is to turn off the character alignment feature.

The Column Definition settings sheet identifies 24 columns from A to X. The type of column is preset for **2**, which is a **numeric** column. If we want a column to be one of the other three types, we change it here. An important concept to remember is that **column A** in the settings sheet corresponds to the *first* tab you set. Think of a column as those numbers that align themselves under the tab.

```
Math Definition        Use arrow keys to position cursor

Columns                A B C D E F G H I J K L M N O P Q R S T U V W X

Type                   Z Z Z Z Z Z Z Z Z Z Z Z Z Z Z Z Z Z Z Z Z Z Z Z

Negative Numbers       ( ( ( ( ( ( ( ( ( ( ( ( ( ( ( ( ( ( ( ( ( ( ( (

Number of Digits to    2 2 2 2 2 2 2 2 2 2 2 2 2 2 2 2 2 2 2 2 2 2 2 2
  the Right (0-4)

Calculation      1
  Formulas       2
                 3
                 4

Type of Column:
       0 = Calculation    1 = Text    2 = Numeric    3 = Total

Negative Numbers
       ( = Parentheses (50.00)        - = Minus Sign  -50.00



Press Exit when done
```

Figure 14.2 *Column Definition Settings Sheet*
(Alt-F7, 2-Math Def)

```
Tab          L     L     L     L     L
...........................................................
  |  ^  |  ^  |  ^  |  ^  |  ^  |  ^  |

 1"    2"    3"    4"    5"    6"    7"

Column       A     B     C     D     E
```

The area between the left margin and the first tab (3") will be used to enter text that identifies the line items. In the example we're about to create, we'll use the first column (A) to tally subtotals and totals. Word-Perfect calls this type of column **2-numeric**. Since all the columns in the settings sheet are present for 2, we need not make any changes. Press **F7** to Save the settings. Figure 14.3 shows how the example looks.

It returns you to the menu items along the bottom of the screen. If you want to use math now, select item **1-Math On**. Otherwise press F7 again to return to the typing area. We have now Defined our math columns for the example in Figure 14.3.

Now we'll enter some numbers into our example. Turn **Math On (Alt-F7, 1-Math On)**. The message center will say "Math." Position the cursor

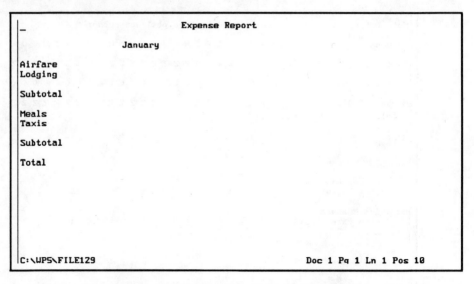

Figure 14.3 *Setting Up a Numeric Worksheet*

```
|_                        Expense Report

                 January

|Airfare              875.00
|Lodging             1258.76

|Subtotal

|Meals              1245.87
|Taxis               126.00

|Subtotal

|Total



|Math                                    Doc 1 Pg 1 Ln 1 Pos 10
```

Figure 14.4 *Entering Numbers with Math Turned On*

past the word "Airfare" and press the **tab** key. Notice that when you type the numbers and enter the decimal, the number aligns itself by the decimal point under the tab marker. All numbers that you enter will align themselves in the column. Entering all our numbers, we will have the columns shown in Figure 14.4.

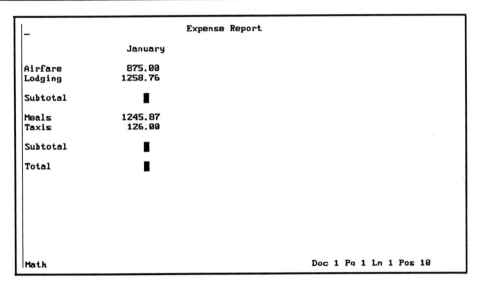

Figure 14.5 *Operator Signs to Add Subtotals and Totals*

14.2 Adding Numbers into Subtotals

To add any contiguous numbers in a column, enter a **plus (+)** sign on the line on which you want the total to appear. Use the **tab** key to enter the column. You can have as many of these subtotals as you wish. To add the subtotals together, you enter an **equals (=)** sign. The menu items in Figure 14.5 were brought up by pressing **Alt-F7**. Whenever we want Word-Perfect to add our subtotals and total, we press **2-Calculate** from this menu (see Figure 14.6).

The + and - operator signs remain on the screen to help you should you want to edit your work, but they do not print.

14.2.1 *One-Line Subtotals and Totals*

If you want to enter a single-line item as a subtotal that will be included in the total, type a **t** before typing the number. During calculation, Word-Perfect treats this number as if it were a subtotal of numbers. In Figure 14.7 we've entered a separate line item for out-of-pocket cash (t200.00) as a single-item subtotal.

You can also use a capital **T** before a single-line item that is a total rather than a subtotal. When the grand total is calculated, the T items will be included (see Figure 14.8).

```
_                              Expense Report

                      January

Airfare                 875.00
Lodging                1258.76

Subtotal              2,133.76█

Meals                  1245.87
Taxis                   126.00

Subtotal              1,371.87█

Total                 3,505.63█




Math                                          Doc 1 Pg 1 Ln 1 Pos 10
```

Figure 14.6 *Worksheet After Calculations*

```
_                              Expense Report

                      January

Airfare                 875.00
Lodging                1258.76

Subtotal              2,133.76+

Meals                  1245.87
Taxis                   126.00

Subtotal              1,371.87+

Cash                  ███████

Total                 3,705.63=




Math                                          Doc 1 Pg 1 Ln 1 Pos 10
```

Figure 14.7 *Single-Line Item as Subtotal*

14.2.2 Calculating Negative Numbers

In Figure 14.8 we created a T (Total) item ("Less Advance") that was to be subtracted from the total. To indicate that the "Advance" should be subtracted, we inserted a **minus (-)** sign between the T and the number. As you can see, WordPerfect correctly subtracted it. We could also have used **parentheses (2000.00)** to denote a negative number. Or, we could have placed an **N** in front of the number to show that it is negative: N2000.00. The advantage of using N is that you can add all the N numbers from a column of figures. To add only the numbers denoted by an N, enter N+ as the operator.

14.2.3 *Math Operators*

As you have seen in the previous examples, WordPerfect uses the **+ (plus)** sign to add each line that becomes a subtotal. Then, once you've created subtotals, either by adding a column of numbers or entering a single-line t number (e.g., t200.00), an **= (equals)** sign adds all the subtotals. Finally, an *** (asterisk)** adds all the totals to produce a grand total. That is the hierarchy that you must follow. In other words, you cannot use an = sign unless you have first used the + sign. Unless there are two or more = signs you cannot create a grand total by using an asterisk.

14.2.4 *Using Other Column Types*

So far we have limited the examples to numbers that appear in a single column, but you'll certainly want to work across columns. We want to position our totals in Figure 14.8 in the adjacent columns (see Figure 14.9).

To accomplish this we must change columns B and D to column-type 3 (Total). Move the cursor to the beginning of the Math table, press **Alt-**

```
|-                      Expense Report

                  January

|Airfare           875.00
|Lodging          1258.76

|Subtotal        2,133.76+

|Meals           1245.87
|Taxis            126.00

|Subtotal        1,371.87+

|Cash            t200.00

|Total           3,705.63=

|Less Advance    █2000.00

|Amount Due      1,705.63█


|Math                                    Doc 1 Pg 1 Ln 1 Pos 10
```

Figure 14.8 *Single-Line Items as Totals*

```
_                          Expense Report

                     January              February

Airfare              875.00               1086.00
Lodging             1258.76               1896.53

Subtotal                +                    +

Meals               1245.87               1693.88
Taxis                126.00                284.00

Subtotal                +                    +

Cash                t200.00               t367.75

Total                        ▮                      ▮




Columns          A         B        C         D        E
C:\WP5\FILE136                             Doc 1 Pg 1 Ln 1 Pos 10
```

Figure 14.9 *Positioning Totals in Adjacent Columns*

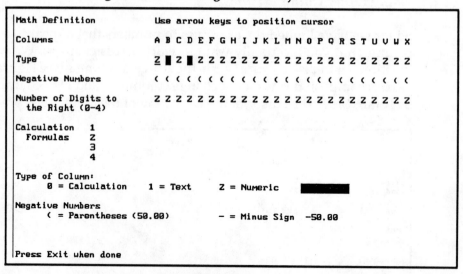

```
Math Definition          Use arrow keys to position cursor

Columns                  A B C D E F G H I J K L M N O P Q R S T U V W X

Type                     Z ▮ Z ▮ Z Z Z Z Z Z Z Z Z Z Z Z Z Z Z Z Z Z Z Z

Negative Numbers         ( ( ( ( ( ( ( ( ( ( ( ( ( ( ( ( ( ( ( ( ( ( ( (

Number of Digits to      Z Z Z Z Z Z Z Z Z Z Z Z Z Z Z Z Z Z Z Z Z Z Z Z
   the Right (0-4)

Calculation      1
  Formulas       2
                 3
                 4

Type of Column:
      0 = Calculation     1 = Text      2 = Numeric    ▮▮▮▮▮▮▮▮▮

Negative Numbers
      ( = Parentheses (50.00)        - = Minus Sign   -50.00



Press Exit when done
```

Figure 14.10 *Setting B and D as "Total" Columns*

F7, then **2-Math Def** to bring up the settings sheet. Using the **Right Arrow** key, move the cursor to column **B** and type **3**. Move to column **D** and type **3**. Press **F7** twice to Save the settings and return to the typing area (see Figure 14.10).

The column type that WordPerfect calls Total will add a column of numbers in the same column or add subtotals or totals in the column adjacent to it. In Figure 14.9 we have used a Total column (B) to add all the

```
                          Expense Report
 _

                  January              February              Totals

Airfare           875.00               1086.00                 ■
Lodging           1258.76              1896.53

Subtotal            +                    +

Meals             1245.87              1693.88
Taxis             126.00               284.00

Subtotal            +                    +

Cash              t200.00              t367.75

Total                        =                    =




Columns           A          B         C         D          E
C:\WP5\FILE138                                    Doc 1 Pg 1 Ln 1 Pos 10
```

Figure 14.11 *Creating Calculation Columns*

subtotals in column A and place the results in column B. (We repeated the instructions for column D.) Remember, Total columns work only on adjacent columns. We could not use column E to add the totals of columns B and D.

14.2.4.1 Formulas in WordPerfect Math Columns

You can work across columns with WordPerfect's calculation columns. Of the 24 available columns, any four can be used to calculate numbers. In Figure 14.11, we'll use column E to add each line item for January and February.

In order to make column E into a calculation column, we'll position the cursor at the beginning of the math table (the cursor should be on the [Math Def] or [Math On] code markers), press **Alt-F7**, then **2-Math Def** to bring up the Math Definition settings sheet (see Figure 14.12).

Using the **Arrow** key, move the cursor to column E and type a 0 (zero). The cursor then jumps to Calculation Formulas where we will enter the formula we need. In our example we want to add columns A and C, so we enter **A+C** and press **F7** twice to return to the typing area.

Once the calculation column is defined, whenever we move the cursor into that column with the Tab key, WordPerfect places an **!** (exclamation mark; see Figure 14.11) that indicates that during calculation the results of a formula will be entered here.

```
Math Definition               Use arrow keys to position cursor

Columns                       A B C D E F G H I J K L M N O P Q R S T U V W X

Type                          2 3 2 3 █ 2 2 2 2 2 2 2 2 2 2 2 2 2 2 2 2 2 2 2 2

Negative Numbers              ( ( ( ( ( ( ( ( ( ( ( ( ( ( ( ( ( ( ( ( ( ( ( (

Number of Digits to           2 2 2 2 2 2 2 2 2 2 2 2 2 2 2 2 2 2 2 2 2 2 2 2
  the Right (0-4)

Calculation    1       █        ███
  Formulas     2
               3
               4

Type of Column:
     0 = Calculation    1 = Text    2 = Numeric    3 = Total

Negative Numbers
     ( = Parentheses (50.00)        - = Minus Sign  -50.00



Press Exit when done
```

Figure 14.12 *Entering Calculation Formulas On the Settings Sheet*

Any of the four basic math operators can be used in a calculation column or combined in a formula. Their symbols are:

+ Add
- Subtract
* Multiply
/ Divide

To multiply columns A and C, enter **A*C**; to divide A by C enter **A/C**.

14.2.4.2 *Entering Formulas that Contain Absolute Values*

In the previous example, we set the formula so that it examined a number in a specified column. If that number changes, the new number is used in the calculation. You may, however, create formulas with numbers as well as with column references (e.g., A+C). For example, if we want to average airfare expenses for January and February and enter the results in column E, our formula would be (A+C)/2, which tells WordPerfect to add the numbers in columns A and C and divide the results by 2. In another example, if the year's budget for airfare is $5000 and we want to keep a running tally of the remaining funds, we could enter 5000-(A+B) or 5000-A-B.

You can group numbers in parentheses, but you cannot use parentheses within parentheses. You can also use negative numbers, which are designated by a minus (-) sign.

14.3 Turning Math Off

WordPerfect's math feature requires a pair of codes to turn it on or off. If the math table is to be included in a longer document, you'll need to turn it off. Press **Alt-F7** and select **1-Math Off**. You can add as many line items as you wish within the math table as long as they fall between the [Math On] and [Math Off] code markers.

Short Cuts and Time Savers: Using Macros

If the word "macro" has gotten a bad name because some software macros are so complicated to build, WordPerfect's macros are a joy to use and will save you countless hours of unnecessary keystroke repetition. All you do to build a macro is to press **Ctrl-F10**. WordPerfect then remembers every subsequent keystroke you enter and can repeat the string anytime you ask. For example, if your company letterhead requires changing the default left and top margins, the following steps are necessary:

Shift-F8
1-Line
7-Margins
Change margin settings
Enter
2-Page
5-Margins
Change margin settings
Enter
Enter

If you turn on **Macro Define** before you enter these keystrokes, you'll never have to enter them again. It is so easy to define macros that a good policy is to build a macro every time you enter any series of command keystrokes. You will quickly collect a macro library that you'll constantly use. There's no limit to the number of macros you can create. Macros can contain text as well as function key commands, and you'll use them for inserting text into your documents as well as for entering codes. Any key that you strike after starting the macro definition will be saved.

15.1 Defining and Naming Macros

Writing a macro requires nothing more than pressing **Ctrl-F10** before you begin entering keystrokes, then pressing **Ctrl-F10** again to turn it off. When you press Ctrl-F10, the message center will ask:

```
Define macro:
```

It wants a name for the macro, and you have a choice. You can give the macro any file name up to 8 characters. It is better to use a name associated with the macro's function, such as "ltrhead" (letterhead).

The second way to name a macro is to press **Alt** and any letter **A-Z**. The third method is to simply press **Enter**. Here are the differences. If a macro has a normal file name of 1 to 8 characters, you retrieve it with that name after pressing **Alt-F10 (Use Macro)**. The prompt says: **Macro:** and you type the name. If you've named the macro with the Alt-A to Z method, you do not have to press Alt-F10 and type the macro name. You simply press **Alt** and the letter, thus saving several keystrokes. The only slight disadvantage to the Alt-A to Z method is that it's more difficult to remember the macro's name. You'll probably have to keep a reference of macros. The third method, pressing Enter to name the macro, Saves the keystrokes only for as long as you're in the program. As soon as you exit, or if you create a second macro, the keystrokes are lost.

15.2 Creating and Using a Macro

To build a macro:

Press **Ctrl-F10**
Macro: Name the macro using one of the methods described above

Description: You may enter up to 39 characters describing what the macro does
Type all the steps for any operation you want to perform
Press **Ctrl-F10** again to turn off macro definition

To use a macro:

Position the cursor where you want the macro commands to begin
Press **Alt-F10**
Type the macro name
Press **Enter**

or, if you have named the macro with the **Alt** method, just press Alt-letter. You can *stop a macro in progress* by pressing **F1 (Cancel)**.

15.2.1 *Entering Data from the Keyboard while a Macro is Operating*

As one of the keystrokes in a macro string, you can enter **Ctrl-PgUp**, which causes the macro to pause. You can then type text or fill in a settings sheet. The macro does not resume its steps until you press **Enter**. At the place in the command string where you want to enter data from the keyboard, press **Ctrl-PgUp**, then **1-Pause**. For example, if we wanted to pause at the Line Format settings sheet, the macro commands are:

Ctrl-F10
Enter   Turns on Macro Definition
Enter

Shift-F8
1-Line   Brings up the settings sheet

Ctrl-PgUp
1-Pause   Pauses the macro

15.3 Uses for Macros

WordPerfect Corporation bills macros as one of the most powerful features in the program, and for "power users" there are unlimited possibilities for automating your word processing environment. As we saw in the chapter on merging, you can insert macro codes in the merge documents, which allows you to set a whole chain of operations in motion. We'll discuss some of the more practical models below, but there are many more uses than these. Power users should consult the Advanced Macro appendix in the WordPerfect documentation.

Before we begin creating sample macros, you should know that in some cases there is no difference in the final result between building a macro and "boilerplating" a file. For example, you can build the macro for setting the margins of your letterhead, or you can create a "blank" file that contains those same settings. With a macro you could write your letter, then invoke the macro anytime. With a blank file, you would bring up the file and then write the letter. The final result is the same. However, there are some operations that are better performed by macros, such as setting the specifications for mailing labels, and some operations better handled by boilerplating files, such as memo formats that contain an automatic date code or weekly newsletters. Here is a list of a few of the many good uses for macros:

1. **Letter writing**

   a. **headings and closings:** If the letters you write use a lengthy heading and closing, such as:

   ```
   Sincerely,


   Henrietta M. Kensey, M.D.
   Director of Medical Research
   Cancer Treatment Center
   ```

   you'll certainly create a macro the first time you type all that.

   b. **Addresses:** If you send letters to the same people frequently and do not use merge to create the address, a macro can save you several lines of repetitive typing. Using **Shift-F5, 2-Date Code**, we entered a code that will automatically insert the current date, then date code:

   ```
   April 7, 1988

   Dr. Patricia Sange
   Greenville County General Hospital
   Communicable Disease Center
   ```

5000 Research Park, Room 523
Greenville, S. C. 29654

Dear Dr. Sange:

    c. Repetitive paragraphs: Perhaps you frequently use one or two sentences or paragraphs. This is a perfect macro application.

    d. Special settings: Margins, paper size, tab settings, column formats, fonts.

2. Printing

Print settings for different jobs can require many key strokes. If you switch from a dot matrix printer to a laser printer for different tasks, you'll want to build a printer selection macro. You might also build a quick-print macro so that Alt-P moves directly through your print menu:

Quick Print (Alt-P)	Quick Stop Printing (Alt-S)
Shift-F7	Shift-F7
1-Full Document	4-Control Printer
Enter	1-Cancel
	Enter
	Enter

Excellent applications for macros are selecting the base font, type size, and spacing.

3. Formatting

    a. Mailing labels: There are so many steps to specifying mailing labels that you'll want to create a macro for each size label you use:

Shift-F8
1-Line   Brings up menu to set left and right margins
7-Margins
Type margin settings
Enter

2-Page
5-Margins   Brings up menu to set top and bottom
                         margins
Type margin settings

8-Paper size
Type label size

Enter   Brings up menu to enter label size
4-Labels
Enter
Enter

b. **Graphics:** There are four different types of graphics boxes you can create. Your macro can either create the empty box whose graphics you'll add later, or it can pause while you enter the graphics file name. The steps for creating the box only are:

Alt-F9
1-Figure
1-Create
F7

To add the name of the graphics file, which we'll merge with the box:

Alt-F9
1-Figure   Creates figure
1-Create
Enter

Ctrl-PgUp
1-Pause   Pauses for you to fill out settings sheet

Alt-F9
1-Figure   Begins merging graphics file
2-Edit

Ctrl-PgUp
1-Pause   Pauses for you to type figure number

Ctrl-PgUp
1-Pause   Pauses for you to type graphics file name

The Ctrl-PgUp sequence is to tell WordPerfect to pause while you enter data from the keyboard (see Section 15.2.1).

4. Sorting, merging, and printing

Merging and printing labels or envelopes for letters that you are sending to selected people in the database is a multistep process that you can automate with macros. First we'll enter the steps for sorting, then the merge steps, and finally the print steps:

Ctrl-F9
2-Sort   Brings up sort settings sheet
Enter
Enter

Ctrl-PgUp   Pauses for you to fill out sort settings sheet and perform action
1-Pause

F7
Y   Saves sorted database under a new file name, "Datasort"
Datasort
Enter

Ctrl-F9   Starts merge operation
1-Merge

Ctrl-PgUp   Pauses for you to enter primary file (Letter) and secondary file (Datasort)
1-Pause

Shift-F7	
1	Enters print job for letters
A (All)	
F7	
N	Clears screen of merged letters
N	
Ctrl-F9	
1-Merge	
Labels	Starts labels merge and names primary file "Labels"
Enter	
Ctrl-PgUp	
1-Pause	Pauses for you to enter secondary file name
F7	
Y	
SortLab	Saves sorted labels under the file name
Enter	"SortLab"
N	
Alt-F10	
Macro:PrintLab	Invokes your macro for printing labels

Obviously, this is a fairly involved macro. You might build a few smaller macros and chain them for the full operation (see Section 15.6). We really have only four operations in this example: (1) merging the database with letters, (2) printing the letters, (3) merging the database into labels, and (4) printing the labels.

This is also a good example of how to design a macro. Plan all the operations you want it to perform and write on paper the keystrokes to achieve it. Then go through those steps to build the macro. Even though this macro example seems complicated, you would have to go through all the steps separately to achieve the same results, so you might as well take the time to build the macro once. This also enables people less familiar with WordPerfect to use the system with much less difficulty.

5. Database records

You can boilerplate your record layout in the macro so that when you've filled out one record WordPerfect will bring up another empty form. This makes data entry faster and more accurate:

Ctrl-F10	Defines and names macro
Alt-R	
^R (name)	Enters field code
Home←	Left arrow positions cursor
Ctrl-PgUp	
1-Pause	Pauses macro for you to enter data
Enter	
^R (address)	
Home←	Repeat these steps for as many fields as
	your database contains
Ctrl-PgUp	
1-Pause	
Enter	
^E	Marks end of record
Enter	Positions cursor for the next record
Alt-letter	Repeats macro
Ctrl-F10	Saves macro

The cursor will stop for you to enter the name. Type the data and press Enter and the cursor moves to the address field. Type the data, press Enter, and the next empty record waits for you to fill it in.

To end a record entry session, press **F1 (Cancel)** after you've entered the last record.

15.4 Macro Comments

When you define a macro, one of the menu items that appears when you press **Ctrl-F10, Ctrl-PgUp** is **4-Comment**. Here you can type a comment that will help you remember specific functions of the macro, which is useful if you want to edit it.

15.5 Editing Macros

If you want to modify a macro, press **Ctrl-F10** and type the macro name (see Figure 15.1).

If you want to totally rewrite the macro, select **1**. If you want to edit portions of it, select **2** (see Figure 15.2). Here's where the macro comment can help if you've written yourself good notes.

When you press **2-Action**, the cursor jumps into the box containing the macro commands. Using the **Arrow** keys, move to the position where you want to add or delete commands. To add commands, use the function keys as if you were creating the macro. Press **F7** twice to return to the typing area.

15.6 Chaining Macros and Advanced Macros

By placing a **start macro** command (Alt-F10 and macro name or Alt-letter) within a macro string, you can command WordPerfect to switch to

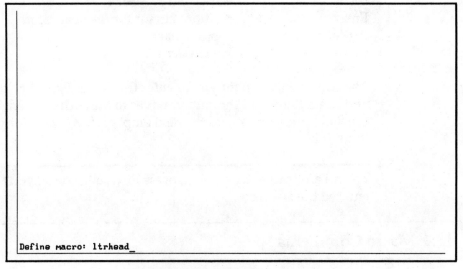

Figure 15.1 *Accessing the Macro Editor*
(Ctrl-F10, Macro Name)

```
Macro: Edit

       File            LTRHEAD.WPM

   1 - Description

   2 - Action

       ┌────────────────────────────────────────────┐
       │ {DISPLAY OFF}{Enter}                         │
       │                                              │
       │                                              │
       │                                              │
       │                                              │
       │                                              │
       │                                              │
       └────────────────────────────────────────────┘

Selection: 0
```

Figure 15.2 *Editing a Macro*
(Ctrl-F10, Macro Name, 2-Edit)

another macro string. However, when the second macro string has been executed, WordPerfect does not switch back to the first string. When WordPerfect has completed any macro, it turns off macro operations. You can chain as many macros as you wish, which is useful for automating such operations as printing:

Macro 1	Type fonts and style
Macro 2	Select laser printer
Macro 3	Print letters
Macro 4	Labels macro
Macro 5	Print labels

If you perform this print job often, you might create a master macro that contains all five macros. Then, by starting the master macro, you would set the entire print job in motion.

Advanced macros allow you to assign variables to either numbers or blocks of text and then perform operations with them. For example, you could assign a paragraph a variable, then tell the macro to perform a function with it. You can also create macros with some programming commands available through the macro editor. While you're in the macro box with codes, press **Ctrl-PgUp** again to produce the list of programming

330 Beacham's WordPerfect 5.0 Handbook

commands. Scroll down the list with the **Arrow** key. If you want to enter one of these commands into the macro, press **Enter**.

The appendix in the documentation, "Advanced Macros," will give you a start on using variables and other advanced features.

CHAPTER 16

Additional Setup
Procedures

The Setup menu (Shift-F1) provides several options that we've not yet discussed.

16.1 Display

The options in the menu in Figure 16.1 affect only text and messages as they appear on the screen. They do not affect how a document looks when printed. Most of the items on the menu in Figure 16.2 are obvious and your selection of them is simply a matter of visual preference. You can turn off displaying document comments (item 3), which is desirable once you have finished using them. You can turn off the permanent display of the file name on the status line (item 4). You can display side-by-side columns on separate screen pages (item 8), which makes them easier to scroll through. They will always, however, be printed side-by-side.

Item **7-Menu Letter Display** changes the size and appearance of the first letter of menu items. The purpose of this is to facilitate selecting menu items by their first letter rather than their number. For example, we brought up the **3-Display** menu by pressing **3**. We could have brought it

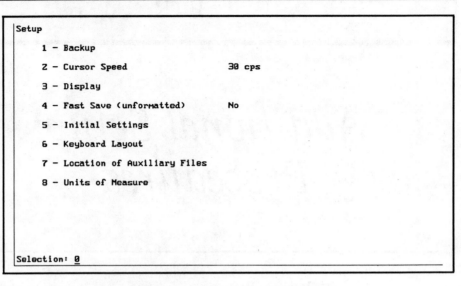

Figure 16.1 *Setup Menu (Shift-F1)*

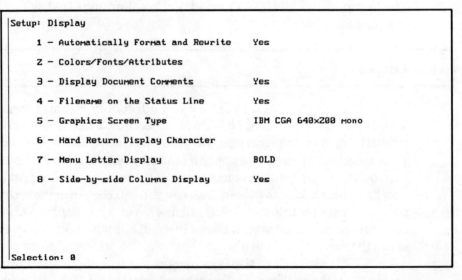

Figure 16.2 *Display Screen Menu*
(Shift-F1, 3-Display)

up by pressing D. Changing the size and appearance of the display letter might make it easier to remember the menu.

16.1.1 *Monitor Display Options*

Item **5-Graphics Screen Type** designates the type of monitor and graphics card your computer is equipped with. WordPerfect supports the standard types (shown in Figure 16.3). If yours is not on this list, you should copy your driver file into the directory that contains the WP.EXE program file.

Item **2-Colors/Fonts/Attributes** allows you to alter the appearance of the screen for presentations (see Figure 16.4). It is not the means for entering codes into your document that determine color printing (see Section 13.10).

Depending on the type of graphics card you designate, WordPerfect lists the colors, fonts, and/or attributes that you can use. You can tell WordPerfect what color you want certain fonts and attributes to be. The column at the far right shows a sample of what your selections will look like.

You may have noticed a second item, **2-Fast Text,** on the menu that led to the color selection. This speeds up WordPerfect's ability to display

```
Setup: Graphics Screen Type

  Text (no graphics)
  Hercules 720x348 mono
  Hercules InColor 720x348 16 color
* IBM CGA 640x200 mono
  IBM EGA 640x350 mono
  IBM EGA 640x200 16 color
  IBM EGA 640x350 4 color
  IBM EGA 640x350 16 color
  IBM VGA 640x480 mono
  IBM VGA 640x480 16 color
  IBM VGA 320x200 256 color
  AT&T 6300 640x400 mono
  Compaq Prtble plasma 640x400 mono
  IBM 8514/A 1024x768 256 color
  MDS Genius2 1280x1024 mono dual
  Multisync 800x560 16 color
  MDS Genius  736x1008 mono portrt
  Hercules 720x348 mono (external)
  WYSE Wy-700 1280X800 mono



1 Select: 1
```

Figure 16.3 *Monitor Screen Types WordPerfect Supports*
(Shift-F1, 3-Display, 5-Graphics Screen Type)

```
Setup: Colors          A B C D E F G H I J K L M N O P
                       A   C D E F G H I   K L M N O P
Attribute              Foreground  Background  Sample
Normal                     H            B        Sample
Blocked                    P            A        Sample
Underline                  H            A        Sample
Strikeout                  C            B        Sample
Bold                       P            B        Sample
Double Underline           F            B        Sample
Redline                    E            B        Sample
Shadow                     B            D        Sample
Italics                    G            B        Sample
Small Caps                 I            B        Sample
Outline                    G            B        Sample
Subscript                  E            D        Sample
Superscript                M            D        Sample
Fine Print                 K            B        Sample
Small Print                L            B        Sample
Large Print                M            B        Sample
Very Large Print           N            B        Sample
Extra Large Print          O            B        Sample
Bold & Underline           P            E        Sample
Other Combinations         A            G        Sample

Switch to switch: Move to copy settings      Doc 1
```

Figure 16.4 *Settings Sheet for Monitor Color/Fonts/*
Attributes (Shift-F1, 3-Display, 2-Color/Fonts/Attributes, 1-Screen Colors)

```
Setup: Initial Settings

     1 - Beep Options

     2 - Date Format                3 1, 4

     3 - Document Summary

     4 - Initial Codes

     5 - Repeat Value              8

     6 - Table of Authorities




Selection: 0
```

Figure 16.5 *Settings Sheet for Changing Some Default*
Items (Shift-F1, 5-Initial Settings)

complex images, but it might cause some fuzziness in the picture. If it does, change Yes to **N**.

16.1.2 *Initial Settings/Changing WordPerfect's Default Settings*

In addition to the default settings that can be changed through various menus in WordPerfect, there are a few you change with this settings sheet. Changes made through Initial Settings become the default for any document you create (see Figure 16.5).

Beep reminds you that you should pay attention to errors, hyphenation, and search failures. Your personal preference might be to beep often or not at all.

Date Format can be changed permanently here or for individual documents through the **Shift-F5 Date/Outline** menu.

To prompt an automatic **Document Summary** when exiting the system or saving a file, select **3-Document Summary** and change item **1-Create on Save/Exit** and change No to **Y**.

Initial Codes changes any default value on the **Shift-F8 (Format)** settings sheet. When you select item **4-Initial Settings**, WordPerfect switches to an empty work area (see Figure 16.6). Now, press **Shift-F8** and go through the steps of changing any setting on the list. For example,

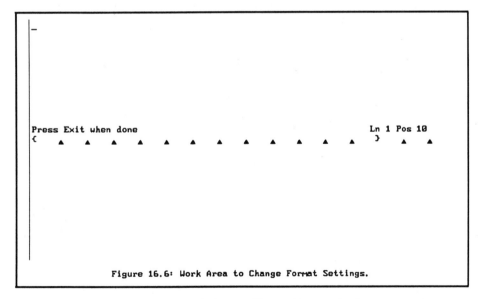

Figure 16.6 *Work Area to Change Format Settings*
(Shift-F1, 5-Initial Settings, 4-Initial Codes)

if you want to change the default hyphenation zone, press **Shift-F8, 1-Line,** and **1-Hyphenation.** Type in the new zone and press **F7** to Save the new default and return to the typing area. The hyphenation zone is permanently set to the new values.

The **Repeat Value** is the number of times WordPerfect repeats an operation, such as erasing to the end of a line. You may change the **8** to any number.

Table of Authorities changes the style so that you can select **dot leaders, underlining,** and **blanks** to the end of the line.

16.1.3 *Keyboard Layout*

WordPerfect's default keyboard is laid out for the general English-speaking user's needs. For specialized users WordPerfect has provided several optional keyboard layouts, as well as the capability to "map" your personalized keyboard. Mapping a keyboard is essentially the same process as building a macro and is performed through the **Edit macro** work area.

To select one of WordPerfect's alternate keyboards, press **Shift-F1** and select **6-Keyboard Layout** to bring up the list of definitions (see Figure 16.7). Move the cursor to your choice and press **1-Select,** then **F7** to return to Save your selection. This becomes the default keyboard until you select another one. If you want to return to WordPerfect's default keyboard,

```
Setup: Keyboard Layout

   ALTRNAT
   ENHANCED
   MACROS


















1 Select: 2 Delete: 3 Rename: 4 Create: 5 Edit: 6 Original: N Name search: 1
```

Figure 16.7 *Keyboard Definitions*
(Shift-F1, 6-Keyboard Definitions)

select **6-Original** from this same menu or press **Ctrl-6** from the typing area.

You may edit any of these keyboard definitions by moving the cursor to the key you want to edit and selecting **5-Edit**. This places you in the edit area where you can add, move, or delete key definitions (see Figure 16.8).

Move the cursor to the key you want to edit and press **1-Edit**. This moves you to the editing area, which you'll recognize as the same edit area for macros (see Figure 16.9).

2-Action moves the cursor to the box where you can complete your editing.

Creating a keyboard definition is the same process. Select **4-Create**, then give your customized keyboard a name (see Figure 16.10). You may now define as many keys as you wish. Use **1-Edit** to edit them. Press F7 to Save them.

16.1.4 *Location of Files*

If you want to store certain auxiliary files under different directories or in different drive locations, you can specify the path through item **7-Location of Files** in the setup menu (see Figure 16.11). Press the number corresponding to your choice and enter the path, such as D:\WORDS.

```
Keyboard: Edit

  Name: MACROS

  Key              Description                              Macro

  Alt-E            Get to Main Editing Screen               11
  Alt-T            Transpose 2 visible characters           7
  Alt-I            Insert a line.                           2
  Alt-P            Move Down by Paragraph                   16
  Alt-A            Print the address to an envelope         19
  Alt-S            Move Down by Sentence                    14
  Alt-D            Delete a line                            3
  Alt-F            Find the Bookmark                        10
  Alt-G            Send GO to printer                       4
  Alt-C            Capitalize 1st letter of current word    8
  Alt-B            Restore the previous block               6
  Alt-N            Edit the Next or Previous Note.          5
  Alt-M            Insert Bookmark                          9
  Alt-F9           List Files from Graphics Key             1
  Ctrl-D           Generate Standard Documents              12
  Ctrl-F           Make Font Changes                        17
  Ctrl-G           Glossary Macro - Expand Abbreviations    18

Key: 1 Edit: 2 Delete: 3 Move: 4 Create:  Macro: 5 Save: 6 Retrieve: 1
```

Figure 16.8 *Editing Key Definitions*
(Shift-F1, 6-Keyboard Layout, 5-Edit)

```
Key: Edit

      Key           Ctrl-S

  1 - Description    Move Up by Sentence

  2 - Action

     ┌─────────────────────────────────────────────────────────────┐
     │ <DISPLAY OFF>                                                 │
     │ {IF}{STATE}&4~              {;}Only·at·editing·screen~        │
     │    {IF}{STATE}&128~         {;}Block·state~                   │
     │    {Word Left}                                                │
     │    {Search Left}.{Esc}                                        │
     │    {Word Right}                                               │
     │ {ELSE}                                                        │
     │    <DISPLAY OFF>                                              │
     │    {Word Left}                                                │
     │    {Move}s{Cancel}         {;}End·of·sentence~               │
     │    {Goto}{Goto}            {;}Other·side~                     │
     │ {END IF}                                                      │
     │ {END IF}                                                      │
     └─────────────────────────────────────────────────────────────┘

Selection: 0
```

Figure 16.9 *Key Edit Area*
(Shift-F1, 6-Keyboard Layout, 5-Edit, 1-Edit, 2-Action)

```
Keyboard: Edit

  Name: MACROS

  Key              Description                    Macro












Key: 1 Edit: 2 Delete: 3 Move: 4 Create:  Macro: 5 Save: 6 Retrieve: 1
```

Figure 16.10 *Settings Sheet to Create Key Layouts*
(Shift-F1, 6-Keyboard Layout, 4-Create, Type Keyboard Name, Enter)

16.1.5 Units of Measure

If you want to work with units other than inches, you can change your
base system to the metric system or to typesetters' points. Selecting item
8 brings up this menu (see Figure 16.12).

```
Setup: Location of Auxiliary Files

     1 - Backup Directory

     2 - Hyphenation Module(s)

     3 - Keyboard/Macro Files

     4 - Main Dictionary(s)

     5 - Printer Files                    C:\WP5

     6 - Style Library Filename

     7 - Supplementary Dictionary(s)

     8 - Thesaurus




Selection: 0
```

Figure 16.11 *Settings Sheet for the Location of*
Auxiliary Files (Shift-F1, 7-Location of Files)

```
Setup: Units of Measure

     1 - Display and Entry of Numbers        "
           for Margins, Tabs, etc.

     2 - Status Line Display                 u

Legend:

     " = inches
     i = inches
     c = centimeters
     p = points
     u = WordPerfect 4.2 Units (Lines/Columns)




Selection: 0
```

Figure 16.12 *Units of Measure Settings Sheet*
(Shift-F1, 8-Units of Measure)

You can change the display for WordPerfect's various menus and setting sheets by selecting item **1**, and you can change the status line display by selecting item **2**. Whatever unit you select, the number in the status line is the horizontal distance from the left margin and the vertical distance from the top line.

```
C>grab

 ┌────────────────────────────────────────────────────────────────┐
 │ Screen Capture Utility                    Release 1.0  October 1, 1987 │
 │                                                                  │
 │ Copyright (c) WordPerfect Inc., 1987, All rights reserved        │
 └────────────────────────────────────────────────────────────────┘
Screen capture utility successfully installed
Activation (hot key) sequence is "<ALT><SHIFT><F9>"
Output goes to active directory at time of capture
Output file name is "GRAB.WPG"
For help, type "grab /h"

C>_
```

Figure 16.13 *Installing Screen Capture*

16.2 Screen Capture

There are some screen images that you cannot print using Screen-Print. WordPerfect provides a utility that makes it possible for you to capture images from the screen.

If you're working on a hard disk computer, copy the **GRAB.COM** utility file from the **Fonts/Graphics** disk. You must load the GRAB.COM file into memory each time you want to use it. At the **C:** or **A:** prompt, type **GRAB**. Then boot DOS. A message will tell you that the screen capture program has been successfully installed (see Figure 16.13).

When you want to capture a screen, press **Alt-Shift-F9**. The screen capture is transmitted to a file called **GRAB.WPG**. WordPerfect begins numbering the GRAB files sequentially, such as GRAB1.WPG, GRAB2.WPG.

You will not be able to print a GRAB screen capture. Using the *Word-Perfect Library* software, which is sold separately from *WordPerfect 5.0*, you copy the GRAB file to a "clipboard" image, then print it.

16.3 Character Sets

Character Set 0

```
       0 1 2 3 4 5 6 7 8 9 0 1 2 3 4 5 6 7 8 9 0 1 2 3 4 5 6 7 8 9
                          1                   2
  0
 30         !  "  ?  $  %  &  '  (  )  *  +  ,  -  .  /  0  1  2  3  4  5  6  7  8  9  :  ;
 60      <  =  >  ?  @  A  B  C  D  E  F  G  H  I  J  K  L  M  N  O  P  Q  R  S  T  U  V  W  X  Y
 90      Z  [  \  ]  ^  _  `  a  b  c  d  e  f  g  h  i  j  k  l  m  n  o  p  q  r  s  t  u  v  w
120      x  y  z  {  ¦  }  ~
```

Character Set 1

```
       0 1 2 3 4 5 6 7 8 9 0 1 2 3 4 5 6 7 8 9 0 1 2 3 4 5 6 7 8 9
                          1                   2
  0    `  ´  ¯  ^  ˇ  _  /  ´  ¨  ˉ  '  ,  ,   ,  ,  °  ˙  "   ,  ˇ  ˊ  —  ˜  ß  ı  ȷ  Á  á  Â  â
 30    Ä  ä  À  à  Å  å  Æ  æ  Ç  ç  É  é  Ê  ê  Ë  ë  È  è  Í  í  Î  î  Ï  ï  Ì  ì  Ñ  ñ  Ó  ó
 60    Ô  ô  Ö  ö  Ò  ò  Ú  ú  Û  û  Ü  ü  Ù  ù  Ÿ  ÿ  Ã  ã  Đ  đ  Ø  ø  Õ  õ  Ý  ý  Ð  ð  Þ  þ
 90    Ă  ă  Ā  ā  Ą  ą  Ć  ć  Č  č  Ĉ  ĉ  Ċ  ċ  Ď  ď  Ě  ě  Ė  ė  Ē  ē  Ę  ę  Ǵ  ǵ  Ğ  ğ  Ĝ  ĝ
120    Ģ  ģ  Ĝ  ĝ  Ġ  ġ  Ĥ  ĥ  Ħ  ħ  -ı  ı  ī  Ī  ī  Ĳ  ĳ  Ĩ  Ĩ  ĩ  Ĳ  ĳ  Ĵ  ĵ  Ķ  ķ  Ĺ  ĺ  Ĺ  ĺ  Ļ  ļ
150    Ł  ŀ  Ł  ł  Ń  ń  Ņ  ṅ  Ň  ň  Ņ  ņ  Ő  ő  Ō  ō  Œ  œ  Ŕ  ŕ  Ř  ř  Ŗ  ŗ  Ś  ś  Š  š  Ş  ş
180    Ŝ  ŝ  Ť  ť  Ţ  ţ  Ŧ  ŧ  Ŭ  ŭ  Ů  ů  Ū  ū  Ų  ų  Ù  ù  Ũ  ũ  Ŵ  ŵ  Ŷ  ŷ  Ź  ź  Ž  ž  Ż  ż
210    Ŋ  ŋ  Ď  ď  Ĺ  ĺ  Ñ  ñ  Ř  ř  Š  š  Ť  ť  Ÿ  ÿ  Ỳ  ỳ  Ď  ď  O' o'  U'  u'
```

Character Set 2

```
       0 1 2 3 4 5 6 7 8 9 0 1 2 3 4 5 6 7 8 9 0 1 2 3 4 5 6 7 8 9
                          1                   2
  0    .  ..  ˙  .   '  ^  ▬  —  K  .  ˀ  '   ,  ˴  ˌ  ˩  ˥  ´  ˊ  ˎ  ˌ  ˎ  ˡ  �‿  ˌ  ´  ˝
```

Character Set 3

```
        0 1 2 3 4 5 6 7 8 9 0 1 2 3 4 5 6 7 8 9 0 1 2 3 4 5 6 7 8 9
                            1                   2
 0  ▒ ▌ ▌ ▌ ▌ ▌ ▪ ▌ ▪ ─ ─ │ ┌ ┐ ┘ └ ├ ┬ ┤ ┴ ┼ ─ ─ │ ┌ ┐ ┘ └ ├ ┬
30  ┌ ┐ ┘ └ ┌ ┐ ┘ └ ├ ┬ ┤ ┴ ┼ ─ ─ ' ─ · ─ ' · · ─ ─ │ │
60  ├ ├ ├ ├ ┬ ┬ ┬ ┬ ┤ ┤ ┤ ┤ ┴ ┴ ┴ ┴ ┼ ┼ ┼ ┼ ┼ ┼ ┼ ┼ ┼ ┼
```

Character Set 4

```
        0 1 2 3 4 5 6 7 8 9 0 1 2 3 4 5 6 7 8 9 0 1 2 3 4 5 6 7 8 9
                            1                   2
 0  ● ○ ■ • ⋆ ¶ § ¡ ¿ « » £ ¥ ₨ ƒ ª º ½ ¼ ¢ ² ⁿ ® © ¤ ¾ ³ ' ' ·
30  " " " – — ‹ › ○ □ † ‡ TM SM ℞ ● ○ ■ ■ □ □ – ﬀ ¶ ¶ ¶ ¶ … $ ₣ ₲
60  ₠ £ , „ ⅓ ⅔ ⅛ ⅜ ⅝ ⅞ Ⓜ Ⓟ Ⓤ % ‰ ‰ № — ¹
```

Character Set 5

```
        0 1 2 3 4 5 6 7 8 9 0 1 2 3 4 5 6 7 8 9 0 1 2 3 4 5 6 7 8 9
                            1                   2
 0  ♥ ♦ ♣ ♠ ♂ ♀ ☼ ☺ ● ♪ ♫ ■ ⌂ ‼ √ ↕ ⌐ ⌐ □ ⊡ ━ ☞ ☜ ✔ □ ⊠ ☹ # ♭ ♮
30  ☞ ⊘ 𝔁 ₡ _
```

Character Set 6

```
        0 1 2 3 4 5 6 7 8 9 0 1 2 3 4 5 6 7 8 9 0 1 2 3 4 5 6 7 8 9
                            1                   2
  0  − ± ≤ ≥ ∝ / ∕ \ + | ⟨ ⟩ ~ ≈ ≡ ∈ ∩ ‖ Σ ∞ ¬ → ← ↑ ↓ ↔ ↕ ▶ ◀ ▲
 30  ▼ · · ° • Å ′ μ − × ∫ ∏ ∓ ∇ ∂ ′ ″ − ℯ ℓ ℏ ℑ ℜ ℘ ⇄ ⇆ ⇒ ⇐ ⇑ ⇓
 60  ⇔ ⇕ ↗ ↘ ↖ ↙ ∪ ⊂ ⊃ ⊆ ⊇ ∋ ∅ ⌈ ⌉ ⌊ ⌋ ≪ ≫ ∠ ⊗ ⊕ ⊖ ⊕ ⊙ ∧ ∨ ⊻ ⊤ ⊥
 90  ⌒ ⊢ ⊣ □ ■ ◇ ◆ ⟦ ⟧ ≠ ≢ ∴ ∵ ∷ ∮ ℒ ℭ ℨ ℘ ○ △ ◇ ★ ‴ ⨿ ≅ ≐ < ≤ >
120  ≥ ∃ ∀ ⋘ ⋙ ⊎ ⊊ ⊒ ⊓ ⊔ ⊏ ⊐ ⊑ ⊒ ⊐ ⊐ △ ▽ ◁ ▷ ⋈ ⌣ ⌢ ○ → ← ⇀ ↼ →
150  ⇁ ↽ ⇀ ⇁ ↿ ↾ ⇃ ⇂ ↦ ⇉ ⇇ ∪ ∩ ⊂ ⊃ ◎ ⊛ ⊝ ℧ ⊿ ◁ ◁ ▷ △ ▽ ± ∓ ⋽ ⋾ ⊠ ⋇
180  ⊨ ≜ ∮ ℓ ★ ≼ ≾ ≽ ≿ ⊀ ≁ ≇ ≄ ⋠ ≴ ⋡ ≵ ⋪ ⋫ ⋬ ⋭ ⊬ ⊭ ⊮ ⊯ ∤ ∦ ⋢ ⊣ ∋ ⅃
210  ↻ ℰ ℑℭ ℭℐ ℐℕℝ ℤℒ
```

Character Set 7

	0	1	2	3	4	5	6	7	8	9	10	1	2	3	4	5	6	7	8	9
0							Σ	Π	Ц	∫	∮									
20		{	{	{	{		{			}	}	}								
40																				
60		∪	∩	φ								Σ	Π	Ц	∫	∮	√	√		
80	√	√	√			→	←					⇒	⇐	=	↑	↓		⇑	⇓	
100	(	(	(	(	(	(		)	)	)	)					[	[	[		
120		]	]	]	]				⟨	⟨	⟨	⟨	⟩	⟩	⟩					
140					∪	∩	⊎	⊎	⊔	⊔	∧	∧	∨	∨	⊗	⊗	⊕	⊕	⊙	⊙
160								^	^	⌢	~	~	~							
180	⊖	⊖	⊕	⊕	⟦	⟦	⟦	⟦				⟧	⟧	⟧	⟧				→	→
200				⇀	⇁	↽	↼			⇒	⇐	=	⇒	⇒	⇐	⇐	=	↿	↾	⇃
220		π	π																	

Character Set 8

```
      0 1 2 3 4 5 6 7 8 9 0 1 2 3 4 5 6 7 8 9 0 1 2 3 4 5 6 7 8 9
   0  Α α Β β Β Β Γ γ Δ δ Ε ε Ζ Ζ Η η Θ θ Ι ι Κ κ Λ λ Μ μ Ν Ξ ξ
  30  Ο ο Π π Ρ ρ Σ σ Σ ς Τ τ Υ υ Φ φ Χ χ Ψ ψ Ω ω ά ΄ ή ί ϊ ö ύ ΰ
  60  ώ ε θ κ ϖ ρ Υ φ ω ; ; ΄ ΄ ΄ ΄ ΄ ΄ ΄ ΄ ΄ ΄ ΄ ΄ ΄ ΄ ΄ ΄ ΄ ΄
  90  ΄ ΄ ΄ ΄ ΄ ΄ ΄ ά â ᾇ ᾅ ᾆ ᾄ ᾆ ᾆ ᾆ ᾇ ᾇ ᾇ ᾆ ᾆ ᾆ ᾇ ᾇ ᾆ ᾇ ᾇ ᾇ ὲ έ έ ἔ
 120  ἐ ἑ ἔ ή ῆ ῇ ῃ ῇ ῇ ῇ ῆ ῇ ῇ ῇ ῇ ῇ ῇ ῇ ῇ ῇ ῇ ῇ ῇ ι ί ῖ ΐ ῗ ΐ ΐ
 150  ΐ ΐ ΐ ΐ ΐ ὸ ὀ ὄ ὄ ὄ ὄ ὄ ὄ ὺ ῦ ῦ ῦ ῦ ῦ ῦ ῦ ῦ ῦ ῦ ῦ ῦ ω ώ ῶ ῷ
 180  ω ώ ῶ ῷ ῷ ῷ ῷ ῷ ῷ ῷ ῷ ῷ φ φ ΄ ΄ ϛ Ϝ ϙ ϡ
```

Character Set 9

```
      0 1 2 3 4 5 6 7 8 9 0 1 2 3 4 5 6 7 8 9 0 1 2 3 4 5 6 7 8 9
   0  כ ב ת ש ר ק צ ף פ ע ס נ מ ם ל כ ך י ט ח ז ו ה ד ג ב א
  30  פ ΄ ΄ ΄ ΄ ΄ ΄ ΄ ΄ ΄ ΄ ΄ ΄ ΄ ΄ ΄ ΄ ΄
```

Character Set 10

```
      0 1 2 3 4 5 6 7 8 9 0 1 2 3 4 5 6 7 8 9 0 1 2 3 4 5 6 7 8 9
   0  А а Б б В в Г г Д Д Е е Ё ё Ж ж З з И и Й й К к Л Л М м Н н
  30  О о П п Р р С с Т т У у Ф Х х Ц ц Ч ч Ш ш Щ ш Ъ ъ Ы ы Ь ь
  60  Э э Ю ю Я я Ґ ґ Ђ ђ Ѓ ѓ Є є Ѕ ѕ І і Ї ї Ј ј Љ љ Њ њ Ћ ћ Ќ ќ
  90  Ў ў Џ џ ҍ ҍ Ѳ ѳ ѵ Ѫ ѫ
```

Character Set 11 (Hiragana)

```
      0 1 2 3 4 5 6 7 8 9 0 1 2 3 4 5 6 7 8 9 0 1 2 3 4 5 6 7 8 9
   0  ぁ い う ぇ ぉ っ ゃ ゅ ょ     か け あ い う え お か き く け こ が ぎ ぐ げ ご さ し す
  30  せ そ ざ じ ず ぜ ぞ た ち つ て と だ ぢ づ で ど な に ぬ ね の は ひ ふ へ ほ ば び ぶ
  60  べ ぼ ぱ ぴ ぷ ぺ ぽ ま み む め も や ゆ よ ら り る れ ろ わ を ん 〔 〕 【 】 「 」 「
  90  」 . 。 、 ゝ ゞ 〃 ー ゛ ゜
```

Character Set 11 (Katakana)

```
      0 1 2 3 4 5 6 7 8 9 0 1 2 3 4 5 6 7 8 9 0 1 2 3 4 5 6 7 8 9
   0  ァ ィ ゥ ェ ォ ッ ャ ュ ョ ヮ ヵ ヶ ケ ア イ ウ エ オ カ キ ク ケ コ ガ ギ グ ゲ ゴ サ シ ス
  30  セ ソ ザ ジ ズ ゼ ゾ タ チ ツ テ ト ダ ヂ ヅ デ ド ナ ニ ヌ ネ ノ ハ ヒ フ ヘ ホ バ ビ ブ
  60  ベ ボ パ ピ プ ペ ポ マ ミ ム メ モ ヤ ユ ヨ ラ リ ル レ ロ ワ ヲ ン 〔 〕 【 】 「 」 「
  90  」 . 。 、 ヽ ヾ 〃 ー ゛ ゜
```

16.4 Clip-Art Images

AIRPLANE.WPG

AND.WPG

ANNOUNCE.WPG

APPLAUSE.WPG

ARROW1.WPG

ARROW2.WPG

AWARD.WPG

BADNEWS.WPG

BOOK.WPG

BORDER.WPG

CHECK.WPG

CLOCK.WPG

CONFIDENTIAL
CONFIDEN.WPG

FLAG.WPG

GAVEL.WPG

GOODNEWS.WPG

NEWSPAPR.WPG

PRESENT.WPG

HAND.WPG

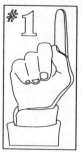

NO1.WPG

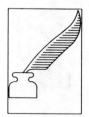

QUILL.WPG

HOURGLAS.WPG

PC.WPG

RPTCARD.WPG

KEY.WPG

PENCIL.WPG

THINKER.WPG

MAPSYMBL.WPG

PHONE.WPG

USAMAP.WPG

16.5 Printers Supported by WordPerfect 5.0

Alphapro 101
Alps ALQ 200
Alps ALQ 300
Alps P2000
Alps P2100
Alps P2400C
Apple Imagewriter II
Apple Laserwriter +
AST TurboLaser
AST TurboLaser/PS
Brother HR-15XL
Brother HR-20
Brother HR-35
C.Itoh C-310 P
C.Itoh C-310 XP
C.Itoh C-715
C.Itoh C-815
C.Itoh D10-40
C.Itoh Prowriter Jr. Plus
Canon LBP-8 A1
Canon LBP-8 A2
Centronics 351
Centronics GLP II
Citizen 120D
Citizen MSP-15
Citizen MSP-25
Citizen Premiere 35
Citizen Tribute 224
Cordata LP300X
Cosmo World Adeus CP-2000
Daisy   Systems'   M45-Q
(QUME)
Daisywriter 2000
Data General 4558 Laser
Data General 6321 Daisywheel
Dataproducts LZR 1230
Dataproducts LZR 2630

Dataproducts P132 (Color)
Dataproducts SPG 8050
Destiny Laseract I
Diablo 620
Diablo 630
Diablo 630 ECS
Diablo 635
Diablo 6Advantage D801F
Diconix 150
Digital LA-100
Digital LA-50
Epson EX-800
Epson FX-286e
Epson FX-86e
Epson CQ-3500
Epson LQ-1050
Epson LQ-2500
Epson LX-800
Florida Data Office Sys 130
Fortis DM1310
Fortis DM2015
Fortis DX-21
Fortis DX-25
Fortis DX-41
Fujitsu DL2400C
Fujitsu DL2600
Fujitsu DL3400
Fujitsu DPL24D
Fujitsu DX2200
Fujitsu SP 320
GTC Blaser
HP 2603A Daisywheel
HP DeskJet
HP LaserJet
HP LaserJet 2000
HP LaserJet 500
HP LaserJet Series II

HP LaserJet
HP PaintJet
HP QuietJet
HP RuggedWriter
HP ThinkJet
IBM Personal Pageprinter
IBM Proprinter II
IBM Proprinter X24
IBM Proprinter XL
IBM Proprinter XL24
IBM Quietwriter III
JDL-850 EWS Series
Kyocera F-1010
Mannesmann Tally MT180
Mannesmann Tally MT290
  w/IBM
Mannesmann Tally MT910
NEC Pinwriter P2200
NEC Pinwriter P5
NEC Pinwriter P6
NEC Pinwriter P7
NEC Spinwriter 3550
NEC Spinwriter 8830
NEC Spinwriter 8850
NEC Spinwriter Elf 360
Nissho NP-2410
Nissho NP-910
Okidata Laserline 6
Okidata ML 192 Plus
Okidata ML 192
Okidata ML 292
Okidata Pacemark 2410
Olympia Compact RO
Olympia ESW 2000
Olympia Startype
Panasonic KX-P10801
Panasonic KX-P1091
Panasonic KX-P10911
Panasonic KX-P1092
Panasonic KX-P10921
Panasonic KX-P1093

Panasonic KX-P1524
Panasonic KX-P1492
Panasonic KX-P1595
Panasonic KX-P3131
Panasonic KX-P3151
Primage 90-GT
Printronix S7024
QMS Kiss Laser
QMS PS Jet+
Quadram Quadlaser
Qume LaserTen
Qume LaserTen Plus
Qume LetterPro Plus
Ricoh LP4080R
Ricoh PC Laser 6000
Silver-Reed EXP 800
Star NB-15
Star NB24-15
Star ND-15
Star SG-10
Talaris T810
Tandy Laser LP1000
TI 855
TI 857
TI Omni Laser 2115
TI Omni Laser 2015
Toshiba P321SL
Toshiba P351C
Toshiba P351SX
Toshiba PageLaser 12
Xerox 4045

Index

A

ASCII characters, 109
ASCII. *See* Text In/Out feature
Asterisk (*), marking files, 106-107
Automatic reference, 206-215
    endnotes/footnotes, use as target,
      212-214
    entering markers separately, 210-212
    markers, types of, 207
    marking both reference and target, 215
    multiple references, same target, 212
      placing reference markers, 208-210
    tie-ins for referencing, 206-207
      replacing old reference numbers, 212

B

Backspace key, 16, 17
    options for deleting, 33-34
Backup, 51-54
    automatic, 22
    from hard disk, 52
    importance of, 51
    original document backup, 54

    timed document backup, 52-54
    See also Saving.
Binding feature, 293-294
    BK extension, retrieving files, 54
Block features, 26-33
    blocking, process of, 25-26
    bold, 26-27
      new text, 27-28
      turning off, 28
    case of letters, changing, 28
    cut/copy/move, 28-29
    deleting text, 30
    print block, 31-32
    protecting blocks, 32-33
    saving blocked text, 31
    underline, 26-27
      new text, 27-28
      turning off, 28
Blocks
    block protect, 291
    printing, 96
    search and replace, 62
    spell checking, 72
Bold (F6), 26-27
    new text, 27-28

punctuation, customizing, 202
starting number, assigning, 202
starting outline, 198-199
turning off, 200
Overstriking text, 247

P

Page breaks, 251
Page formatting (advanced)
  block protect, 291
  conditional end of page, 290-291
  hard spaces, 291
  printing, 291
    binding feature, 293
    color printing, 302-304
    font styles, 298-299, 300-303
    from specified position, 291-292
    kerning, 296
    leading, changing, 295
    odd/even pages, 292
    paper size/type option, 293-294
    pitch, 295, 296-298
    printer commands, 304-305
    type size, 298-299
    working while printing, 294
  windows/orphans, 290
Page numbering, 48-50
Pages, deleting, 18-19
Paper size/type option, 293-294
Paragraph box types, graphics boxes,
  264-265
Paragraph numbering, 203-206
  deleting paragraphs/markers, 205
  moving paragraphs, 205
  starting of, 203-204
  value of, 206
Paragraph sort, 153-154
Parallel port (LPT port), 82-83
Password

locking files, 123-124
  removing, 124
Percentage (%) change, graphics boxes,
  277
Pitch, 295, 296-298
  refining settings, 295-298
Primary file, 130, 131
  merge codes, 144-145
  See also Database.
Printers
  commands, entering, 303-305
  laser printers, initializing, 84
  set-up, 80-88
    parallel port (LPT port), 82-83
    selecting printer, 80-82
    serial port (COM port), 83-84
    Standard Printer default, 80, 85
  switching between printers, 84-85
  typeface selections, 86-87
    changing font choices, 87-88
Printing, 79-104
  advanced
    binding feature, 293
    color printing, 302-304
    font styles, 298-299, 300-303
    from specified position, 291-292
    kerning, 296
    leading, changing, 295
    odd/even pages, 292
    paper size/type option, 293-294
    pitch, 295, 296-298
    printer commands, 304-305
    type size, 298-299
    working while printing, 294
  blocks, 31-32, 96
  cautions about, 79
  database
    merged documents, 147
    sending text to printer, 147
  from disks, 91

About the Authors

Walton and Deborah Beacham began using WordPerfect in their publishing business soon after its realease and they wrote the first book on Word-Perfect in 1983. Their book, *Using WordPerfect,* is one of the most widely read computer application books in personal computing history. They have subsequently written books on other word processing software, Manuscript, DisplayWrite, and WordStar. They continue to use Word-Perfect on a daily basis to manage large databases, to produce mail merges and to edit manuscripts.

Deborah combines her practical use of WordPerfect with an extensive personal computer background. In 1983, she was an information center consultant teaching end users Lotus 1-2-3, followed by experience as a computer hardware/software consultant. In 1985, she joined Lotus Development Corporation where for two and a half years she marketed Lotus' full software product line. She worked closely with end users to help them understand the full power and uses of their Lotus software. In 1988, she left Lotus to become MarketingDirector for Beacham Publishing, a major publisher of reference books and instructional videos for high school and university libraries.

Walton, who holds four college degrees, has authored and edited dozens of books. His experience from telve years of teaching English and writing in universities, combined with his background in engineering and business, give him a unique eye for software applications, as well as a gift for writing clear, polished books. In addition to writing computer books and scholarly books on literrary criticism, he also writes novels, poems, and children's books.